Learn Python with Projects

"For my grandmother who left me too soon, but I always miss her and still feel the love and warmth, my parents who valued education and give their full support, my first boss, who taught me the value of programming and knowledge transfer, my husband, who has been my most profound inspiration, my 20,000+ students and readers for their inspiration and encouragement, and finally, my dear pet, three Beagles and one Chihuahua, for providing the entertainment and stress relief."

Learn Python with Projects

Table of Contents

FIGURES PART I V

TABLES PART I VI

SYNTAXES PART I VII

FIGURES PART II VIII

TABLES PART II XI

EQUATIONS PART II XII

PART I   THE BASICS XIV

   CHAPTER 1 INTRODUCTION 1
      Installing Python 2
      Installing Packages or Modules 6
      Installing a Package 6
      Program Python Using Visual Studio Code 8
      Advantages of VS Code 10
      virtual environment 17
          Exercises 20
   CHAPTER 2 DATA TYPES 21
      Integers 22
      Floats 22
      Strings 25
      Boolean 26
          Exercises 57
   CHAPTER 3 LISTS, DICTIONARIES, SETS, TUPLES 58
      Lists 58
      Dictionaries 68
      Sets 71
      Tuples 81
          Exercises 85
   CHAPTER 4 OPERATORS 86
      Arithmetic Operators 87
      Comparison Operators 91
      Logical Operators 93
      Identity operators 97
      Membership operators 99
      Bitwise operators 100
      Assignment operators 108
          Exercises 110

Learn Python with Projects

CHAPTER 5 CONDITIONAL STATEMENTS 111
   if 112
   if..else 113
   if..elif..else 118
   while..loop 121
   with…as 126
   continue 126
   while..else 129
   for..loop 131
   elif 137
   pass 137
      Exercises 138
CHAPTER 6 FUNCTIONS 139
   define function 139
   calling a function 140
   define a function with *parameter 142
   defining a function with **parameter 144
   defining a function with default values to parameters 145
   defining a function with return 147
   Lambda Functions 149
   defining a function with return value of the lambda function   151
      Exercises 154
CHAPTER 7 MODULES 155
   create module 156
   using module 156
   using variable in module 156
   using function in module 157
   using dictionary in module 158
   rename module 158
   using random module 159
   using datetime module 165
   The datetime Module 165
   datetime module formatting when calling the strftime() or strptime() function. 166
      Exercises 171
CHAPTER 8 STRING FORMATTING 172
      Exercises 177
CHAPTER 9 OBJECT- ORIENTED PROGRAMMING 178
   Create Class and Object 179
   parent and child 183
   Overrides 188
   Polymorphism 189
   Inheriting Multiple Classes 192

Association	199
Aggregation	200
Composition	201
Exercises	212
CHAPTER 10 TRY... EXCEPTION	213
Exercises	216
CHAPTER 11 FILE MANAGEMENT WITH...AS AND JSON	217
Open File	217
Create	218
Write File	219
with...as	219
Create File	220
Delete File	221
Delete Folder	222
JSON	223
loads	223
open	224
convert Python to JSON	225
Exercises	228

PART II SOFTWARE DEVELOPMENT PROJECTS — **229**

PROJECT I GAME	232
free games	232
Pygame	236
Installing Pygame	237
Using the Example program to create a new game	238
Display the background as the desired image.	253
Drawing Geometric Shapes	255
Drawing a Rectangle	257
Programming Keyboard Controls	259
Programming Mouse Controls	263
PROJECT II WEB APPLICATION	268
To access virtual environment	268
Check python version	269
Check Django suitable version	269
install django	269
create web project	270
runserver	270
Migrate	272
Start Application	272
Create HTML	275
Use SQLite database	282
record multiple entries	286

edit data		288
change back		289
Display as Links		294
Create, Read, Update, Delete : CRUD		299
PROJECT III DATA ANALYSIS		316
matplotlib		316
To access virtual environment		317
Example Program: Histogram		324
Example Program: Pie Chart		327
Example Program: Bar Chart		328
Example Program: Retrieving Data from a CSV File		335
Map graphing		337
PROJECT IV ARTIFICIAL INTELLIGENCE (AI)		344
Examples of artificial intelligence usage		346
Machine Learning		348
Neural Networks		348
Perceptron Algorithm		349
Developing artificial intelligence programs using Python		351
Mathematical tools		353
Statistics		353
1)	Mean(μ)	353
2)	Median	354
3)	Mode	356
4)	Standard Deviation	357
5)	Percentiles	360
Creating data for testing		361
6)	Creating a Uniform distribution	361
7)	Creating normally distributed	364
data analysis		365
8)	Scatter Plot analysis	365
9)	Linear Regression analysis	367
10)	Polynomial Regression Analysis	374
11)	Multiple Regression Analysis	380
12)	Categorical Data Analysis	385
Data mining tools		389
13)	A decision tree	389
14)	Hierarchical Clustering	395
15)	K-Means	398
16)	Association rules	403
Teaching and testing tools		417
Files used in projects/Exercise Solutions		424
ABOUT THE AUTHOR		**A**

Learn Python with Projects

Figures Part I

Figure 1- 1: download window for the latest version of 3
Figure 1- 2: 1st python installation window for macOS . 4
Figure 1- 3: 2nd Python installation window for macOS 4
Figure 1- 4: 3rd python installation window for macOS 5
Figure 1- 5: folder showing installed python files 5
Figure 1- 6: Visual Studio Code Download Window 8
Figure 1- 7: 1st installation window of Visual Studio Code 9
Figure 1- 8: 2nd installation window of Visual Studio Code 10
Figure 1- 9: Starting Visual Studio Code 11
Figure 1- 10: Visual Studio Code Welcome Screen 11
Figure 1- 11: folder created to keep files for Python software development 12
Figure 1- 12: Visual Studio Code asking for permission to use the folder 12
Figure 1- 13: Visual Studio Code starting window 13
Figure 1- 14: Visual Studio Code menu 13
Figure 1- 15: Visual Studio Code terminal window 14
Figure 1- 16: Visual Studio Code menu bar 14
Figure 1- 17: Visual Studio Code file submenu 15
Figure 7- 1: Visual Studio Code displaying all modules available of python for programmer 164
Figure 7- 2: module randint() is used 164
Figure 7- 3:random. randint() will appear in program 164
Figure 9-1: UML representation of a class 180
Figure 9-2: UML representation of the "animal" class 182
Figure 9-3:UML representation of an inheritance relationship. 184
Figure 9-4: UML representation an inheritance relationship with multiple classes.......... 192

v

Figure 9-5: Class diagram of animals in the zoo that show an inheritance relationship with multiple classes....................................... 193
Figure 9-6: UML representation of an association relationship. 199
Figure 9-7: UML representation an aggregation relationship. 200
Figure 9- 8: UML representation a composition relationship. 202
Figure 9-9: Class diagram of animals in the zoo with an association relationship. 202
Figure 9-10: Class diagram of animals in the zoo with an aggregation relationship. 205
Figure 9- 11: Class diagram of animals in the zoo with a composition relationship. 209

Tables Part I

Table 2-1: Functions Used In Data Type Conversion For Python 23
Table 2-2 : Frequently Functions Used in String Type Data for Python 27
Table 3- 1: Functions Used in Lists for Python 61
Table 3- 2: Functions Used in Dictionaries for Python . 70
Table 3- 3: Functions Used in Sets for Python.............. 71
Table 3- 4: Functions Used in Tuples for Python 83
Table 3- 5: Differences between lists, dictionaries, sets and tuples 84
Table 4- 1: Arithmetic Operators................................. 87
Table 4- 2: Order of Operations 89
Table 4- 3: BMI results meaning................................... 90
Table 4- 4:Comparison Operators 91
Table 4- 5: AND Truth Table 93

Table 4- 6: OR Truth Table 94
Table 4- 7: XOR Truth Table 94
Table 4- 8: NOT Truth Table 94
Table 4- 9: Logical Operators 95
Table 4- 10: Identity Operators 97
Table 4- 11: Membership Operators 99
Table 4- 12: Bitwise Operators 101
Table 4- 13: Assignment Operators 108
Table 5- 1: Symbols for Flow Chart 114
Table 5- 2: Comparison operators 116
Table 7- 1: Frequently Used Functions of Random
           Provided by Python 160
Table 7- 2: Command Format enclosed in brackets
           strftime() or strptime() 166
Table 11- 1:Python to JSON conversion table 223

Syntaxes Part I

Syntax 3-1: Create Lists 1 59
Syntax 3-2: Index number of element in List 59
Syntax 3-3: Negative index of element in List 60
Syntax 3-4: Combining Two Lists 67
Syntax 3-5: Create Lists 2 67
Syntax 3-6: Create Dictionaries 68
Syntax 3-7: Create Sets 71
Syntax 3-8: Create Tuples 81
Syntax 5- 1: if statement 112
Syntax 5- 2: if..else statement 113
Syntax 5- 3: if..elif..else statement 118
Syntax 5- 4: while..loop statement 121
Syntax 5- 5: while..loop with break statement 123
Syntax 5- 6: while..loop with break and continue
           statement 127

Syntax 5-7: while..else statement 130
Syntax 5-8: for..loop statement 131
Syntax 5-9: for..loop with break statement 132
Syntax 7-1: create python file 156
Syntax 7-2: use a module 156
Syntax 7-3: use a variable in module 156
Syntax 7-4: use a function in module 157
Syntax 7-5: use a dictionary in module 158
Syntax 7-6: rename a module 159
Syntax 8-1: String formatting for Strings 172
Syntax 8-2: String format for decimal values 173
Syntax 8-3: format to display multiple values inside a string 174
Syntax 8-4: format with variables inside the string ... 175
Syntax 9-1: Creating a class in python 180
Syntax 9-2: Creating an object in python 181
Syntax 9-3: Display an object in python 182
Syntax 9-4: Creating a child class in python 185
Syntax 9-5: Creating an object in a child class in python 185
Syntax 9-6: Adding attributes or methods to a child class 186
Syntax 9-7: Create a child class that have multiple parent classes in python 194
Syntax 9-8: Create an association between class1 and class2 with method in python 200

Figures Part II

Figure Project I-1: freegame.snake 235
Figure Project I-2: snake.py for developer 236
Figure Project I-3: Pygame Aliens 238
Figure Project I-4: Pygame PoisonRains 253

Figure Project I- 5: Replaced background Image......... 254
Figure Project I- 6:Drawing geometric shapes 257
Figure Project I- 7: Pygame defines rectangles 257
Figure Project I- 8: a drawn rectangle 259
Figure Project I- 9:Initial keyboard controls screen.... 260
Figure Project I- 10:Lines drawn with keyboard controls
.... 263
Figure Project I- 11:Mouse Control Game 264
Figure Project I- 12:Mouse Control Game Press 266
Figure Project II- 1: Created ExampleWebPython folder
.... 270
Figure Project II- 2: Django Server running on a virtual machine... 271
Figure Project II- 3: Members folder found in ThaiFruits
.... 273
Figure Project II- 4: 127.0.0.1:8000/country/ 282
Figure Project II- 5:country page................................ 292
Figure Project II- 6: country page after use CSS 294
Figure Project II- 7: country page with link 298
Figure Project II- 8:after click link China.................... 299
Figure Project II- 9: Django administration login page300
Figure Project II- 10: After login success 301
Figure Project II- 11: Country added to admin page .. 302
Figure Project II- 12: click to add country 302
Figure Project II- 13:add country page...................... 303
Figure Project II- 14:country data management 304
Figure Project II- 15: after click country for edit or delete
.... 305
Figure Project II- 16: change the title........................ 306
Figure Project II- 17: ADMIN INTERFACE has shown .. 314
Figure Project II- 18:Select Theme to change page.... 315
Figure Project III- 1::Line Graph example................... 319
Figure Project III- 2:Line graph with custom font....... 321
Figure Project III- 3:Line graph with added markers.. 323

Figure Project III- 4 : Line graph with grid 324
Figure Project III- 5:Histogram 326
Figure Project III- 6:PNG image of histogram............. 326
Figure Project III- 7: Pie Chart 327
Figure Project III- 8: Bar Chart..................................... 329
Figure Project III- 9:Comparative bar graph............... 331
Figure Project III- 10 : Using subplot to create a dashboard................................... 333
Figure Project III- 11: Using subplot to create a dashboard 2................................. 335
Figure Project III- 12: graph from a CSV file 337
Figure Project III- 13:Map graphing example 1 341
Figure Project III- 14:Map graphing example 2 343
Figure Project IV- 1: Various AI Levels 345
Figure Project IV- 2: Neural Networks........................ 348
Figure Project IV- 3: Example Uniform distribution histogram.. 363
Figure Project IV- 4: Example Normal data distribution histogram.. 364
Figure Project IV- 5: Example Scatterplot analysis of age versus weight lifted 366
Figure Project IV- 6: Example Scatterplot analysis of age versus weight lifted with a line graph 369
Figure Project IV- 7: Example Scatterplot analysis of age versus weight with line graph....... 373
Figure Project IV- 8: Example Scatterplot analysis of Income vs. Online Purchases with 2 degrees of Polynomial regression 376
Figure Project IV- 9: Example Scatterplot analysis of Income vs. Online Purchases with 3 degrees of Polynomial regression 378
Figure Project IV- 10: Example Decision Tree for car sales 391

Figure Project IV- 11: Example Scatterplot graph for hierarchical clustering 395
Figure Project IV- 12: Example automatic hierarchical clustering 397
Figure Project IV- 13: Example The Kmeans Elbow Method 401
Figure Project IV- 14: Example Scatterplot graphs showing various number of clusters 403
Figure Project IV- 15: Example Size of Total, Training and Testing Data 419
Figure Project IV- 16: Example Polynomial regression of training data 420

Tables Part II

Table Project II- 1: Django vs python versions 269
Table Project IV- 1: Example Nominal Data 351
Table Project IV- 2: Example Ordinal Data.................. 352
Table Project IV- 3: Example Discreet Data 352
Table Project IV- 4: Example Continuous Data 353
Table Project IV- 5: Example Height of Student Table for finding Average........................... 353
Table Project IV- 6: Example Student height Table (amount of data is odd) 354
Table Project IV- 7: Example Student height Table after sorting 354
Table Project IV- 8: Example Student height Table (amount of data is even) 355
Table Project IV- 9: Example Student height Table after sorting 355
Table Project IV- 10: Example Student height Table for finding mode 356

Table Project IV- 11: Frequency of Example student height 356
Table Project IV- 12: Standard Deviation Example Data Table 358
Table Project IV- 13: Standard Deviation Example Data Table 2 359
Table Project IV- 14: For Find Percentiles Example Data Table 360
Table Project IV- 15: Example Maximum weight lifted by subject weight 365
Table Project IV- 16: Example Maximum weight lifted by subject weight 367
Table Project IV- 17: Example Weight vs Age 372
Table Project IV- 18: Example Income vs. Online purchases 374
Table Project IV- 19: Example Income, installment, Purchase 381
Table Project IV- 20: Example Income, Installment, No of children, Purchase 384
Table Project IV- 21: Example Data table for categorical data analysis 386
Table Project IV- 22: Example Education levels data classified with get_dummies 387
Table Project IV- 23: Example Data table for decision tree 389
Table Project IV- 24: Example Decision tree nodes 393
Table Project IV- 25: Example Hierarchical clustering data table 395
Table Project IV- 26: Example Sample data table for association rules 404

Equations Part II

Equation Project IV- 1: Standard deviation 358

Equation Project IV- 2: Gini Impurity Formula 392
Equation Project IV- 3: Distortion 398
Equation Project IV- 4: Inertia 398
Equation Project IV- 5: distance 398
Equation Project IV- 6: Support 406
Equation Project IV- 7: Confidence 407
Equation Project IV- 8: Lift 408
Equation Project IV- 9: Leverage 409
Equation Project IV- 10: Zhang's Metric 411

Part I

The Basics

In this part, readers will be able to learn the basic of Python programming. , creating a foundation for general programming languages, which is applicable for programming in any language.

Chapter 1 Introduction : Readers learn to Install Python.Including Python packages, modules. and Code editor (Visual Studio Code).
Chapter 2 Data Types : Readers learn of data types defined in the Python programming language, among others.
Chapter 3 Lists/Dictionaries/Sets/Tuples : Python has lists, dictionaries, sets and tuples, all of which are used to define as much data as desired to be stored in a single

variable, making it possible to work with large amounts of data using just a few lines of code.

Chapter 4 Operators : In Python, operators are generally used perform operations on values and variables using for logical and mathematical operations.

Chapter 5 Conditional Statements : Conditional statements allow programmers to specify conditions that use the value of a variable or the result of a comparison to perform a desired statement. Python has a number of interesting techniques for using them.

Chapter 6 Functions : In this chapter, readers learn how to define and call functions, as well as pass and return data.

Chapter 7 Modules : Readers learn how to create their own modules and how to import other modules.

Chapter 8 String Formatting : Readers can use String formatting to format strtings within strings, causing variable values to be passed into the strings.

Chapter 9 Object-oriented programming (OOP) : Python is an object-oriented programming language. Readers will learn to create classes (with method or attributes), objects and relationships between classes (Inheritance, Association, Composition, and Aggregation)

Chapter 10 Try...Exception : Python has a try...exception that reader can use to easily catch errors.

Chapter 11 File Management, with...as and JSON : Reader will learn how to use functions for creating, reading, updating and deleting files,with..as, and to read and write JSON files.

Learn Python with Projects

Chapter 1
Introduction

Python is a popular programming language created by Guido van Rossum and launched in 1991. It can be used to build web applications, servers, in combination with other software to create workflows, connect to a relational database system that uses Structured Query Languages (SQLs) such as Oracle, DB2 or MySQL, as well as connect to non-relational database systems (NoSQL) such as MongoDB. This is explained in detail in the Advanced Python Programming Textbook.

Advantages of the Python language include:
1. Being able to handle a lot of data and perform complex mathematical calculations.
2. Rapid prototyping or development of production-ready software
3. Works on different OSs (Windows, Mac, Linux, Raspberry Pi, etc.)
4. Simple grammar similar to English, making it easy to program.
5. It contains syntax that allows programmers to write programs with a smaller number of lines compared to other programming languages.
6. Works on interpreter systems, so codes can be executed as soon as it is written, which means prototyping can be done quickly.
7. Able to act in a procedural, object-oriented or function-oriented manner.
8. Python uses a line break to complete a command, as opposed to other programming languages that often use semicolons or brackets. Relying on indents using spaces to define boundaries, such as loop boundaries, functions, and classes, other programming languages often use brackets for this purpose.

Installing Python
Many PCs and Macs have Python pre-installed. To check, launch the Terminal App on Mac, or Command Line on the PC and enter the command below.

For Mac or Linux OSs, go to the terminal, the console will appear to enter the command, with the host name appearing differently depending on the name defined. The author uses the name "VariitSris", so the following line of command will be displayed.

VaritSris>

To find out if the machine has Python installed and which version, use the following command:

VaritSris> python3 --version

Python 3.12.3

Note: For Windows operating systems, go to the Command Line and use the py --version command.

If not installed, go to:

https://www.python.org/downloads

To download the latest version of python according to your operating system, as shown in Figure 1- 1: download window for the latest version of python.

Figure 1- 1: download window for the latest version of python

Download the appropriate version for your operating system (in this example we will install on macOS) using the following steps:

1. Select macOS to download. You should receive file python-3.12.3-macos11.pkg. Double click the file. The result is shown in Figure 1-2.

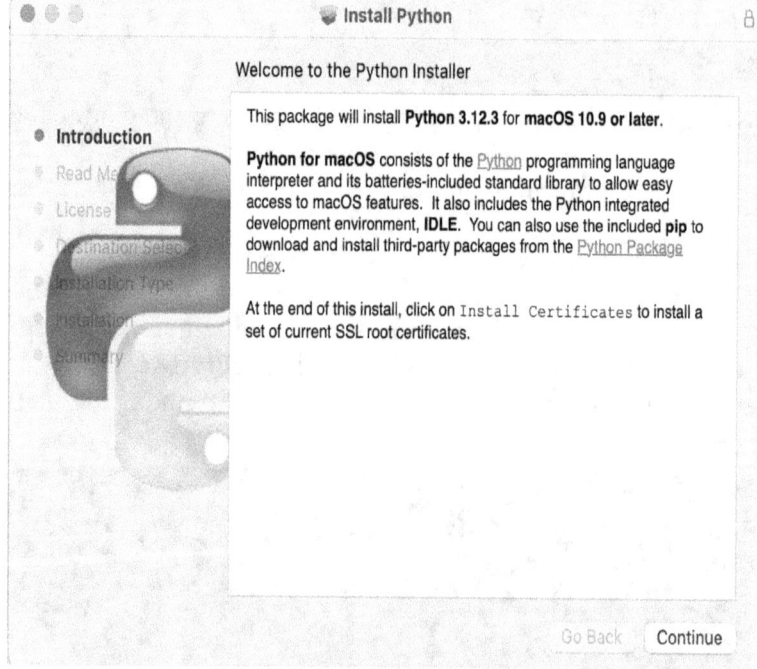

Figure 1- 2: 1st python installation window for macOS

2. Click `Continue`, result is shown as Figure 1-3.

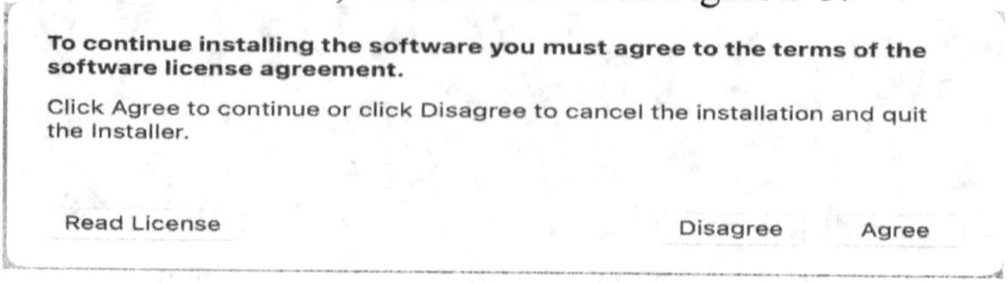

Figure 1- 3: 2nd Python installation window for macOS

3. Click Agree , result is shown as Figure 1-4.

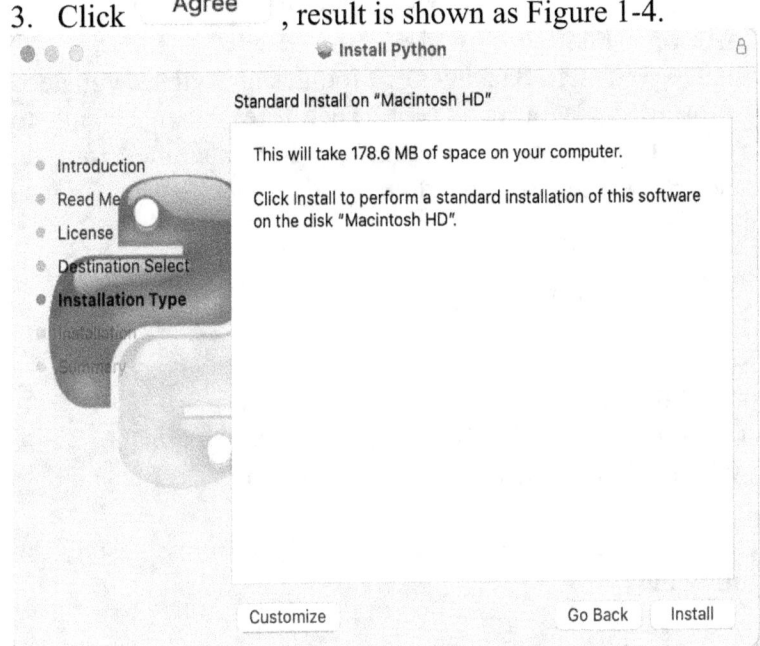

Figure 1- 4: 3rd python installation window for macOS

4. Click Install
5. You will find various files for programming with python. The result is shown as Figure 1-5.

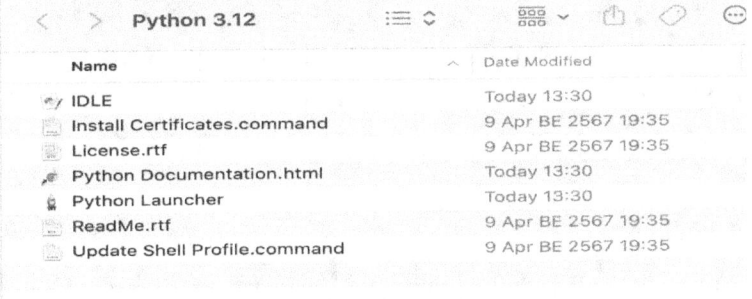

Figure 1- 5: folder showing installed python files

Now you are ready to program with python!

Installing Packages or Modules

To install Packages or Modules for Python, you need an installer program or "pip." Therefore, it is necessary to check if pip is already installed. For machines running macOS, Linux or Windows operating systems, use command:

> VaritSris>pip3 –version

Results
pip 24.0 from /Library/Frameworks/Python.framework/Versions/3.12/lib/python3.12/site-packages/pip (python 3.12)

If not, for Mac or Linux operating systems, install the following:

> VaritSris> python -m ensurepip –upgrade

> VaritSris>python get-pip.py

Note: For Windows operating systems, use py -m ensurepip –upgrade, then py get-pip.py

Installing a Package

After installing pip, try installing the "numpy" package

> VaritSris>pip3 install numpy

Results
Collecting numpy
 Downloading numpy-1.26.4-cp312-cp312-macosx_10_9_x86_64.whl.metadata (61 kB)
──────────────────────────────── 61.1/61.1 kB 1.2 MB/s eta 0:00:00

Learn Python with Projects

Downloading numpy-1.26.4-cp312-cp312-macosx_10_9_x86_64.whl (20.3 MB)

──────────────── 20.3/20.3 MB 6.0 MB/s eta 0:00:00

Installing collected packages: numpy
Successfully installed numpy-1.26.4
To check which packages or modules are installed, use the following command:

```
VaritSris>pip3 list
```

Results

```
Package    Version
-------    -------
numpy      1.26.4
pip        24.0
```

To use Terminal to program Python, follow these steps:

```
VaritSris>python3
```

Results

Python 3.12.3 (v3.12.3:f6650f9ad7, Apr 9 2024, 08:18:48)
[Clang 13.0.0 (clang-1300.0.29.30)] on darwin
Type "help", "copyright", "credits" or "license" for more information.

>>>

When using the command print('Hello')
>>> print('Hello')

Results

Hello

Program Python Using Visual Studio Code

To use visual studio code in programming python, go to the following link to download the appropriate installer, according to your operating system:

https://code.visualstudio.com/download

to download the appropriate installer, according to your operating system. Visual Studio Code is supported on Windows, Linux and Mac, as shown :

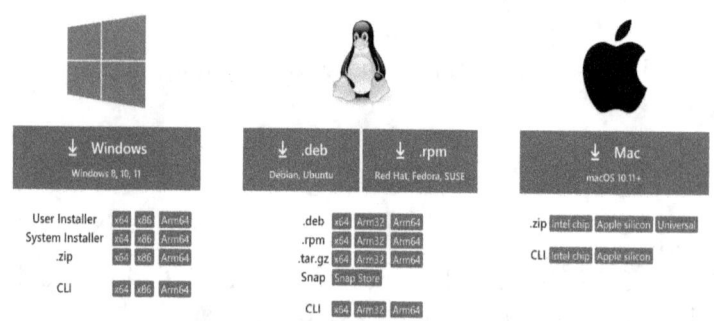

Figure 1- 6: Visual Studio Code Download Window

Click to download the appropriate installer and the installation file will be shown.

VSCode-darwin-....zip

Double click the downloaded file to show :

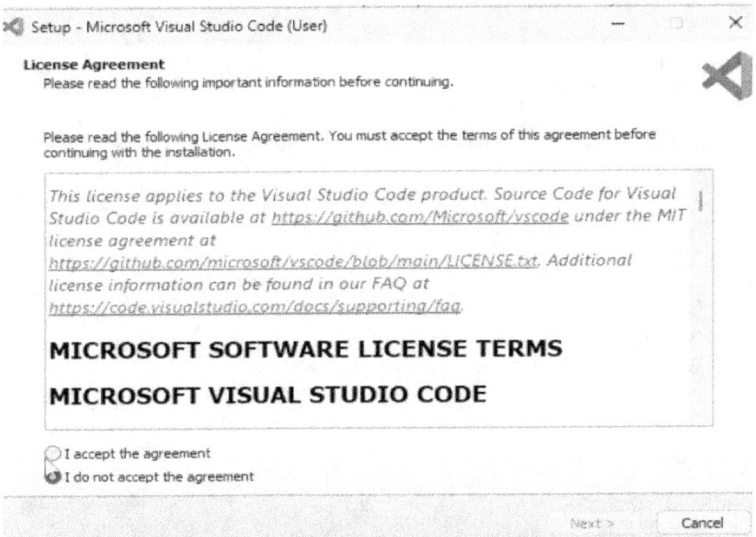

Figure 1- 7: 1st installation window of Visual Studio Code

Select `I accept the agreement` to allow the installation to begin, the next button should become visible. Click `Next >` To set the desired installation path for Visual Studio Code. In this case, you can use Microsoft's the default path: `C:\Users\appzs\AppData\Local\Programs\Microsoft VS Code`

click `Next >`. The result is shown as Figure 1-8.

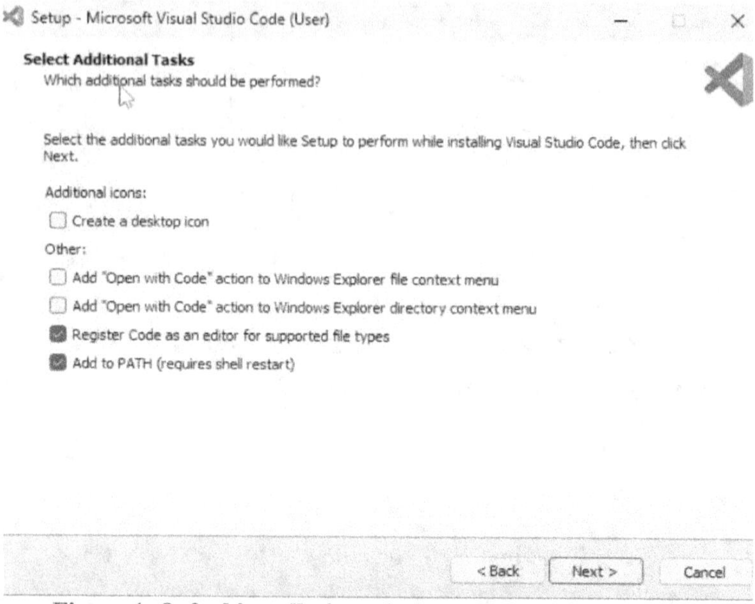

Figure 1-8: 2nd installation window of Visual Studio Code

Advantages of VS Code
1. The "IntelliSense" feature helps programmers by predicting what program code will be written in Python language. This is like having an assistant, making it easier for programmers to perform tasks such as entering code, show parameter information, quick information, member lists, variable names, and code hints, as well as clearly separating by colors that the programmer can adjust as desired (Color Themes).
2. Built-in Python debugging support makes editing programs easy.
3. It is open source and can be used free of charge.
4. Its Secure Shell (SSH) is designed for connecting to other computers within a network and is highly secure. Working with multiple machines and networks, will be discussed in detail in the Advanced Python Programming Textbook.

VSCODE Has its own terminal that runs python, so we need to create a work folder to keep all programming files. For this textbook, we will use the folder "ExamplePythonCode." Click VSCODE, 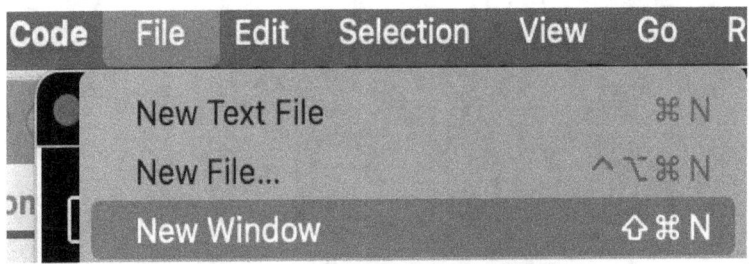 then File->New Window as show in Figure 1-9.

Figure 1- 9: Starting Visual Studio Code

And the following new window will appear in Figure 1-10.

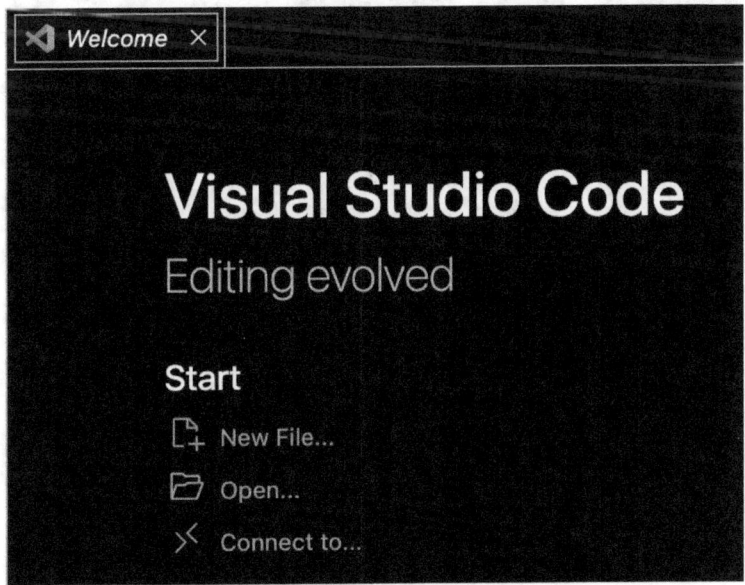

Figure 1- 10: Visual Studio Code Welcome Screen

Learn Python with Projects

Click open, then open the newly created folder used to keep our python files as in Figure 1-11.

Figure 1- 11: folder created to keep files for Python software development

Select and open the ExamplePythonCode folder and the following window will appear in Figure 1-12.

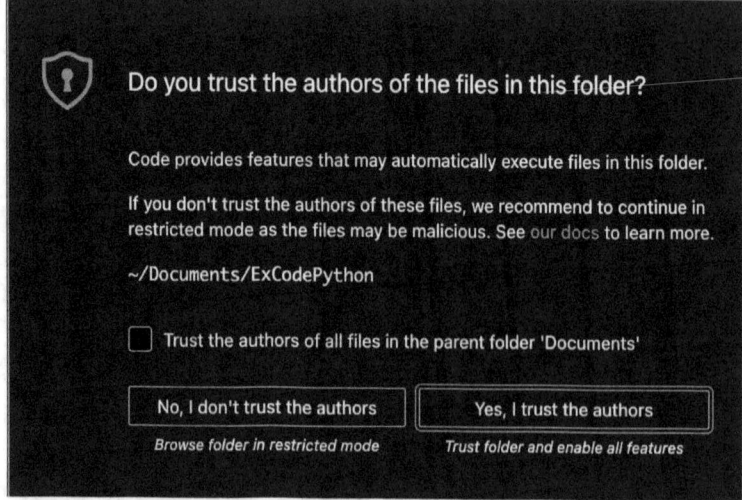

Figure 1- 12: Visual Studio Code asking for permission to use the folder

Choose **Yes, I trust the authors** to confirm that you trust the authors, since you created this folder yourself. When selected this screen will be shown in Figure 1-13.

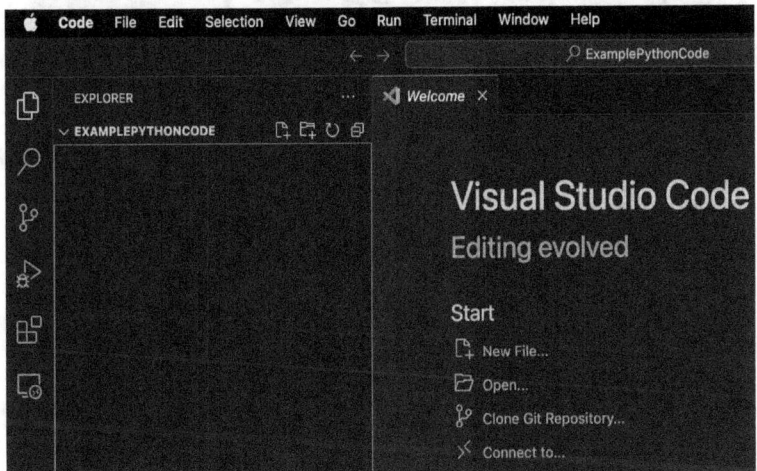

Figure 1- 13: Visual Studio Code starting window

A new menu, **Terminal**, will appear, and can be used instead of **>_** in Figure 1-14.

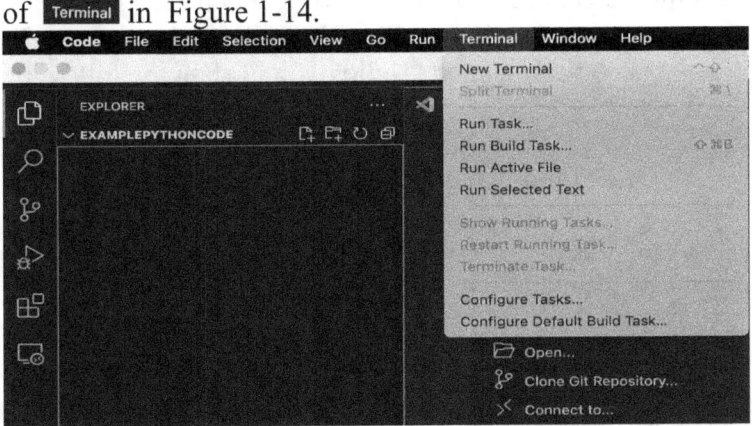

Figure 1- 14: Visual Studio Code menu

Then select "New terminal." A new terminal window will appear as shown in Figure 1-15.

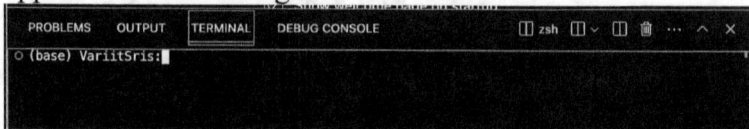

Figure 1- 15: Visual Studio Code terminal window

To write a program, click the space below EXAMPLEPYTHONCODE to reveal these icons in Figure 1-16.

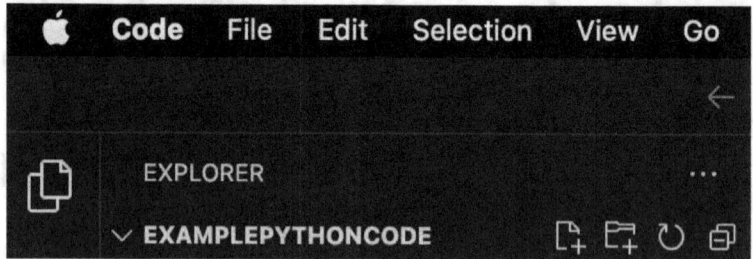

Figure 1- 16: Visual Studio Code menu bar

means creating a new file, while means creating a new folder under EXAMPLEPYTHONCODE. Start by creating a new file named "Hello.py" and enter the following instructions:

print("Hello "+input("What is your name?"))

Select File->Autosave in Figure 1-17, so that any changes are saved automatically.

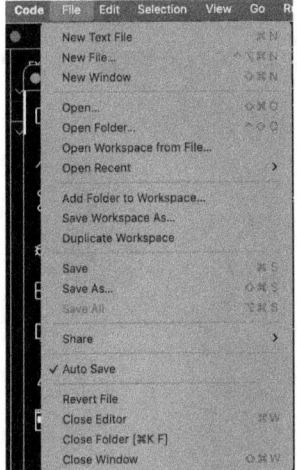

Figure 1- 17: Visual Studio Code file submenu

After that, select the terminal window and enter the following instructions:

VaritSris>python Hello.py

Results

What is your name?

Enter VariitSris

What is your name?VariitSris

Results

Hello VariitSris

The Code input('What is your name?') is using the text "What is your name?" To query its user to enter information. Changing the program text to

```
print("Welcome "+input("What is your name?")+ " to Thailand")
```

Then running Hello.py
```
    VaritSris>python3 hello.py
```

Results

What is your name? VariitSris

Results

Welcome VariitSris to Thailand

Example
```
print('No.of Character '+
str(len(input('What is your name? '))))
```

Results

What is your name? VariitSris

No.of Character 10

Example
```
name = "Jack"

print(name)

name = "Angela"

print(name)

name = input("What is your name?")

length = len(name)
```

print(length)

Results
   Jack
   Angela
   What is your name?VariitSris
   10

virtual environment

In case you want to use multiple versions of Python and mutiple projects on single machine
   The methods and steps for using a virtual environment vary according to different operating systems. For this textbook, let's use macOS as an example.
1. Install brew
   /bin/bash -c "$(curl -fsSL https://raw.githubusercontent.com/Homebrew/install/HEAD/install.sh)"
2. Update brew
   brew update
3. Install pyenv
   brew install pyenv
4. Install python. Required version for use in Part II, use python 3.9.16
   pyenv install 3.9.16
   Note :
   In case you want to develop other software projects that use packages or modules. If appropriate for your project, you must check which version of Python is appropriate and install to match that version.
5. Install pyenv-virtualenv
   brew install pyenv-virtualenv

Learn Python with Projects

6. Give the environment an appropriate name for your project so it is make easy to remember. For Part II, the environment names are set as follows.
   <u>Game</u>
   pyenv virtualenv 3.9.16 PyGame
   <u>Web Application</u>
   pyenv virtualenv 3.9.16 PyWebApp
   <u>Data Analysis</u>
   pyenv virtualenv 3.9.16 PyDataAnalysis
   <u>AI</u>
   pyenv virtualenv 3.9.16 PyAI
   The command used to create a virtual environment with python version is shown as follows.
   pyenv virtualenv <python_version> <environment_name>
7. To access that environment, use the command.
   pyenv activate <environment_name>
   If there is an error, it will show as follows.

   Failed to activate virtualenv.

   Perhaps pyenv-virtualenv has not been loaded into your shell properly.
   Please restart current shell and try again.

   Use the following command to resolve the error:
   eval "$(pyenv init -)"
   eval "$(pyenv virtualenv-init -)"
8. Check python version.
   Inside the environment.
   python –version
   <u>Result</u>
   Python 3.9.16
   Outside the environment.
   <u>Result</u>
   The `python' command exists in these Python versions:

Learn Python with Projects

   3.9.16
   3.9.16/envs/PyAI
   3.9.16/envs/PyDataAnalysis
   3.9.16/envs/PyGame
   3.9.16/envs/PyWebApp
   PyAI
   PyDataAnalysis
   PyGame
   PyWebApp

9. Exit environment.
   source deactivate

10. uninstall environment.
    pyenv uninstall <environment_name or python version>

Exercises

1. Show the results of running print("Hi,"+input("My name is "))
2. Write a program that queries the user's name and address, and displays the name and address of the user.

Chapter 2
Data Types

Python has the following Data Types:
- Integers
  Data that is any whole number, such as 342,456,2513
- Floats
  Data that is any numbers with decimal places, such as 1.2 or 3.54
- Strings
  Characters enclosing quotes, such as "What"
- Boolean
  Can only be True or False

- Lists/Dictionaries/Sets/Tuples
  (Examples and programming functions in Chapter 3)

To determine the correct data class that will function as such, you must use variables to configure the data class you need.

Integers

If you want to determine the number of students (NoOfStudent) as a whole number (integer) of 150, then program:
NoOfStudent = 150

Floats

If you want to determine the Student's Grade point average (GradeStudent) as a decimal (float) of 2.75, then Program:
GradeStudent = 2.75

In case of decimals within the data, it will not be added to the sum as integer data, so all data needs to be configured as float data.

For example:

    print(float(1.2)+float(3))

This will convert all data to Float first before running.

Results
    4.2

For example:

    print(float(1.2)+int(3.6))

This will combine the decimals of 1.2 with just the integer of 3.

Results
   4.2

   print(float(1.2)+float(3.6))

This will add all integer and decimal data between 1.2 and 3.6.
Results
   4.8

For examples of functions, refer to Table 2-1: Functions Used In Data Type Conversion For Python.

Table 2-1: Functions Used In Data Type Conversion For Python

Functions Used in Data Type Conversion for Python		
Function	Description	Example

int()	Make the value in brackets an integer, perform calculations with integers. Results in an integer value.	x=int(1.7)
		print(x)
		print(type(x))
		`1`
		`<class 'int'>`
		Where value in brackets is a whole number.

float()	Make the value in brackets a decimal, perform calculations with decimals. Results in a decimal value.	x=float(5)
		print(x)
		print(type(x))
		`5.0`
		`<class 'float'>`
		Where values in brackets is decimal.

Functions Used in Data Type Conversion for Python

Function	Description	Example

str()	Make the value in brackets a String. Display results as a character.	x=str(5)
		print(x)
		print(type(x))
		`5`
		`<class 'str'>`

bool()	Make the value in brackets Boolean	x= bool("test")
		print(x)
		print(type(x))
		`True`
		`<class 'bool'>`
		num= bool(1034)
		print(num)
		print(type(num))
		`True`
		`<class 'bool'>`
		list= bool(["apple", "cherry", "banana"])
		print(list)
		print(type(list))
		`True`
		`<class 'bool'>`
		`False` values are
		bool(False)
		bool(None)
		bool(0)
		bool("")
		bool(())
		bool([])
		bool({})

Strings
In case of String Class Data
Determine the student's name (StudentName) as Character strings by using quotation marks. either "" or ' ' will work.

StudentName ='Jane' or StudentName ="Jane"

String Functions
String values have the following functions:
print("What"[0]) Results: W
print("What"[2]) Results: a
print("12"+"34") Results 1234 (as a string)

We can also find the number of characters in the string:

num_char = len(input("What is your name? "))

print("Your name has "+str(num_char)+" characters.")

Results
What is your name? VariitSris
Your name has 10 characters.

We can combine string values, but if the value is not a string value but an integer, you convert its class into string like this:

num_char = len(input("What is your name? "))

print(type(num_char))

print("Your name has "+str(num_char)+" characters.")

Results
What is your name? VariitSris
<class 'int'>
Your name has 10 characters.

print(str(1.2)+str(3)) to convert values to string

Results
    1.23

Boolean

Boolean has a value of True or False only, as in the example.

Finding a value in a string whether it exists or not. If there is a result, it will be True, if it is not there, it will be False.

> sentence = "Anna is beautiful girl"
>
> print("Anna" in sentence)
>
> Result
> True

> sentence = "Anna is beautiful girl"
>
> print("Jane" not in sentence)
>
> Result
> True
> For examples of functions, refer to

Table 2-2: Frequently Functions Used in String Type Data for Pytho

Table 2- 2: Frequently Functions Used in String Type Data for Python

Frequently Functions Used in String Type Data for Python		
Function	Description	Example
capitalize()	Capitalizes first character	sentence = "anna is a beautiful girl" print(sentence.capitalize()) Results Anna is a beautiful girl
casefold()	Make all characters lowercase	sentence = "aNNa Is a beaUtiful Girl" print(sentence.casefold()) Results anna is a beautiful girl
center()	Centers all characters according to the number of characters in brackets.	sentence = "Anna is beautiful " print(sentence.center(40)) Results Anna is beautiful

Frequently Functions Used in String Type Data for Python		
Function	**Description**	**Example**
count()	Find the number of words or letters in brackets of a string	sentence = "Anna is a beautiful girl. " print(sentence.count("a")) Results 3
		sentence = "Anna is a beautiful girl. She has a child. She has two dogs." print(sentence.count("has")) Results 2
		sentence = "Anna is a beautiful girl. She likes to eat bananas. And likes to give bananas to her friends. She grows bananas in her garden" print(sentence.count("a")) Results 14
		sentence = "Anna is a beautiful girl. She likes to eat bananas,

Frequently Functions Used in String Type Data for Python		
Function	**Description**	**Example**
		and likes to give bananas to her friends. She grows bananas in her garden" print(sentence.count("bananas")) Results 3
endswith()	Find out if the end of a string includes words enclosed in brackets at the end of the string. If there is, the result is True. If not, False is displayed.	Find if the value "sentence" ends with ".". sentence = "Anna is a beautiful girl. She likes to eat bananas, and likes to give bananas to her friends. She grows bananas in her garden" print(sentence.endswith(".")) Results False

Frequently Functions Used in String Type Data for Python		
Function	**Description**	**Example**
		sentence = "Anna is a beautiful girl. She likes to eat bananas, and likes to give bananas to her friends. She grows bananas in her garden" print(sentence.endswith("her garden")) Results True
expandtabs()	Set the space as defined in the brackets of the string.	Set the space as defined in the brackets of the string, using \t between spaces (tab) sentence = "Anna\tis\ta\tbeautiful\tgirl." print(sentence.expandtabs(2)) Results Anna is a beautiful girl

Frequently Functions Used in String Type Data for Python

Function	Description	Example
find()	Searches for value enclosed in brackets, if found, returns a return value. The first position in the string is 0 until all the letters in the string are checked. Works like index(), except that if not found, -1 is returned.	Finds a value enclosed in brackets, The first position in the string is 0. sentence = "Anna is a beautiful girl. She likes to eat bananas, and likes to give bananas to her friends. She grows bananas in her garden." findPosition = sentence.find("A") print(findPosition) Results 0
		sentence = "Anna is a beautiful girl. She likes to eat bananas. And likes to give bananas to her friends. She grows bananas in her garden." findPosition = sentence.find("She") print(findPosition) Results

Learn Python with Projects

Frequently Functions Used in String Type Data for Python		
Function	Description	Example
		26 First found in position 26. sentence = "Anna is a beautiful girl. She likes to eat bananas, and likes to give bananas to her friends. She grows bananas in her garden." findPosition = sentence.find("xxx") print(findPosition) Results -1

Frequently Functions Used in String Type Data for Python		
Function	Description	Example
index()	Searches for value enclosed in brackets, if found, returns a return value. The first position in the string is 0 until all the letters in the string are checked. Works like find(), except that if not found, error is returned.	Finds a value enclosed in brackets, The first position in the string is 0. sentence = "Anna is a beautiful girl. She likes to eat bananas. And likes to give bananas to her friends. She grows bananas in her garden." indexPosition = sentence.index("A") print(indexPosition) Results 0 sentence = "Anna is a beautiful girl. She likes to eat bananas, and likes to give bananas to her friends. She grows bananas in her garden." indexPosition = sentence.index("She ") print(indexPosition)

Frequently Functions Used in String Type Data for Python

Function	Description	Example
		Results 26 First found in position 26. sentence = "Anna is a beautiful girl. She likes to eat bananas, and likes to give bananas to her friends. She grows bananas in her garden." indexPosition = sentence.index("xxx") print(indexPosition) Returns Results ValueError: substring not found

Frequently Functions Used in String Type Data for Python		
Function	Description	Example
format()	Format decimal places. e.g.: .2f, displays 2 decimal places, rounded up. .0f displays an integer.	To display the amount decimal value, sentence = "Yesterday, Anna bought bananas for {amount:.2f} baht." print(sentence.format(amount=50)) Results Yesterday, Anna bought bananas for 50.00 baht. If the next decimal is 5 or more, it will round up. 50.558 rounds to 50.56 sentence = "Yesterday, Anna bought bananas for {price:.2f} baht." print(sentence.format(price=50.558)) Results Yesterday, Anna bought bananas for 50.56 baht.

Learn Python with Projects

Frequently Functions Used in String Type Data for Python		
Function	Description	Example
		to add comma separators, use ,.2f sentence = "Yesterday, Anna bought bananas for {price:,.2f} baht." print(sentence.format(price=12250.558))

Learn Python with Projects

Frequently Functions Used in String Type Data for Python		
Function	Description	Example
		Results Yesterday, Anna bought bananas for 12,250.56 baht. You can also add currency signs in front sentence = "Yesterday, Anna bought bananas for ${price:,.2f} baht." print(sentence.format(price=12250.558)) Results Yesterday, Anna bought bananas for $12,250.56 baht.
isalnum()	If all the characters in a string are alphanumeric, meaning alphabet letter (a-z) and numbers (0-9), returns True.	sentence = "Yesterday, Anna bought bananas for 50 baht." print(sentence.isalnum()) Results False Since it includes space, "," and "."

Frequently Functions Used in String Type Data for Python		
Function	Description	Example
		sentence = "YesterdayAnnaboughtbananasfor50baht" print(sentence.isalnum()) Results True
isalpha()	If all the characters in a string are alphabet letters (a-z)(A-Z) only, returns True.	sentence = "Yesterday, Anna bought bananas for 50 baht." print(sentence.isalpha()) Results False Since it includes space, "," and "." sentence = "YesterdayAnnaboughtbananasfor50baht" print(sentence.isalpha()) Results False Since it includes the number 50

Frequently Functions Used in String Type Data for Python		
Function	Description	Example
		sentence = "YesterdayAnnaboughtbananasforbaht" print(sentence.isalpha()) Results True
isdecimal()	If all the characters in a string are decimals only, returns True.	sentence = "Yesterday, Anna bought bananas for 50 baht." print(sentence.isdecimal()) Results False not decimal sentence = "3341341" print(sentence.isdecimal()) Results True
isdigit()	If all the characters in a string are digits only, returns True.	sentence = "Yesterday, Anna bought bananas for 50 baht." print(sentence.isdigit())

Frequently Functions Used in String Type Data for Python

Function	Description	Example
	Note: Digits are values with numbers 0, 1, 2, 3, 4, 5, 6, 7, 8, 9 in a string. e.g. 25, 45672 etc.	Results False Not a Digit sentence = "3341341" print(sentence.isdigit()) Results True sentence = "33,413.41" print(sentence.isdigit()) Results False Not all digits. contains "," and "."
islower()	If all the characters in a string are lowercase only, returns True.	sentence = "Yesterday, Anna bought bananas for 50 baht." print(sentence.islower()) Results False

Frequently Functions Used in String Type Data for Python		
Function	Description	Example
		Contains Uppercase Y and A sentence = "yesterday, anna bought bananas for 50 baht." print(sentence.islower()) <u>Results</u> True sentence = "33,413.41" print(sentence.islower()) <u>Results</u> False Numbers cannot be lowercase
isupper()	If all the characters in a string are uppercase only, returns True.	sentence = "Yesterday, Anna bought bananas for 50 baht." print(sentence.isupper()) <u>Results</u> False Contains Uppercase Y and A

Frequently Functions Used in String Type Data for Python		
Function	Description	Example
		sentence = "yesterday, anna bought bananas for 50 baht." print(sentence.isupper()) Results False sentence = "YESTERDAY, ANNA" print(sentence.isupper()) Results True
upper()	Change all character in string to uppercase	sentence = "Yesterday, Anna bought bananas for 50 baht." print(sentence.upper()) Results YESTERDAY, ANNA BOUGHT BANANAS FOR 50 BAHT.

Frequently Functions Used in String Type Data for Python		
Function	Description	Example
isnumeric()	If all the characters in a string are numeric only, returns True. Note: Numeric are values with numbers 0, 1, 2, 3, 4, 5, 6, 7, 8, 9 in a string. e.g. 25, 45672 etc.	sentence = "Yesterday, Anna bought bananas for 50 baht." print(sentence.isnumeric()) Results False sentence = "3451" print(sentence.isnumeric()) Results True sentence = "-33,413.41" print(sentence.isnumeric()) Results False Contains "-", "," and "."
isprintable()	If all the characters in a string are printable only, returns True.	sentence = "Yesterday, Anna bought bananas for 50 baht." print(sentence.isprintable())

Frequently Functions Used in String Type Data for Python		
Function	Description	Example
		Results True sentence = "Yesterday, \n Anna bought bananas for 50 baht." print(sentence.isprintable()) Results False Contains \n, a character for creating a new line. sentence = "Yesterday, \n Anna bought bananas for 50 baht." print(sentence) Results Yesterday, Anna bought bananas for 50 baht.
isspace()	If all the characters in a string are spaces only, returns True.	sentence = "Yesterday, Anna bought bananas for 50 baht." print(sentence.isspace())

Frequently Functions Used in String Type Data for Python		
Function	Description	Example
		Results False sentence = " " print(sentence.isspace()) Results True
istitle()	If all words in a text start with an uppercase letter, AND the rest of the word are lower case letters, returns True.	sentence = "Yesterday, Anna Bought Bananas For 50 Baht." print(sentence.istitle()) Results True sentence = "YESTERDAY, Anna bought bananas for 50 baht." print(sentence.istitle()) Results False

Frequently Functions Used in String Type Data for Python		
Function	Description	Example
title()	Capitalize all words in the string.	sentence = "Yesterday, Anna bought bananas for 50 baht." print(sentence.title()) Results Yesterday, Anna Bought Bananas For 50 Baht.
lower()	Change all characters in string to lowercase.	sentence = "Yesterday, Anna bought bananas for 50 baht." print(sentence.lower()) Results yesterday, anna bought bananas for 50 baht.

Frequently Functions Used in String Type Data for Python		
Function	Description	Example
replace()	Find and replace instances of a word in string.	sentence = "Yesterday, Anna bought bananas for 50 baht." print(sentence.replace("bananas", "apples")) Results Yesterday, Anna bought apples for 50 baht. sentence = "Anna is beautiful girl. She likes to eat bananas. And likes to give bananas to her friends. She grows bananas in her garden." print(sentence.replace("bananas", "apples",1)) Results Anna is a beautiful girl. She likes to eat apples, and likes to give bananas to her friends. She grows

Frequently Functions Used in String Type Data for Python		
Function	Description	Example
		bananas in her garden.

Replace only the first instance by adding ,1 |
| rfind() | From the rightmost, finds the last occurrence of the specified value in a string. Returns -1 if the value is not found. | sentence = "Anna is a beautiful girl. She likes to eat bananas. And likes to give bananas to her friends. She grows bananas in her garden."
print(sentence.rfind("bananas"))

<u>Results</u>
104
sentence = "Anna is a beautiful girl. She likes to eat bananas. And likes to give bananas to her friends. She grows bananas in her garden." |

Frequently Functions Used in String Type Data for Python		
Function	Description	Example
		print(sentence.rfind("apples")) Results -1 Returns -1 if the value is not found sentence = "Anna is a beautiful girl. She likes to eat bananas. And likes to give bananas to her friends. She grows bananas in her garden." print(sentence.rfind("bananas",50,100)) to search between 50 and 100 Results 70
rindex()	From the rightmost, finds the last occurrence of the specified value in a string. Functionally identical to	Finds the last occurrence of the specified value. sentence = "Anna is a beautiful girl. She likes to eat bananas. And likes to give bananas to her

Frequently Functions Used in String Type Data for Python		
Function	Description	Example
	rfind(), but returns "ValueError: substring not found" instead if the value is not found.	friends. She grows bananas in her garden." indexPosition = sentence.rindex("A") print(indexPosition) Results 52 sentence = "Anna is beautiful girl. She likes to eat bananas. And likes to give bananas to her friends. She grows bananas in her garden." indexPosition = sentence.rindex("She ") print(indexPosition) Results 94 Found in last position 94. sentence = "Anna is a beautiful girl. She likes to eat bananas. And likes to give bananas to her

Frequently Functions Used in String Type Data for Python		
Function	Description	Example
		friends. She grows bananas in her garden." indexPosition = sentence.rindex("xxx") print(indexPosition) Returns Results ValueError: substring not found
split()	Split words in a string.	sentence = "Anna is a beautiful girl. She likes to eat bananas. And likes to give bananas to her friends. She grows bananas in her garden." splitSentence = sentence.split() print(splitSentence) Results ['Anna', 'is', 'a', 'beautiful', 'girl.', 'She', 'likes', 'to', 'eat', 'bananas,', 'and', 'likes', 'to', 'give', 'bananas', 'to', 'her', 'friends.',

Frequently Functions Used in String Type Data for Python		
Function	Description	Example
		'She', 'grows', 'bananas', 'in', 'her', 'garden.']
splitlines()	Split lines in a string. requires /n to create line breaks.	sentence = "Anna is a beautiful girl. \nShe likes to eat bananas. And likes to give bananas to her friends. \nShe grows bananas in her garden." splitLinesSentence = sentence.splitlines() print(splitLinesSentence) Results ['Anna is a beautiful girl.', 'She likes to eat bananas, and likes to give bananas to her friends.', 'She grows bananas in her garden.']

Frequently Functions Used in String Type Data for Python		
Function	Description	Example
startswith()	Check if The value in brackets is the first value of the string.	Check if "Hello" is the first value of the string. sentence = "Anna is a beautiful girl. \nShe likes to eat bananas. And likes to give bananas to her friends. \nShe grows bananas in her garden." startswithSentence = sentence.startswith(" Hello") print(startswithSentence) Results False sentence = "Anna is a beautiful girl. \nShe likes to eat bananas. And likes to give bananas to her friends. \nShe grows bananas in her garden." startswithSentence = sentence.startswith(" Anna") print(startswithSentence)

Frequently Functions Used in String Type Data for Python		
Function	Description	Example
		Results True sentence = "Anna is a beautiful girl. \nShe likes to eat bananas. And likes to give bananas to her friends. \nShe grows bananas in her garden." startswithSentence = sentence.startswith(" Anna is a beautiful") print(startswithSente nce) Results True
strip()	Remove spaces at the beginning and at the end of the string before combining with other string values.	Remove spaces at the beginning and at the end of the string. fruit = " bananas " print(fruit.strip()) sentence="She likes to eat "+fruit.strip()+". And likes to give "+fruit.strip()+" to her friends."

Frequently Functions Used in String Type Data for Python		
Function	Description	Example
		print(sentence) Results bananas She likes to eat bananas. And likes to give bananas to her friends.
rstrip()	Remove any spaces at the end of the stringbefore combining with other string values.	fruit = " bananas " print(fruit.rstrip()) sentence="She likes to eat "+fruit.rstrip()+". And likes to give "+fruit.rstrip()+" to her friends." print(sentence) Results ....bananas She likes to eat bananas. And likes to give bananas to her friends.

Frequently Functions Used in String Type Data for Python		
Function	Description	Example
swapcase()	Swap uppercase characters with lowercase, and vice versa.	sentence = "Yesterday, Anna bought bananas for 50 baht." print(sentence.swapcase()) Results yESTERDAY, aNNA BOUGHT BANANAS FOR 50 BAHT.
zfill()	adds 0 at the beginning of the number, until it reaches the length Specified in brackets.	To add 0 In front of the number 20 to reach the length specified, which is 5 digits sentence = "20" print(sentence.zfill(5)) Results 00020

Exercises

1. 23.42 is what python data type?
2. "I love Thailand." is what python data type?
3. What python data type has the value "true"?
4. What value is returned with: print(int(4.3)+int(3.5))? What data type is it?
5. Write a program to display 'a' from the string "How are U?"

   information = "Where is the best place in Thailand?"

6. Write a program to display the "information" string but all uppercase.
7. Write a program to count all the 'e's in the "information" string.
8. Write a program to find 'place' in the "information" string.

   BKKPeople = "In 2016, Bangkok had an estimated population of 9 million according to data from the 2010 census."

9. write a program to display the estimated population as 8.28 million
10. Write a program to split all the words in the "BKKPeople" string.

Chapter 3
Lists, Dictionaries, Sets, Tuples

Lists

A **List** is what python uses instead of arrays to store multiple values, sorted alphabetically in ascending order, in a single variable that can change values and store repeating values.

One syntax for creating a list is Syntax 3-1.

Syntax 3-1: Create Lists 1

```
ListName = [value₁, value₂,...,valueₙ]

Note
    N is number of value in List.
```

To store multiple fruits (fruit) including "Orange, Apple, Mango, Mangosteen, Rambutan, Durian, Pineapple, Papaya" in a single variable as a list, proceed as follows:

fruit = ["orange","mango","mangosteen","rambutan", "durian", "pineapple","papaya"]
print(fruit)

Results
['orange', 'mango', 'mangosteen', 'rambutan', 'durian', 'pineapple', 'papaya']

Using the data kept in the list requires an index number, starting with the number 0, followed by 1, 2, 3, up until the last index. The syntax for index number of element in List is Syntax 0-1.

Syntax 3-2: Index number of element in List

```
listname=[listname[0],listname[1],listname[2],...,
         listname[len(listname)-1]]
```

Example
print(fruit[0])

Results
orange

print(fruit[1])

Results
mango

If you want the last index value in the list, we need to know the total number of items in a list with this function: len(List)

Example
print(len(fruit))

Results
7

Therefore, if you want to return the last value in the list, then we need to use **fruit[6]** as the last value is always len(List)-1 with the first index being 0.
In case you don't want to search with len(List), alternatively we could use negative indexes, with -1 as the last index as shown in Syntax 3-3.

Syntax 3-3: Negative index of element in List

```
listname=[listname[-len(listname)],....,listname[-2],listname[-1]]
```

print(fruit[-1])

Results
papaya
If the index is -3, it will return the 3rd item from the end.

print(fruit[-3])

Results
durian
For functions, refer to .

Table 3-1: Functions Used in Lists for Python.

Functions Used in Lists for Python		
Function	**Description**	**Example**
append()	Append the new value at the end of the list. Duplicates can only be added one value at a time.	fruit = ["orange","mango","mangosteen","rambutan","durian","pineapple","papaya"] fruit.append("strawberry") print(fruit) Results ['orange', 'mango', 'mangosteen', 'rambutan', 'durian', 'pineapple', 'papaya', 'strawberry']
clear()	Clear the list. No values kept.	Clear the "fruit" list of all values. fruit = ["orange","mango","mangosteen","rambutan","durian","pineapple","papaya"] fruit.clear() print(fruit) Results []

Functions Used in Lists for Python		
Function	Description	Example
copy()	Copy the list and submit the value.	Copy "fruit" with "copy_fruit" fruit = ["orange","mango","mangosteen","rambutan","durian","pineapple","papaya"] copy_fruit=fruit.copy() print(copy_fruit) Results ['orange', 'mango', 'mangosteen', 'rambutan', 'durian', 'pineapple', 'papaya', 'strawberry']
count()	Count the number of times a value is in the list and submit the result.	Count the number of "cherry" in the "fruit" list fruit = ["orange","mango","mangosteen","rambutan","durian","pineapple","papaya"] NoOfCherry = fruit.count("cherry") print(NoOfCherry) Results 0

Functions Used in Lists for Python		
Function	**Description**	**Example**
extend()	Add the values from one list to another.	Extend the values in the "fruit" list With the values in "chineseFruit" fruit = ["orange","mango","mangosteen", "rambutan","durian","pineapple", "papaya"] chineseFruit = ["loquat","lychee"] fruit.extend(chineseFruit) print(fruit)
extend()		Results ['orange', 'mango', 'mangosteen', 'rambutan', 'durian', 'pineapple', 'papaya', 'strawberry', 'loquat', 'lychee']
index()	Returns Index number of a value.	Find the index of value "mango" fruit = ["orange","mango","mangosteen", "rambutan","durian","pineapple", "papaya"] indexOfMango=fruit.index("mango") print(indexOfMango) Results 1

Functions Used in Lists for Python		
Function	**Description**	**Example**
insert()	Insert a value into a list by specifying its index number.	Add "strawberry" as the first value in the list. fruit = ["orange","mango","mangosteen", "rambutan","durian","pineapple", "papaya"] fruit.insert(0, "strawberry") print(fruit) Results ['strawberry', 'orange', 'mango', 'mangosteen', 'rambutan', 'durian', 'pineapple', 'papaya']
pop()	Removes a value from the list using its index.	To remove the value indexed as 0, "orange" from the "fruit" list. fruit = ["orange","mango","mangosteen", "rambutan","durian","pineapple", "papaya"] fruit.pop(0) print(fruit) Results ['mango', 'mangosteen', 'rambutan', 'durian', 'pineapple', 'papaya']

Functions Used in Lists for Python		
Function	**Description**	**Example**
remove()	Removes the specified value from the list.	To remove the value "orange" from the list fruit = ["orange","mango","mangosteen", "rambutan","durian","pineapple","papaya"] fruit.remove("orange") print(fruit) Results ['mango', 'mangosteen', 'rambutan', 'durian', 'pineapple', 'papaya']
sort()	Sort the values alphabetically or numerically in ascending order.	Tube the values alphabetically in ascending order of fruit list: fruit = ["orange","mango","mangosteen", "rambutan","durian", "pineapple","papaya"] fruit.sort() print(fruit)
		Results ['durian','mango', 'mangosteen','orange','papaya', 'pineapple', 'rambutan'] If the values within the list have multiple languages, upper and lowercase, as well as numbers, the values will be sorted by numbers value, then all the uppercase values, then all lowercase values, and

65

Functions Used in Lists for Python		
Function	**Description**	**Example**
		finally any other languages. listSort = ["orange","mango", "mangosteen", "Apple","Tomato", "Peach","5","4","2", "6"] listSort.sort() print(listSort) Results ['2', '4', '5', '6', 'Apple', 'Peach', 'Tomato', 'mango', 'mangosteen', 'orange']
join()	Join the values in the list and display.	to display values in the fruit list separated by / fruit = ["orange","mango","mangosteen", "rambutan","durian","pineapple","papaya"] print("/".join(fruit)) Results orange/mango/mangosteen/rambutan/durian/pineapple/papaya

To combine two lists together, use syntax 3-4.

Syntax 3-4: Combining Two Lists

```
ListName₁ = [ListName₁[0],ListName₁[1],...,
           ListName₁[len₁-1]]
ListName₂ = [ListName₂[0],ListName₂[1],...,ListName₂[len₂-1]]
ListName₃ = [ListName₁, ListName₂]
                        Results
ListName₃ = [[ListName₁[0],ListName₁[1],...,
           ListName₁[len₁-1]],[ListName₂[0],ListName₂[1],...,
           ListName₂[len₂-1]]
Note
• len1 is number of value in ListName1
• len2 is number of value in ListName2
• Number of value in ListName3 is len1 + len2
```

Example:
fruit = ["orange","mango","mangosteen","rambutan", "durian","pineapple", "papaya"]
vegetable = ["tomato","avocado","bean","pepper", "pumpkin"]
plant = [fruit,vegctable]
print(plant)

Results
[['orange', 'mango', 'mangosteen', 'rambutan', 'durian', 'pineapple', 'papaya'], ['tomato', 'avocado', 'bean', 'pepper', 'pumpkin']]

Another way to create lists is with Syntax 3-5.

Syntax 3-5: Create Lists 2

```
ListName = list((value₁, value₂,...,valueₙ))

Note
  N is number of value in List
```

Example:
fruit = list(("orange","mango","mangosteen","rambutan","durian", "pineapple", "papaya"))
print(fruit)

Results
['orange', 'mango', 'mangosteen', 'rambutan', 'durian', 'pineapple', 'papaya']

Dictionaries
Dictionaries in Python are data kept in pairs, using the syntax key:value, as shown in Syntax 3-6.

Syntax 3-6: Create Dictionaries

DictionaryName={'key$_1$':'value$_1$','key$_2$':'value$_2$',..., 'key$_N$':'value$_N$'}

Note
N is number of value in Dictionary

Dictionaries are useful in collecting related data, such as student name and gender, and using the same indexes to call the related data in a database. They're written using curly braces {} separated by colons.
student_gender = {'Ammy':'Female','Jame':'Male','Mike':'Male','Minnie':'Female'}
print(student_gender)
print(student_gender['Jame'])

Results
{'Ammy': 'Female', 'Jame': 'Male', 'Mike': 'Male', 'Minnie': 'Female'}
Male

In case of student age:
student_age = {'Ammy':'16','Jame':'12','Mike':'17','Minnie':'14'}
print(student_age)
print(student_age['Jame'])

Note that key values cannot repeat. If it does, then only the last key and value will be referenced.
For example:
student_age = {'Ammy':'16','Jame':'12','Mike':'17','Minnie':'14', 'Minnie':'18','Minnie':'19'}
print(student_age)
print(student_age['Minnie'])

Results
{'Ammy': '16', 'Jame': '12', 'Mike': '17', 'Minnie': '19'}
19
And since duplicate keys do not count, the len command will result as:
print(len(student_age))

Results
4

We can, however, store a list of values within the same key, for example, to store a student's name, age, then a list grades in three years:
student = {'Name':'Jame','Age':18,'Grade':['A','C','F']}
print(student)
print(student['Grade'])

Results
{'Name': 'Jame', 'Age': 18, 'Grade': ['A', 'C', 'F']}
['A', 'C', 'F']
To show their first-year grade:
print(student['Grade'][0])

Results
A

For functions, refer to Table 3- 2: Functions Used in Dictionaries for Python

Table 3- 2: Functions Used in Dictionaries for Python

Functions Used in Dictionaries for Python		
Function	Description	Example
clear()	Clears the dictionary. No values kept.	student=dict(Name = "Jame", Age = 18, Grade =['A','C','F']) print(student) student.clear() print(student) Results {'Name': 'Jame', 'Age': 18, 'Grade': ['A', 'C', 'F']} {}

Sets

Sets in Python are multiple items stored under a single variable. Items <u>cannot</u> be repeated, are randomly ordered and <u>cannot</u> be changed. To create a set, use Syntax 3-7.

Syntax 3-7: Create Sets

> SetName = {value$_1$, value$_2$, value$_3$,...,value$_N$}
> **Note**
> N is number of value in Set

```
student={'Ammie','Ann','Minnie','Jame','Mike','Ann'}
print(student)
```

Results
{'Minnie', 'Ann', 'Jame', 'Ammie', 'Mike'}

For functions, refer to Table 3-3: Functions Used in Sets for Python 3-3.

Table 3-3: Functions Used in Sets for Python

Functions Used in Sets for Python		
Function	Description	Example
add()	Add values into the set must be a value not already contained in the set, otherwise it will not be added.	fruit = {"apple","banana", "cherry","orange", "mango","mangosteen","rambutan","durian", "pineapple", "papaya"} fruit.add("papaya") print(fruit) Results {'cherry', 'mango', 'rambutan', 'papaya', 'banana', 'apple', 'mangosteen', 'durian', 'pineapple', 'orange'}

Functions Used in Sets for Python		
Function	**Description**	**Example**
		fruit = {"apple","banana","cherry","orange", "mango", "mangosteen", "rambutan", "durian", "pineapple", "papaya"} fruit.add("strawberry") print(fruit) Results {'orange', 'durian', 'mango', 'banana', 'strawberry', 'pineapple', 'cherry', 'papaya', 'apple', 'rambutan', 'mangosteen'}
clear()	Clear the set of all values.	fruit = {"apple","banana","cherry","orange", "mango","mangosteen","rambutan","durian", "pineapple","papaya","papaya"} fruit.clear() print(fruit) Results set()
copy()	Copy the set.	fruit = {"apple","banana","cherry","orange", "mango","mangosteen","rambutan","durian", "pineapple","papaya","papaya"} Copy_fruit=fruit.copy() print(Copy_fruit) Results

Functions Used in Sets for Python

Function	Description	Example
		{'mango', 'papaya', 'durian', 'cherry', 'banana', 'pineapple', 'rambutan', 'orange', 'apple', 'mangosteen'}
difference()	Display the differences between two sets.	interfruit = {"apple","banana","cherry","orange", "mango", "mangosteen", "rambutan", "durian", "pineapple", "papaya","papaya"} Thaifruit = {"banana","orange","mango", "mangosteen", "rambutan", "durian", "pineapple", "papaya"} print(interfruit.difference(Thaifruit)) <u>Results</u> {'cherry', 'apple'} Since the interfruit set has apple, cherry, Which does not appear in Thaifruit, whereas print(Thaifruit.difference(interfruit)) <u>Results</u> set() Since all fruits in Thaifruit are in interfruit.

Functions Used in Sets for Python

Function	Description	Example
difference_update()	Show the different values between two sets. Differences will be cleared.	interfruit = {"apple","banana", "cherry","orange", "mango", "mangosteen", "rambutan","durian", "pineapple", "papaya","papaya"} Thaifruit = {"banana","orange","mango", "mangosteen", "rambutan","durian","pineapple", "papaya"} interfruit.difference_update(Thaifruit) print(interfruit) **Results** {'apple','cherry'}
discard()	Clears the values in brackets from the set	fruit = {"apple","banana", "cherry","orange", "mango", "mangosteen", "rambutan","durian", "pineapple","papaya","papaya"} fruit.discard("apple") print(fruit) **Results** {'pineapple', 'orange', 'mangosteen', 'rambutan', 'cherry', 'durian', 'banana', 'papaya', 'mango'}
intersection()	Display like values between 2 or more sets.	fruit1 = {"apple","banana","mangosteen", "rambutan","durian","pineapple", "papaya"} fruit2 = {"apple","mango","mangosteen",

Functions Used in Sets for Python		
Function	Description	Example
		"rambutan","durian","pineapple", "papaya"} print(fruit1.intersection(fruit2))
		Results
		{'papaya', 'pineapple', 'durian', 'apple', 'rambutan', 'mangosteen'}
		fruit1 = {"apple","banana","mangosteen", "rambutan","durian","pineapple","papaya"}
		fruit2 = {"mangosteen","rambutan","durian", "pineapple","banana"}
		fruit3 = {"rambutan","banana"} print(fruit1.intersection(fruit2,fruit3)) print(fruit2.intersection(fruit1,fruit3)) print(fruit3.intersection(fruit1,fruit2))
		Result of each computation will be the same, as follows:
		Results
		{'banana', 'rambutan'} {'banana', 'rambutan'} {'banana', 'rambutan'}

Learn Python with Projects

Functions Used in Sets for Python		
Function	**Description**	**Example**
intersection_update()	Display like values between 2 or more sets, then remove all other values from the set preceding .intersection_update	fruit1 = {"apple","banana","mangosteen", "rambutan","durian","pineapple","papaya"} fruit2 = {"apple","mango","mangosteen","rambutan", "durian","pineapple","papaya"} fruit1.intersection_update(fruit2) print(fruit1) Results {'mangosteen', 'rambutan', 'apple', 'pineapple', 'durian', 'papaya'} fruit1 = {"apple","banana","mangosteen", "rambutan","durian","pineapple","papaya"} fruit2 = {"mangosteen","rambutan", "durian","pineapple","banana"} fruit3 = {"rambutan","banana"} fruit1.intersection_update(fruit2,fruit3) print(fruit1)

Functions Used in Sets for Python		
Function	**Description**	**Example**
		Result of each computation will be the same, as follows: {'rambutan', 'banana'}
isdisjoint()	Find the same value between two sets. If there is none, return true, if not, false.	fruit1 = {"apple","banana","mangosteen", "rambutan","durian","pineapple","papaya"} fruit2 = {"apple","mango","mangosteen", "rambutan","durian","pineapple","papaya"} print(fruit1.isdisjoint(fruit2))] Results False Contains like values. fruit1 = {"apple","banana","mangosteen", "rambutan","durian","pineapple","papaya"} fruit2 = {"mango"} print(fruit1.isdisjoint(fruit2)) Results True

Functions Used in Sets for Python

Function	Description	Example
issubset()	check whether the first set is a subset of the second. If yes, return true, if not then false.	fruit1 = {"apple","banana","mangosteen", "rambutan","durian","pineapple","papaya"} fruit2 = {"banana","mangosteen","rambutan", "durian","pineapple"} print(fruit1.issubset(fruit2)) <u>Results</u> False print(fruit2.issubset(fruit1)) <u>Results</u> True
issuperset()	check whether the first set is a superset of the second. If yes, return true, if not then false.	fruit1 = {"apple","banana","mangosteen", "rambutan","durian","pineapple","papaya"} fruit2 = {"banana","mangosteen","rambutan", "durian","pineapple"} print(fruit1.issuperset(fruit2))
		<u>Results</u> True print(fruit2.issuperset(fruit1)) <u>Results</u> False

Functions Used in Sets for Python		
Function	**Description**	**Example**
pop()	Removes a value from the set. (Random)	fruit1 = {"apple","banana","mangosteen", "rambutan","durian","pineapple","papaya"} fruit1.pop() print(fruit1) Results {'pineapple', 'banana', 'mangosteen', 'rambutan', 'apple', 'papaya'} Removed value is "durian"
remove()	Removes value specified in brackets from the set.	fruit1 = {"apple","banana", "mangosteen", "rambutan","durian","pineapple","papaya"} fruit1.remove("papaya") print(fruit1) Results {'mangosteen', 'rambutan', 'apple', 'pineapple', 'durian', 'papaya'}
symmetric_difference ()	Display the differences between both sets.	fruit1 = {"apple","banana","mangosteen", "rambutan","durian", "pineapple","papaya", "mango"} fruit2 = {"banana","mangosteen", "rambutan","durian", "pineapple","strawberry"} print(fruit1.symmetric_difference(fruit2))

Learn Python with Projects

\multicolumn{3}{c}{Functions Used in Sets for Python}		
Function	**Description**	**Example**
union()	Combine the values of two or more sets, Removing all duplicates.	Results {'strawberry', 'apple', 'papaya', 'mango'} fruit1 = {"apple","banana","mangosteen", "rambutan","durian","pineapple","papaya", "mango"} fruit2 = {"banana","mangosteen", "rambutan","durian","pineapple","strawberry"} print(fruit1.union(fruit2)) Results {'papaya', 'durian', 'mangosteen', 'pineapple', strawberry', 'banana', 'rambutan', 'apple', 'mango'}
union()		fruit1 = {"apple","banana","mangosteen", "rambutan","durian","pineapple","papaya"} fruit2 = {"mangosteen","rambutan", "durian", "pineapple","banana"} fruit3 = {"rambutan","banana"} print(fruit1.union(fruit2,fruit3)) Results {'mangosteen', 'banana', 'papaya', 'durian', 'apple', 'rambutan', 'pineapple'}

Learn Python with Projects

Functions Used in Sets for Python		
Function	**Description**	**Example**
update()	Updates the set by adding values from another set without creating duplicates	fruit1 = {"apple","banana","mangosteen", "rambutan","durian","pineapple","papaya", "mango"} fruit2 = {"banana","mangosteen","rambutan", "durian","pineapple","strawberry"} fruit1.update(fruit2) print(fruit1)
		Results
		{'pineapple', 'papaya','mangosteen', 'banana', 'durian', 'apple', 'mango', 'rambutan', 'strawberry'}

Tuples

Tuples in python are used to store multiple items ordered under a single variable. It is <u>unchangeable</u>, but <u>does</u> allow duplicates. To write tuples, use Syntax 3-8.

Syntax 3-8: Create Tuples

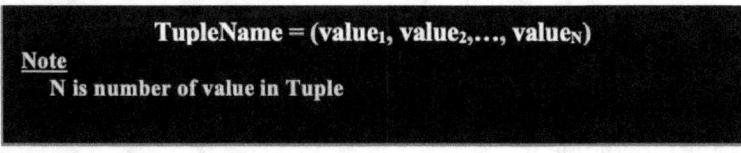

Example
fruit = ("apple","banana","cherry","orange","mango","mangosteen", "rambutan","durian","pineapple", "papaya")

print(fruit)

Results
('apple', 'banana', 'cherry', 'orange', 'mango', 'mangosteen', 'rambutan', 'durian', 'pineapple', 'papaya')

With duplicates:
fruit = ("apple", "banana","cherry","orange","mango","mangosteen", "rambutan","durian","pineapple","papaya", "papaya")

print(fruit)
Results
('apple', 'banana', 'cherry', 'orange', 'mango', 'mangosteen', 'rambutan', 'durian', 'pineapple', 'papaya')

Therefore, when using len() to count the number of items, all items will be counted.
print(len(fruit))

Results
11

There are two different data types to keep a variable as a single item. These are:
Case 1
As a tuple
student = ("Jame",)
print(type(student))

Results
<class 'tuple'>

Case 2
As a String
student = ("Jame")
print(type(student))

For functions, refer to Table 3- 4: Functions Used in Tuples for Python

Table 3- 4: Functions Used in Tuples for Python

Functions Used in Tuples for Python		
Function	Description	Example
count()	Count the instances of the bracketed value in the tuple.	fruit = ("apple","banana", "cherry","orange", "mango","mangosteen", "rambutan","durian", "pineapple","papaya","papaya") print(fruit.count("papaya")) Results 2
index()	Find the first indexed location of the bracketed value in the tuple, Starting from 0.	fruit = ("apple","banana","cherry","orange", "mango","mangosteen","rambutan","durian", "pineapple","papaya","papaya") print(fruit.index("papaya")) Results 9 fruit = ("apple","banana", "cherry","orange", "mango", "mangosteen", "rambutan","durian", "pineapple","papaya","papaya") print(fruit.index("apple")) Results 0

Table 3- 5: Differences between lists, dictionaries, sets and tuples

Item	List	Dictionary	Set	Tuple
Changeable	✓	✓	X	X
Orderable	✓	✓	X	✓
Duplicates	✓	X	X	X
Indexable	✓	✓	X	✓

Note: ✓ Yes   X No

Exercises

1. Create a list to store the names and telephone numbers of at least 5 members and display them.
2. Display the name of the 3rd member.
3. Add at least 2 members.
4. Make a copy of the members list named copyMember.
5. Display the number of members.
6. Insert a new value for the 3rd member.
7. Display results of copyMember.pop(2)
8. Display the phone numbers of all members.
9. Write a program that uses issubset().
10. Create a tuple of the members.

Chapter 4
Operators

Python has the following operators:

- Arithmetic operators
- Comparison operators
- Logical operators
- Identity operators
- Membership operators
- Bitwise operators
- Assignment operators

Arithmetic Operators

Used in basic calculations, Table 4-1 contains all the arithmetic operators used by Python.

Table 4-1: Arithmetic Operators

Arithmetic Operators		
Arithmetic Operator	**Meaning**	**Example**
+	Add	x = 8 y = 3 print(x + y) Results 11
-	Subtract	x = 8 y = 3 print(x - y) Results 5
*	Multiply	x = 8 y = 3 print(x * y) 24
/	Divide	x = 8 y = 3 print(x / y) Results

Arithmetic Operators		
Arithmetic Operator	**Meaning**	**Example**
		2.6666666666666665

//	Floor Division (Integer only, discarding remainders and decimals.)	x = 8
		y = 3
		print(x // y)
		2

**	Exponentiation (power of)	x = 8 y = 3 print(x ** y) Results 512
%	Modulus (finds remainder)	x = 8 y = 3 print(x%y) Results 2

Arithmetic statements follow Table 4-2: Order of Operations, from left to right, bracketed values first.

Table 4-2: Order of Operations

Order	Operation
First	() Bracketed values
Second	** Exponents
Third	% Modulo, * Multiply, / Divide, // Floor Divide
Fourth	+ Add, - Subtract

Example 1

print(5+2**2+8/4*10%3%2)

The result of the order of operations are as follows: Starting from the second order, which is exponents, 2 To the power of 2 equals 4. Next or third order operations from left to right: 8 divided by 4 equals 2, 2 multiplied by 10 equals 20, then modulo operations, 20 divided by 3 leaves remainder 2, 2 divided by 2 leaves remainder 0. Finally, do additions from the fourth order: 5 plus 4 plus 0 equals 9.0

Results
9.0

Example 2

print(5+2/2*5+8)

Start with the third order: 2 divided by 2 equals 1, 1 multiplied by 5 equals 5. Then the addition: 5 plus 5 plus 8 equals 18.0

Results
18.0

print(5+2**2/2*5+8)

Start with exponents: 2 to the power of 2 equals 4. 4 divided by 2 equals 2. 2 multiplied by 5 equals 10. 5 plus 10 plus 8 equals 23.

Results
23.0

Adding brackets will change the order of operations. For example:

print((5+2)**2/(2*5)+8)

Starting with bracketed values: 5 plus 2 equals 7, 2 times 5 equals 10. 7 to the power of 2 equals 49. 49 divided by 10 equals 4.9. 4.9 plus 8 equals 12.9.

Results
12.9

Example 3

Let's say we want to use python to calculate body mass index (BMI) to display whether the person is underweight, normal or overweight, using the formula weight(kg) divided by height(m) to the power of 2, we can determine the results using Table 4- 3: BMI results meaning:

Table 4- 3: BMI results meaning

BMI	Category
below 18.5	Underweight
between 18.5 and 22.9	Normal
above 22.9	Overweight

Weight_kg = float(input('Your Weight(Kg) is '))
Height_m = float(input('Your Height(M) is '))
print('Your BMI is '+str(Weight_kg/Height_m**2))

Learn Python with Projects

Results
Your Weight(Kg) is 80
Your Height(M) is 1.8
Your BMI is 24.691358024691358
and if you want the text to display only 2 decimal places, add this code:

```
Weight_kg = float(input('Your Weight(Kg) is '))
Height_m = float(input('Your Height(M) is '))
BMI=round(float(Weight_kg/Height_m**2),2)
print('Your BMI is '+str(BMI))
```

Results
Your Weight(Kg) is 50
Your Height(M)is 1.50
Your BMI is 22.22

Comparison Operators

Used in comparing statements, Table 4-4 contains all the comparison operators used by Python.

Table 4- 4:Comparison Operators

Comparison Operators		
Comparison Operator	Meaning	Example
==	equal	x = 8 y = 3 print(x == y) Results False

Comparison Operators		
Comparison Operator	**Meaning**	**Example**
!=	not equal	x = 8 y = 3 print(x != y) <u>Results</u> True
>	more than	x = 8 y = 3 print(x > y) <u>Results</u> True
<	less than	x = 8 y = 3 print(x < y) <u>Results</u> False
>=	greater or equal to	x = 8 y = 3 print(x >= y) <u>Results</u> True x = 8 y = 8

Comparison Operators		
Comparison Operator	**Meaning**	**Example**
		print(x >= y) Results True
<=	lesser or equal to	x = 8 y = 3 print(x <= y) Results False x = 8 y = 8 print(x <= y) Results True

Logical Operators

Logical operators combine two conditional propositions. They return true or false under the following tables:

For AND operators, use Table 4- 5: AND Truth Table

Table 4- 5: AND Truth Table

AND Truth Table		
p	**q**	**p and q**
True	True	True
True	False	False
False	True	False
False	False	False

For OR operators, use Table 4- 6: OR Truth Table.

Table 4-6: OR Truth Table

OR Truth Table		
p	q	p or q
True	True	True
True	False	True
False	True	True
False	False	False

For XOR operators, use Table 4-7: XOR Truth Table.

Table 4-7: XOR Truth Table

XOR Truth Table		
p	q	p ^ q
True	True	False
True	False	True
False	True	True
False	False	False

For NOT operators, use Table 4-8: NOT Truth Table.

Table 4-8: NOT Truth Table

NOT Truth Table	
p	Not p
True	False
False	True

Note: Statements are either true or false, where symbol p Represents the first proposition or sq represents the second.

For example:
a = 5
b = 6
p proposes a<b, which is True
q proposes a=b, which is False
Considering the table,

p and q, True and False, Result is False
p or q , True and False, Result is True
not p, not True, result is False

Examples in Table 4- 9: Logical Operators

Table 4- 9: Logical Operators

Logical operators	
Logical Operator	**Example**
and	x = 8 y = 3 print(x == y and x>y) Results False x==y is false x>y is True When checking the AND Truth Table, Result is False.
or	x = 8 y = 3 print(x == y or x>y) Results True x==y is false x>y is True

Logical operators	
Logical Operator	**Example**
	When checking the OR Truth Table, Result is True.
not	x = 8 y = 3 print(not(x == y or x>y)) <u>Results</u> False x==y is false x>y is True When checking the OR Table, Result is True, adding not, result is False. print(not(x == y and x>y)) <u>Results</u> True

Logical operators	
Logical Operator	**Example**
	x==y is false x>y is True When checking the And Table, Result is False adding not, result is True.

Identity operators

Identity operators as shown in Table 4- 10: Identity Operators.

Table 4- 10: Identity Operators

Identity Operators	
Identity operator	**Example**
is	x = 8 y = 3 print(x is y) <u>Results</u> False x = 8 y = 8

Identity Operators	
Identity operator	**Example**
	print(x is y) <u>Results</u> True x = 8 y = "8" print(x is y) <u>Results</u> False
is not	x = 8 y = 3 print(x is not y) <u>Results</u> True x = 8 y = 8 print(x is not y) <u>Results</u> False

Identity Operators	
Identity operator	**Example**
	x = 8 y = "8" print(x is not y) <u>Results</u> True

Membership operators

Membership operators as shown in Table 4- 11: Membership Operators

Table 4- 11: Membership Operators

Membership Operators		
Membership operator	**Meaning**	**Example**
in	is a member of	fruit = ["strawberry", "mango", "banana"] print("banana" in fruit) <u>Results</u> True

Membership Operators		
Membership operator	**Meaning**	**Example**
		print("papaya" in fruit) Results False
not in	is not a member of	fruit = ["strawberry", "mango", "banana"] print("banana" not in fruit) Results False print("papaya" not in fruit) Results True

Bitwise operators

Bitwise operators as shown in Table 4- 12: Bitwise Operators

Table 4-12: Bitwise Operators

Bitwise Operators		
Bitwise operator	**Meaning**	**Example**
&	And (for bits), that is, Converting both values in the logical operator into bits (binary) before performing said logical operator for each digit.	x = 8 y = 3 print(x & y) <u>Results</u> 0 This will compare each of the 16 digits, one by one, using the AND truth table, where 0 is false and 1 is true. 8 in binary is 0000000000001000 3 in binary is 0000000000000011 Using the AND logic operator for each bit: 0000000000001000 0000000000000011 --------------------------- 0000000000000000 Therefore, result is <u>Results</u>

Bitwise Operators

Bitwise operator	Meaning	Example
		0
|	Or (for bits), that is, Converting both values in the logic operator into bits (binary) before performing said logical operator for each digit.	x = 8 y = 3 print(x | y) <u>Results</u> 11 This will compare each of the 16 digits, one by one, using the OR truth table, where 0 is false and 1 is true. 8 in binary is 0000000000001000 3 in binary is 0000000000000011 Using the OR logic operator for each bit: 0000000000001000 0000000000000011 --------------------------- 0000000000001011

Bitwise Operators		
Bitwise operator	Meaning	Example
		Therefore, result is <u>Results</u> 11
^	Xor (for bits), that is, Converting both values in the logic operator into bits (binary) before performing said logical operator for each digit.	x = 5 y = 6 print(x^y) <u>Results</u> 3 This will compare each of the 16 digits, one by one, using the XOR truth table, where 0 is false and 1 is true. 5 in binary is 0000000000000101 6 in binary is 0000000000000110 Using the XOR logic operator for each bit: 0000000000000101 0000000000000110

Bitwise Operators		
Bitwise operator	**Meaning**	**Example**
		-------------------------- 0000000000000011 Therefore, result is Results 3 In Contrast to using the OR logic operator for each bit: 0000000000000101 0000000000000110 -------------------------- 0000000000000111 Results 7
~	Not (for bits), that is, Converting the value into bits (binary) before performing said logical operator for each digit.	x = 5 print(~x) Results -6 This will compare the 16 digits, one by one,

Bitwise Operators

Bitwise operator	Meaning	Example
		using the NOT truth table, where 0 is false and 1 is true. 5 in binary is 0000000000000101 As a NOT, 0 converts to 1, while 1 becomes 0, like so: 1111111111111010 is Results -6
<<	After Converting the value into bits (binary) Move all the digits to the left equal to the number specified after <<, replacing all displaced digits with 0.	x = 5 print(x << 2) Results 20 Convert x into 16 digit binary. 5 in binary is 0000000000000101 then move 2 digits to the left:

Bitwise Operators		
Bitwise operator	**Meaning**	**Example**
		0000000000010100 Results 20
>>	After Converting the value into bits (binary) Move all the digits to the right equal to the number specified after >>, replacing all displaced digits with 0.	x = 5 print(x >> 2) Results 1 Convert x into 16 digit binary. 5 in binary is 0000000000000101

Bitwise Operators		
Bitwise operator	Meaning	Example
		then move 2 digits to the right: 00000000000001 is Results 1

Assignment operators

Assignment operators as shown in Table 4-13: Assignment Operators

Table 4-13: Assignment Operators

Assignment Operators		
Assignment	**Example**	**Equivalent Result**
=	x=7	x=7
+=	x+=7	x=x+7
-=	x-=7	x=x-7
*=	x*=7	x=x*7
/=	x/=7	x=x/7
//=	x//=7	x=x//7
**=	x**=7	x=x**7
%=	x%=7	x=x%7
&=	x&=7	x=x&7
|=	x|=7	x=x|7
^=	x^=7	x=x^7
>>=	x>>=7	x=x>>7
<<=	x<<=7	x=x<<7

Assignment Examples

num=0
num +=1
print(num)

Results
1

num=0
num +=50
print(num)

Results
50

Deduct values
num=0
num -=50

Results
-50

display the variable using f-String
num=0
num -=50
Logic = True
print(f"num is {num} Logic is {Logic}")

Results
num is -50 Logic is True

Exercises

1. print(15+2**3+9/4*10%3%3) gives what result?
2. Using the formula for BMI in this chapter, Calculate your BMI.
3. If student = ["ant","bee","kai"]
   print("banana" in student) gives what result?
4. If x = 40 y = 35
   - 4.1. print(not(x == y and x>y)) gives what result?
   - 4.2. print(not(x == y and x&y)) gives what result?
   - 4.3. print(x ^ y and x|y) gives what result?
   - 4.4. print(x += y) gives what result?
   - 4.5. print(x //= y) gives what result?
   - 4.6. print(x <<= y) gives what result?

Chapter 5
Conditional Statements

When writing a conditional statement, The program checks whether the statement is true or false. If true, it executes 1.1, then 1.2 (if available) then 1.3 (if available) until all commands are executed. if false, it executes 2.1, then 2.2 (if available) then 2.3 (If available) until all commands are executed. In python, there are additional statements that help us write conditional statements, namely elif with...as and pass accordingly.

Conditional statements in python are as follows:
if..else
while..loop

for..loop
elif
Commands that make writing conditional statements more convenient are:
with...as, continue and pass

if

An **if** statement has the following syntax:

Syntax 5- 1: if statement

```
if condition :
    command₁
    command₂
    ...
    commandₙ
```

Note
  command₁ to commandₙ are executed when condition is True.
  N is the total number of commands executed

if..else

An **if..else** statement has the following syntax:

Syntax 5-2: if..else statement

```
if condition :
    command_{1.1}
    command_{1.2}
    ...
    command_{1.N}
else:
    command_{2.1}
    command_{2.2}
    ...
    command_{2.M}
```

Note
command$_{1.1}$ to command$_{1.N}$ are executed when condition is True.
command$_{2.1}$ to command$_{2.M}$ are executed when condition is False.

N is the total number of commands executed when condition is True.
M is the total number of commands executed when condition is False.

Programming conditional statements is easier if you organize your thoughts with a **flow chart,** which is useful for debugging and software testers checking if the program is running properly. Symbols used in drawing Flow Charts are as Table 5-1.

Table 5-1: Symbols for Flow Chart

Symbol	Meaning
(rounded rectangle)	**Start Program** or **Stop Program**
(oval)	**Connect**
(arrow)	**Direction** - Show work in the direction of arrow
(rectangle)	**Process**
(parallelogram)	**Input Data**
(diamond)	**Decisions** that require conditional statements. Program by stating if, followed by condition. If true, executes the following set of commands, if false, execute commands following else:
(display shape)	**Display**
(document shape)	**Print**

Example Program

Programming to find BMI values and display results begins with designing and drawing a flow chart before coding the program, shown as Figure 5-1.

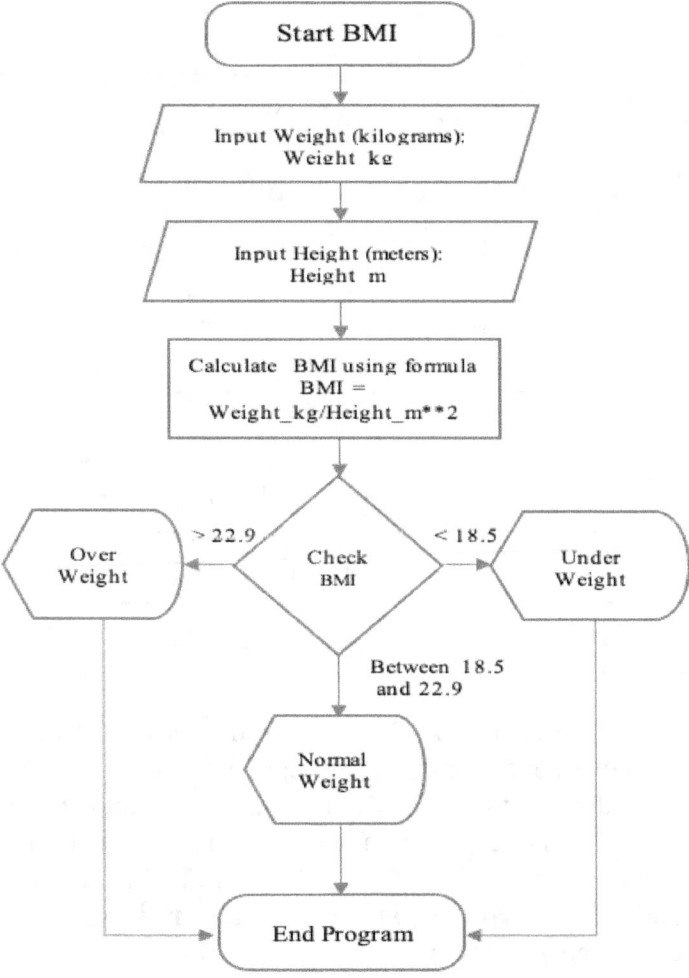

Figure 5- 1: Flow Chart for finding BMI values and displaying results.

Whether a person is over, under or normal weight, when inputting their weight and height, write a flow chart first to make programming easier.

Comparison operators, shown as Table 5-2 : Comparison operators

Table 5- 2: Comparison operators

Comparison Operators	
Comparison Operator	**Meaning**
>	more than
<	less than
==	equal to
>=	greater than or equal to
<=	less than or equal to
!=	not equal to

To calculate the BMI value and know whether the result is over, under or normal weight, write a program using additional conditions of BMI table values to find the result, that is, using if or else, which after if must be a condition that gives the result TRUE or FALSE (FALSE) and when the result is true, it will do command 1 and if it is false, it will do command 2 as follows.

```
Weight_kg   = float(input('Your Weight(Kg) is '))
Height_m    = float(input('Your Height(M) is '))
BMI         = round(float(Weight_kg/Height_m**2),2)
```

```
if BMI > 22.9:
    print("You are overweight")
```

Results
Your Weight(Kg) is 60
Your Height(M)is 1.4
You are overweight

```
Weight_kg   = float(input('Your Weight(Kg) is '))
Height_m    = float(input('Your Height(M) is '))
BMI         = round(float(Weight_kg/Height_m**2),2)
if BMI > 22.9:
    print("You are overweight")
else: print("You are normal or underweight")
```

Results
Your Weight(Kg) is 40
Your Height(M)is 1.60
You are normal or underweight

if..elif..else

In the case of overlapping conditions, an **if..elif..else** command has the following syntax:

Syntax 5- 3: if..elif..else statement

```
if condition₁:
    command₁.₁
    command₁.₂
    ...
    command₁.L
elif condition₂:
    command₂.₁
    command₂.₂
    ...
    command₂.M
else:
    command₃.₁
    command₃.₂
    ...
    command₃.N
```

Note
- commands are executed from 1.1 to 1.L when condition₁ is true.
- L is the total number of commands executed when condition1 is true.
- commands are executed from 2.1 to 2.M when condition₁ is false and condition₂ is true.
- M is the total number of commands executed when condition₁ is false and condition₂ is true.
- commands are executed from 3.1 to 3.N when condition₁ is false and condition₂ is false.
- N is the total number of commands executed when condition₁ is false and condition₂ is false.

Commands can be programmed as if_else as well.

```
Weight_kg   = float(input('Your Weight(Kg) is '))
Height_m    = float(input('Your Height(M) is '))
BMI         = round(float(Weight_kg/Height_m**2),2)
if BMI > 22.9:
```

```
  print("You are overweight")
elif BMI < 18.5:
  print("You are underweight")
else:
  print("You are normal weight")
```

Results

Your Weight(Kg) is 50
Your Height(M)is 1.5
You are normal weight

Results

Your Weight(Kg) is 60
Your Height(M)is 1.4
You are overweight

Results

Your Weight(Kg) is 40
Your Height(M)is 1.60
You are underweight

You can also write the program as nested if_else chains. For example, if condition 1 is this:

```
if BMI < 18.5:
  print("You are underweight")
else:
  print("You are normal")
```

Therefore, you can write the BMI calculation program in this manner:

```
Weight_kg   = float(input('Your Weight(Kg) is '))
Height_m    = float(input('Your Height(M) is '))
BMI         = round(float(Weight_kg/Height_m**2),2)
```

```
if BMI < 22.9:
    if BMI < 18.5:
        print("You are underweight")
    else:
        print("You are normal")
else:
    print("You are overweight")
```

Results

Your Weight(Kg) is 50
Your Height(M)is 1.5
You are normal weight
Your Weight(Kg) is 60
Your Height(M)is 1.4
You are overweight
Your Weight(Kg) is 40
Your Height(M)is 1.60
You are underweight

while..loop

The syntax of the **while..loop** conditional statement has the following syntax:

Syntax 5- 4: while..loop statement

```
i = 0
j = K
while i<j:
    command_{1.1}
    command_{1.2}
    ...
    command_{1.N}
    i += 1
```

where i is the variable used to count the cycles.
j is a numeric variable that defines a cycle equal to K cycles.

Note :
- commands are executed from 1.1 to 1.L when i<j
- N is the total number of commands executed when i<j.

while..loop Is used in case of when you want a program to run for a certain number of cycles until a number of determined cycles is reached.

Example

Programming to display numbers 0-10 begins with designing and drawing a flow chart before coding the program, shown as Figure 5-2.

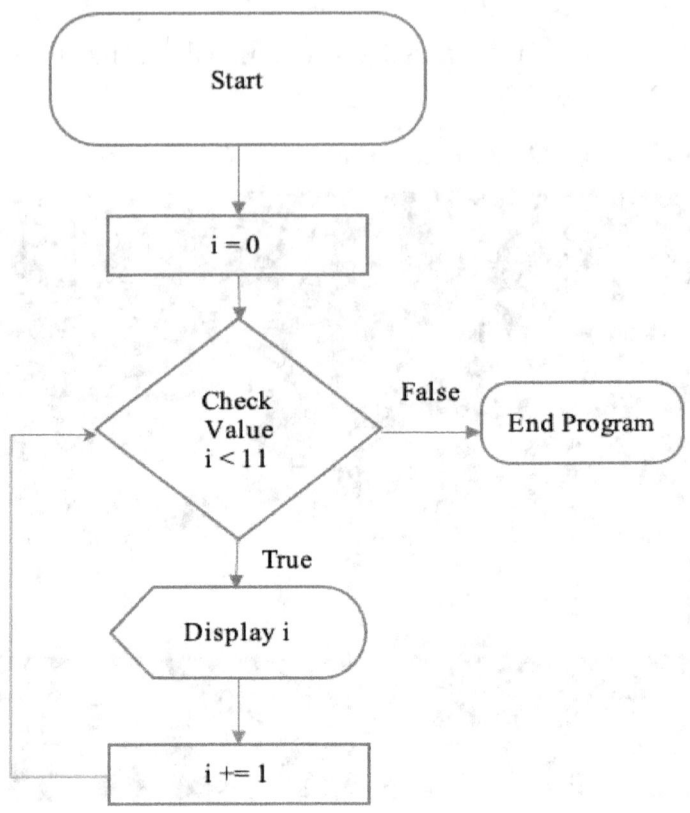

Figure 5- 2: Flow Chart for Displaying number 0 to10

Program for displaying the numbers 0-10

i = 0
while i < 11:
  print(i)
  i += 1
Results

0
1

2
3
4
5
6
7
8
9
10

We can use **break** during the process if there is a condition that requires a break. The syntax of the **while..loop** with **break** as shown in Syntax 5-5

Syntax 5- 5: while..loop with break statement

```
i = 0
j = K
while i<j:
    command₁.₁
    command₁.₂
    ...
    command₁.ₘ
    if condition :
        command₂.₁
        command₂.₂
        ...
        command₂.ₙ
        break
    i += 1
```

where i is the variable used to count the cycles.
j is a numeric variable that defines a cycle equal to K cycles.

Note :
- commands are executed from 1.1 to 1.M when i<j
- M is the total number of commands executed when i<j.
- commands are executed from 2.1 to 2.N and exit after executed when i<j and condition is True.
- N is the total number of commands executed when i<j and condition is True..

Example program:

Programming to display index of "durian" with designing and drawing a flow chart before coding the program, shown as Figure 5-3.

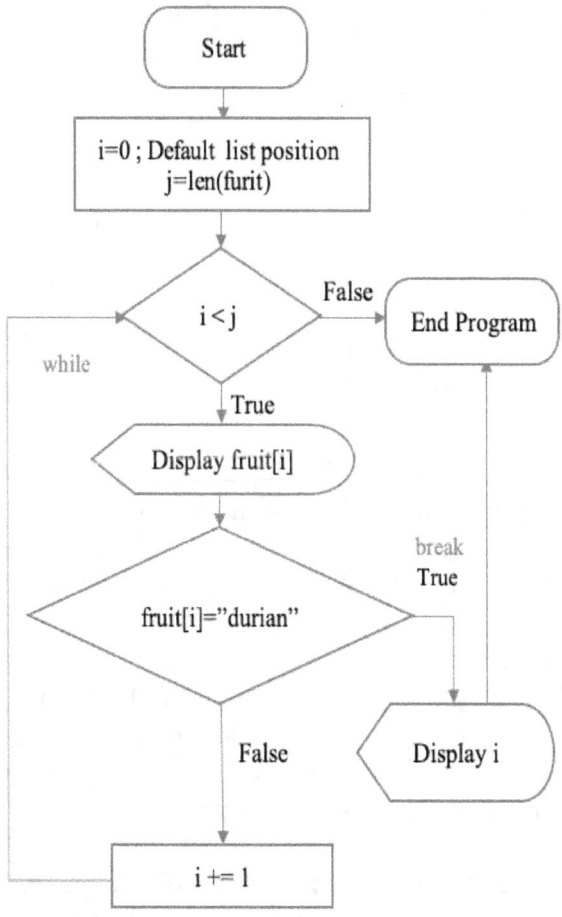

Figure 5- 3: Flow Chart for finding index of "durian" in list

```
fruit = list(("orange","mango","mangosteen","rambutan","durian",
"pineapple","papaya"))
i = 0
j = len(fruit)
while i < j:
  print(fruit[i])
  if (fruit[i] == "durian"):
    print("position of durian is "+str(i))
    break
  i += 1
```

Results
 orange
 mango
 mangosteen
 rambutan
 durian
 position of durian is 4

with...as
with...as is a command that is similar to defining a variable with a different way to code, but yields the same results. Examples of its use could be found in Chapter 11: with...as.

continue
Or if you want to show all the items in the list along with a certain item's position, you can use **continue**, but remember to use **break** to not go beyond the total values in the list, which can cause errors in the display.

We can use **break** and **continue** during the process if there is a condition that requires **break** and **continue**. The syntax of the **while..loop** with **break** and **continue** as shown in Syntax 5-6

Syntax 5-6: while..loop with break and continue statement

```
i=0
j=K
while i<j :
   command_{1.1}
   command_{1.2}
   ...
   command_{1.L}
   i+=1
   if condition_1:
      command_{2.1}
      command_{2.2}
      ...
      command_{2.M}
      break
   if condition_2:
      command_{3.1}
      command_{3.2}
      ...
      command_{3.N}
      continue
```

where i is the variable used to count the cycles.
   j is a numeric variable that defines a cycle equal to K cycles.

Note :
- commands are executed from 1.1 to 1.L when i<j
- L is the total number of commands executed when i<j.
- commands are executed from 2.1 to 2.M and exit after executed when i<j and condition$_1$ is True.
- M is the total number of commands executed and exit the loop when i<j and condition is True.
- commands are executed from 3.1 to 3.N and continue the loop when i<j and condition$_2$ is True.
- N is the total number of commands executed and continue the loop when i<j and condition$_2$ is True.

Example Program:

Programming to display index of "durian" and display all of fruit in list with designing and drawing a flow chart before coding the program, as shown in Figure 5-4.

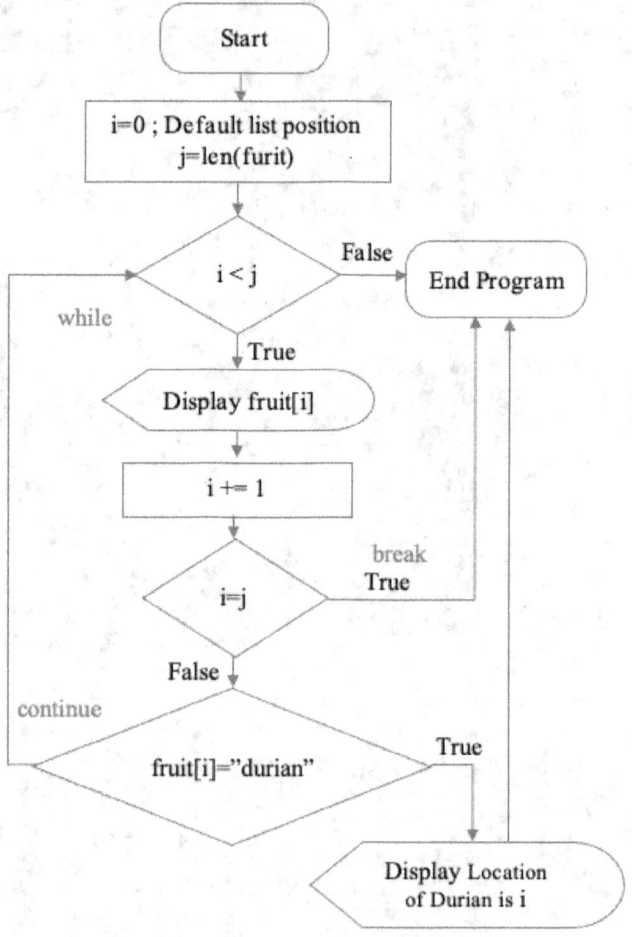

Figure 5- 4: Flow Chart to display index of "durian" and display all of fruit in list

```
fruit =
list(("orange","mango","mangosteen","rambutan","durian",
"pineapple","papaya"))
i = 0
j = len(fruit)
while i < j:
  print(fruit[i])
  i += 1
  if (i == j): break
  if (fruit[i] == "durian"):
    print("Location of Durian is "+str(i))
    continue
```

Result
orange
mango
mangosteen
rambutan
Location of Durian is 4
durian
pineapple
papaya

while..else

We can use **else** during the process if there is a condition that requires **else**. With this, after completing the designated number of loops, will execute commands after **else**. The syntax of the **while** with **else**, as shown in Syntax 5-7:

Syntax 5- 7: while..else statement

```
i = 0
j = K
while i<j:
    command_1.1
    command_1.2
    ...
    command_1.M
    i += 1
else :
    command_2.1
    command_2.2
    ...
    command_2.N
```

where i is the variable used to count the cycles.
    j is a numeric variable that defines a cycle equal to K cycles.

Note :
- commands are executed from 1.1 to 1.M when i<j
- M is the total number of commands executed when i<j.
- commands are executed from 1.1 to 1.N when i>=j
- N is the total number of commands executed when i>=j.

Example

```
fruit = list(("orange","mango","mangosteen","rambutan","durian", "pineapple","papaya"))
i = 0
j = len(fruit)
```

```
while i < j:
 print(fruit[i])
 i += 1
else :
 print("End of fruit list")
```

Results
 orange
 mango
 mangosteen
 rambutan
 durian
 pineapple
 papaya
 End of fruit list

for..loop

The syntax of **for..loop** is as follows:

Syntax 5- 8: for..loop statement

> **for variable in list :**
>   **command$_1$**
>   **command$_2$**
>   **...**
>   **command$_N$**
>
> Note :
> - commands are executed from 1 to N every value in list and executed with variable that is value in list.
> - N is the total number of commands executed first to last value in list.

For..loop is for when you want to write a command to cycle through the desired command from the first value in the list (position 0) until the last value in the list (position len(list)-1).

```
fruit = list(("orange","mango","mangosteen","rambutan","durian", "pineapple","papaya"))
for n in fruit:
  print(n)
```

Results
orange
 mango
 mangosteen
 rambutan
 durian
 pineapple
 papaya

We can use a break during processing if there are conditions that require a break.

The syntax of **for..loop with break** is as follows:

Syntax 5- 9:for..loop with break statement

```
for variable in list :
    command₁.₁
    command₁.₂
    ...
    command₁.ₙ
    if condition
        command₂.₁ :
        command₂.₂
        ...
        command₂.ₘ
        break
Note :
    •   commands are executed from 1.1 to 1.N from value the first to
        the last value in list.Unless the condition is True the loop will
        stop.
    •   N is the total number of commands executed from value the first
        to the last value in list.Unless the condition is True the loop will
        stop.
    •   commands are executed from 2.1 to 2.M when condition is True
        and stop looping.
```

Example Programs:

If you wish to break once you find "mango" in the list:

```
fruit = list(("orange","mango","mangosteen","rambutan","durian", "pineapple","papaya"))
for n in fruit:
  print(n)
  if n == "mango":
    print(len(fruit))
    break
```

Results
 orange
 mango
 7

If you wish to break once you find "mango", as well as display its position in the list:

```
fruit = list(("orange","mango","mangosteen","rambutan","durian", "pineapple","papaya"))
p = 0
for n in fruit:
  print(n)
  p=p+1
  if n == "mango":
    print(p)
    break
```

Results
 orange
 mango
 2

Caution: Indentations

Caution: Indentations matter for commands, and will have different effects on how statements are executed. For example:

For if...else

Example A

```
m = 2
n = m = 2
n = 33
if m > n:
   print("m>n")
   print("m is more n")
print("results as stated")
```

Results
results as stated

Example B

```
m = 2
n = 33
if m > n:
   print("m>n")
print("m is more n")
print("results as stated")
```

Results

m is more than n
results as stated

Because in example A, print("m is more n") **is within if, whereas example B has** print("m is more n") **outside** if.

For while..loop

Example A

```
i = 0
while i < 11:
  i += 1
  print(i)
```
Results
1
2
3
4
5
6
7
8
9
10
11

Example B

```
i = 0
while i < 11:
  i += 1
print(i)
```

Results
11

Because in example A, print(n) **is within** while**, whereas example B has** print(n) **outside** while.

For for..loop

Example A

```
fruit = list(("orange","mango","mangosteen","rambutan","durian", "pineapple","papaya"))
p = 0
for n in fruit:
 if n == "mango":
   continue
 print(n)
```

Results

orange
mango
mangosteen
rambutan
durian
pineapple
papaya

Example B

```
fruit = list(("orange","mango","mangosteen","rambutan","durian", "pineapple","papaya"))
p = 0
for n in fruit:
 if n == "mango":
   continue
print(n)
```

Results

papaya

Because in example A, print(n) **is within** for**, whereas example B has** print(n) **outside** for.

elif

    elif checks if the condition preceding **if** is not true, executes **elif** commands instead.

Example
```
num1 = 2
num2 = 10
if num2>num1:
  print("num2 is more than num1")
elif num1 == num2:
  print("num2 is equal to num 1")
else:
  print("num1 is more than num2")
```
Results num2 is more than num1

pass

    pass check if the condition is true, will not display anything.

Example
```
num1 = 2
num2 = 10
if num2>num1:
  pass
elif num1 == num2:
  print("num2 is equal to num 1")
else:
  print("num1 is more than num2")
```
Results
Nothing is displayed

Exercises

1. Draw a flowchart, then write a program to check the conditions for variable values with positive integers displays '+', negative integers displays '-' and displays '0' when variable values have a value of 0.
2. Repeat Exercise 1, but only use the comparison operator > in programming.
3. Repeat Exercise 1, but only use the comparison operator >= in programming.
4. Repeat Exercise 1, but only use the comparison operator != in programming.
5. Repeat Exercise 1, but use while…loop in programming, where it accepts 5 values to display.
6. Repeat Exercise 1, but use while…loop in programming to only allow input of values less than 100 in the display. If the variable has a value greater than 100, exit the program and display the variable value.
7. Repeat Exercise 1, but use while…else in programming to only allow input of values less than 100 in the display. If the variable has a value greater than 100, exit the program and display the variable value.
8. Repeat Exercise 1, but use for…loop in programming to only allow input of values less than 100 in the display. If the variable has a value greater than 100, exit the program and display the variable value.

Chapter 6
Functions

Creating a function for Python is creating a block of program code that runs when it is called and can pass data called parameters into the function. The function can return data as a result.

define function

The following is the syntax for defining a function in Python:

Syntax 6-1: defining a function

> **def functionName(parameter$_1$,...,parameter$_M$) :**
>   **command$_1$**
>   **...**
>   **command$_N$**
>
> Call Function
>
> **functionName(argument$_1$, argument$_2$,..., argument$_M$)**
>
> Note :
> - commands are executed from 1 to N, with or without parameters when the function is called.
> - M is the number of parameters. which may have a value of 0.
> - N is the total number of commands executed when the function is called.
> - arguments are values passed in a sequence of parameters in a function that are defined when the function is called from 1 to M.

Where parameter$_1$,...,parameter$_N$ are **arguments**. Whether arguments are present or not depends on whether perimeters are needed.

calling a function

To call a function, use the following syntax:

Syntax 6-2: calling a function

> Call Function
>
> **functionName(argument$_1$, argument$_2$,..., argument$_M$)**
>
> Note :
> - commands are executed from 1 to N, with or without parameters when the function is called.
> - M is the number of arguments and parameters. which may have a value of 0.
> - arguments are values passed in a sequence of parameters in a function that are defined when the function is called from 1 to M.

Where $value_1,\ldots,value_M$ are **arguments**. Whether arguments are present or not depends on whether perimeters are needed to execute that function.

Example Function Programs
```
def favoriteFruit():
  print("My favorite fruit is "+"orange")
favoriteFruit()
```

Results

My favorite fruit is orange

when the argument $parameter_1$ is fFruit
```
def favoriteFruit(fFruit):
  print("My favorite fruit is "+fFruit)

favoriteFruit("apple")
```

Results

My favorite fruit is apple

favoriteFruit("orange")

Results

My favorite fruit is orange

If you want to add a *parameter* to include the name of the person as well.

def favoriteFruit(fName,fFruit):

print("The fruit "+fName+" likes most is "+fFruit)

favoriteFruit("ส้ม","orange")
Results

The fruit Som likes most is orange

favoriteFruit("Sansuay","mango")

Results
The fruit Sansuay likes most is mango

Caution: include all *parameters* so it can function without errors.

define a function with *parameter

For Python, in cases where we don't know the exact number of arguments to be passed to our function, place a asterisk (*) in front of parameter. The *parameter must be a tuple.

    The following is the syntax for defining a function with *parameter in Python:

Syntax 6-3: defining a function with *parameter

```
def functionName(parameter₁,...,parameterL,
                *parameter₁,...,*parameterM) :
    command₁
    ...
    commandN
```

Call Function

```
functionName(argument₁, argument₂,..., argumentL,
*argument₁, *argument₂,..., *argumentM)
```

Note :
- commands are executed from 1 to N, with or without parameters and with or without *parameters when the function is called.
- L is the number of parameters. which may have a value of 0.
- M is the number of *parameters. which may have a value of 0.
- *parameter must be tuple.
- N is the total number of commands executed when the function is called.

Example Program

```
def favoriteFruit(*fFruit):
  print("At least 2 of my favorite fruits are "+fFruit[0]+" "+fFruit[1])
favoriteFruit("orange","banana","mango", "watermelon")
```
Results
At least 2 of my favorite fruits are orange banana

```
def favoriteFruit(fName,lName,*fFruit):
  print("At least 2 fruits that"+fName+" "+lName+" likes most are "+fFruit[0]+" "+fFruit[1])
favoriteFruit("Sansuay","Sakunsaendeengam","Orange", "Banana","Mango", "Watermelon")
```
Results
At least 2 fruits thatSansuay Sakunsaendeengam likes most are Orange Banana

To display every item of fruit, write a program like this:

```
def favoriteFruit(fName,lName,*fFruit):
  print("The fruits that "+fName+" "+lName+" likes most are ")
  for name in fFruit:
     print(name)
favoriteFruit("Sansuay","Sakunsaeneengam","Orange", "Banana","Mango","Watermelon")
```
Results
The fruits that Sansuay Sakunsaeneengam likes most are
Orange
Banana
Mango
Watermelon

defining a function with **parameter

If we don't know the number of parameters to pass to the function, use double-asterisks ** before the parameter name.

The following is the syntax for defining a function with **parameter in Python:

Syntax 6- 4: defining a function with **parameter

> **def functionName(**parameter) :**
>   **command$_1$**
>   ...
>   **command$_L$**
>
> Note 1:
> - When using parameters, you must refer to parameters and variables as follows in commands:
>
>   **parameter["variable"]**
>
> Call Function
>
> **functionName(variable$_1$=argument$_1$,**
>   **variable$_2$=argument$_2$,...,**
>   **variable$_M$=argument$_M$)**
>
> Note 2 :
> - commands are executed from 1 to L, with parameters when the function is called.
> - L is the number of commands are executed, when the function is called.
> - M is the number of parameters.

Learn Python with Projects

Example Program

```
def favoriteFruit(**fFruit):
   print("The fruits that "+fFruit["fName"]+" "+
   fFruit["lName"]+" likes most are "   +fFruit["fFruit1"]
   +" "+fFruit["fFruit2"]+" "+fFruit["fFruit3"]
   +fFruit["fFruit4"])
favoriteFruit(fName ="Sansuay",lName
="Sakunsaendeengam",fFruit1="orange",fFruit2="banana",
fFruit3="mango",
fFruit4="watermelon")
```
Results
The fruits that Sansuay Sakunsaendeengam likes most are orange banana mangowatermelon

defining a function with default values to parameters

The following is the syntax for defining a function with default values to parameters in Python:

Syntax 6- 5: defining a function with default values to parameters

```
def functionName(parameter₁ = value₁.₁,
                 parameter₂ = value₁.₂,...,
                 parameter_M = value₁.M) :
   command₁
   ...
   command_N

Call Function

functionName()
functionName(parameter₁ = value₂.₁,
             parameter₂ = value₂.₂,...,
             parameter_M = value₂.M)
```

Note :
- commands are executed from 1 to N, with default values (1.1 to 1.M) assigned to each parameter(1 toM). If no value is passed in the function call but if in calling the function there is a value (2.1 to 2.M) set in any parameterm that value will be used instead.
- N is the number of commands are executed, when the function is called.
- M is the number of parameters, whose values range from 0.

Example Program

```
def favoriteFruit(fName="Sansuay",lName
   ="Sakunsaedeengam",fFruit="orange"):
  print("The fruit that "+fName+" "+lName+" likes is
  "+fFruit)
 favoriteFruit(fName ="Ma",lName
 ="Boonlaimakmay",fFruit="papaya")
 favoriteFruit()
```

Results

The fruit that Ma Boonlaimakmay likes is papaya

The fruit that Sansuay Sakunsaedeengam likes is orange

In python, we can send list data as follows:

```
def favoriteFruit(fFruit):
  for n in fFruit:
    print("My favorite fruit is "+n)

fruit = ["orange","banana","mango","watermelon"]
favoriteFruit(fruit)
```

Results

My favorite fruit is orange
My favorite fruit is banana
My favorite fruit is mango
My favorite fruit is watermelon

defining a function with return

Using **return** returns a value when calling a function. The following is the syntax for defining a function with return in Python:

Syntax 6- 6: defining a function with return

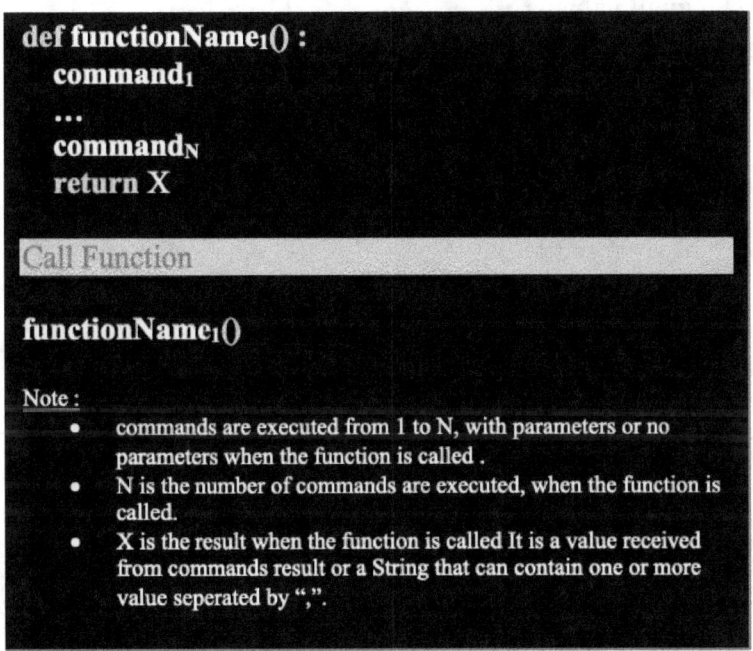

Example

```
def my_function(n):
  print("The input value is "+str(n))
  return "The return value is "+str(10 * n)

print(my_function(20))
print(my_function(5))
```

```
print(my_function(34))
```

Results

The input value is 20
The return value is 200
The input value is 5
The return value is 50
The input value is 34
The return value is 340

Using the returned value as a variable can be done as follows:

Example Program

```
def my_function(n):
  print("The input value is "+str(n))
  return "The return value is "+str(10 * n)

m = my_function(20)
print(m)
```

Results

The input value is 20
The return value is 200

Example Program

```
def cal(a, b):
   result = a + b
   result2 = a - b
   return "result a+b=",result,"result a+b=",result2
def nocal():
```

```
    return "no cal"
print(cal(2,2))
print(nocal())
```

Results

('result a+b=', 4, 'result a+b=', 0)
no cal

Example Program

```
def factorial(x):
   if x == 1:
      return 1
   else:
      return (x * factorial(x-1))

n = 5
print("Factorial value of", n, "is", factorial(n))
```

Results

Factorial value of 5 is 120

Lambda Functions

     A Lambda function in Python is a block of code that runs when executed and can pass data called parameters to the function. A function can return data as a result as a small function written in one line.

     The following is the syntax for defining a Lambda function in Python:

Syntax 6- 7: defining a Lambda function

> variableName = lambda parameter$_1$, parameter$_2$,..., parameter$_M$: command
>
> **Call Function**
>
> variableName(value$_1$, value$_2$,...,value$_M$)
>
> Note :
> - variableName stored result of command.
> - M is the number of parameters.

where parameter$_1$,...,parameter$_N$ are **arguments** which may or may not be present. while the command can use parameters$_1$,..., parameter$_N$.

Example Program

```
sawasdee = lambda : print("Hello")
sawasdee()
```
Results
Hello

```
sawasdee = lambda name: print("Hello "+name)
sawasdee("Sansuay")
```

Results
Hello Sansuay

```
add5 = lambda n : n + 5
print(add5(5))
```
Results
10
```
multi = lambda n,m : n * m
print(multi(5,6))
```
Results

30

defining a function with return value of the lambda function

The following is the syntax for defining a function with return value of the lambda function in Python:

Syntax 6- 8: defining a function with return value of the lambda function

```
def functionName(parameter_{1.1},
                 parameter_{1.2},
                 ...,parameter_{1.L},
                 parameter_{2.1}= value_{2.1},
                 parameter_{2.2}=value_{2.2},
                 ...,parameter_{2.M}= value_{2.M}) :
    command_{1.1}
    ...
    command_{1.N}
    return lambda  parameter_{3.1}, parameter_{3.2},
                   ...,parameter_{3.P}: command_2

variable = functionName(argument_{1.1}, argument_{1.2},
                        ..., argument_{1.L},
                        parameter_{2.1}= value_{3.1},
                        parameter_{2.2}=value_{3.2},
                        ...,parameter_{2.M}= value_{3.M})
```

Note :
- commands are executed from 1.1 to 1.N, with parameters (1.1 to 1.L and 2.1 to 2.M) or without parameters (1.1 to 1.L and 2.1 to 2.M) when the function is called and command_2 is excuted with parameters (3.1 to 3.P) or without parameters (3.1 to 3.P).
- arguments are actual value that are passed to the function in the order their parameters are defined from 1.1 to 1.L.
- The values from 3.1 to 3.M are used instead of the values from 2.1 to 2.M respectively if they were defined then the function was called.
- L is the number of parameters of the function without default value .
- M is the number of parameters of the function with default value.
- N is the number of commands of the function
- P is the number of parameters of the lambda for command_2.

Call Function that return lambda

variable(argument_{3.1}, argument_{3.2},..., argument_{3.P})
Note :
- command_2 are executed when using variable.
- arguments are actual value that are passed to command_2 in the order their parameters are defined from 3.1 to 3.P.

The lambda command can use function parameters as demonstrated in the following

Example programs

```
def funcandlambda(n):
  return lambda m : m * n

callfunclamb = funcandlambda(10)

print(callfunclamb(50))
```

Results

500

Finding exponents
```
def powerVal(n):
  return lambda m : m ** n

power2 = powerVal(2)
power3 = powerVal(3)

print(power2(5))
print(power3(5))
```
Results
25
125

```
def funcandlambda(n,q=5):
  q=4
  n=6
  return lambda m : m * n * q

callfunclamb = funcandlambda(10)
```

```
print(callfunclamb(50))
```
Results
1200

```
def funcandlambda(n,q=5):
  q=4
  n=6
  return lambda m,p : m * n * q * p

callfunclamb = funcandlambda(10)

print(callfunclamb(50,10))
```

Results
12000

Exercises

1. Create a function called sumX to get the values of 5 variables and sum them up and display the result.
2. Create a lambda function to take the values of 5 variables and combine them and display a result.

Chapter 7
Modules

To create a module, go to https://replit.com/ which lets you write Python code through a browser. Once there, you will find a previously created module called "main.py". Let's create a new file and name a new .py module with the following syntax:

create module

Syntax 7- 1: create python file

```
moduleName.py
```

using module

By naming our module my_module.py, we will get a module named my_module. When we want to use it, use the following syntax:

Syntax 7- 2: use a module

```
import moduleName
```

For example, write the my_module.py module as follows:
x = 5
After saving my_module.py in the main.py program, use the **import** my_module command. After that, we can call the defined variable or function saved in that module. The format of the command to call the variables saved in the module is as follows.

using variable in module

Syntax 7- 3: use a variable in module

```
moduleName.variable
```

For example when you need variable x,

```
import my_module

print(my_module.x)
```

Results
5

using function in module
We can add and use functions in a module, and can call the variables saved in the module with the following syntax:

Syntax 7-4: use a function in module

> $moduleName.functionName(parameter_1, parameter_2, ..., parameter_N)$
>
> Note:
>
> N is the number of parameters of the function.

Note: the presence or absence of parameters depends on the functions in the module.

For example, when we program a function to my_module.py as follows:

```
def sawasdee(name):
  print("Hello" + name)
```

When we run my_module and call this function in the program called by writing the program as follows.

```
import my_module
my_module.sawasdee("Sansuay")
```

Results
Hello Sansuay

using dictionary in module

We can also create dictionaries in modules, and call it with the following syntax:

Syntax 7-5: use a dictionary in module

```
moduleName.dictionaryName['key']
```

Example Program
Add a dictionary to the my_module module:

student_gender =

  {'Ammy':'Female','Jame':'Male','Mike':'Male',

  'Minnie':'Female'}

Then, run my_module and call this function as follows:

```
import my_module
print(my_module.student_gender['Jame'])
```

Results
Male

rename module

To rename the module, use the following syntax:

Syntax 7-6: rename a module

```
import moduleName as renamedModule
```

Once the name is changed, the new module name must be used throughout.

Example Program

import my_module as mm
print(mm.student_gender['Jame'])

Results
Male

Python has built-in modules that can be viewed at

> https://docs.python.org/3/py-modindex.html

using random module

To use the random module to randomly pick an integer value between 1 to 10, import random and write the program as follows:

import random
random_int = random.randint(1,10)
print(random_int)

When run, it displays a random value between 1 to 10.

First executed result could be:

2

Second executed result could be:

4

python has created a Python Random Module that has functions that can be used without having to write a new program. You can go see more at:

https://docs.python.org/3/library/random.html

Frequently Python Random Module is shown in Table 7-1

Table 7- 1: Frequently Used Functions of Random Module Provided by Python

Frequently Used Functions of Random Module Provided by Python		
Function	**Description**	**Example**
seed()	Generate a random number based on the bracketed seed value. Will always return the same random number.	To generate a random number with 8 as the seed value with random.seed(8), it will always return 0.2267058593810488 as the same random number Example import random random.seed(8) print(random.random()) <u>Results</u> 0.2267058593810488

Frequently Used Functions of Random Module Provided by Python

Function	Description	Example
randint()	Returns a random number between the given range, including the given integers.	To get a random integer value between 50 and 60: import random print(random.randint(50, 60)) Results 52 print(random.randint(50, 60)) Results 59
randrange()	Returns a random number between the given range, including the first integer but not the last.	To get a random integer value between 50 and 59: import random print(random.randrange(50, 60)) Results 52 print(random.randrange(50, 60)) Results 59

Frequently Used Functions of Random Module Provided by Python		
Function	**Description**	**Example**
choice()	Returns a random element from the given list (see chapter 3)	To return 1 random element from the fruit list: import random fruit = ["orange","mango","mangosteen","rambutan","durian", "pineapple","papaya"] print(random.choice(fruit)) Results pineapple
sample()	Returns a given sample of a list (see chapter 3)	To return a sample of 3 random elements from the fruit list: import random fruit = ["orange","mango","mangosteen","rambutan","durian", "pineapple","papaya"] print(random.sample(fruit,3)) Results ['mango', 'rambutan', 'orange']

Frequently Used Functions of Random Module Provided by Python		
Function	**Description**	**Example**
random()	Returns a random float number between 0.0000000000000 and 1.0000000000000	Returns a random float number between 0.0000000000000000 and 1.0000000000000000 import random print(random.random()) Results 0.8236315525555947
uniform()	Returns a random float number between two given parameters	Returns a random float number between 0.0000000000000000 and 10.0000000000000000 import random print(random.uniform(1, 10)) Results 3.351523796647222

While using programming applications, various functions available in imported modules will be displayed, such as in the case of **import random**. When the function is called, it will be displayed as shown in Fiqure 7-1:

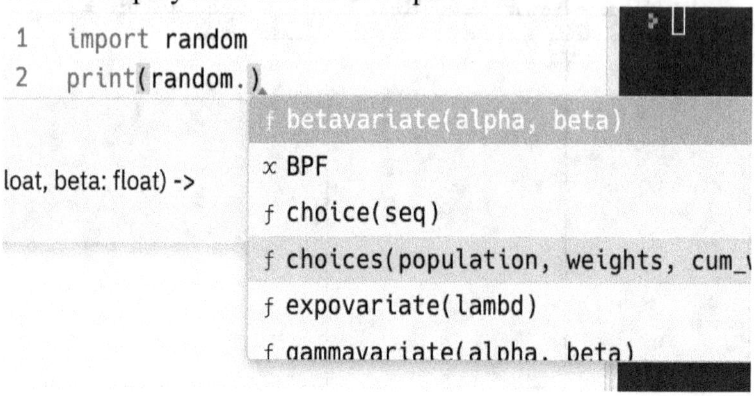

```
1  import random
2  print(random.)
```

loat, beta: float) ->
  f betavariate(alpha, beta)
  x BPF
  f choice(seq)
  f choices(population, weights, cum_
  f expovariate(lambd)
  f gammavariate(alpha, beta)

Figure 7-1: Visual Studio Code displaying all modules available of python for programmer

To use generate a random integer value between 1 and 10, navigate the menu to **randint()** as shown:

  f randbytes(n)
  f randint(a, b)
  ⁂ Random

Figure 7-2: module randint() is used

When clicked, the function will appear in the program.

```
import random
print(random.randint(1,10))
```

Figure 7-3: random. randint() will appear in program

If you want to get a random float value, use **random.random()** instead.

using datetime module

The datetime Module
import datetime

now = datetime.datetime.now()

print(now)
<u>Results</u>
2024-04-27 19:00:18.380691
This Module pulls the current date and time to display in a format we define, provided by Python, when calling the strftime() or strptime() functions is as follows:

datetime module formatting when calling the strftime() or strptime() function.

Command Format enclosed in brackets strftime() or strptime() of datetime Module is shown in Table 7-2

Table 7- 2: Command Format enclosed in brackets strftime() or strptime()

Command Format enclosed in brackets strftime() or strptime()	Displayed result	Example
%d	Date in 2 digits: '01'-'31'	import datetime now = datetime.datetime.now() print(now.strftime("%d ")) Results 07
%m	Month in 2 digits: '01'-'12'	print(now.strftime("%m ")) Results 02
%y	Year in 2 digits:	print(now.strftime("%y ")) Results

Command Format enclosed in brackets strftime() or strptime()	Displayed result	Example
	For example, 2023 displays '23'.	23
%Y	Year in 4 digits: For example, 2023 displays '2023'.	print(now.strftime("%Y")) Results 2023
%H	Time : hours in 12h, value '00'-'12'	print(now.strftime("%H")) Results 07
%I	Time: hours in 24h, value '00'-'23'	print(now.strftime("%I")) Results 07
%M	Time: minutes, value '00'-'59'	print(now.strftime("%M")) Results 38

Command Format enclosed in brackets strftime() or strptime()	Displayed result	Example
%S	Time: seconds, value '00'-'59'	print(now.strftime("%S")) Results 36
%p	AM or PM	print(now.strftime("%p")) Results PM
%f	Time: microseconds, '000000'-'999999'	print(now.strftime("%f")) Results 784460
%A	Days: 'Monday'-'Sunday'	print(now.strftime("%A")) Results Tuesday
%a	Days: 'Mon'-'Sun'	print(now.strftime("%a")) Results Tue

Command Format enclosed in brackets strftime() or strptime()	Displayed result	Example
%B	Months 'January'-'December'	print(now.strftime("%B")) Results February
%b	Months 'Jan'-'Dec'	print(now.strftime("%b")) Results Feb
%j	Order of days in 366 days 001-366	print(now.strftime("%j")) Results 038
%U	Order of weeks in 53 weeks 001-53	print(now.strftime("%U")) Results 06

For Thai dates and times, you must use the replace() command to convert Arabic numbers to Thai numbers. And convert full days, abbreviated days, full months, abbreviated months from English to Thai, as well as converting A.D. to B.E. by adding 543 years.

Download source code and consult at

Learn Python with Projects

https://www.variitsris.org/learning-python/

or scan QR Code

Exercises

1. Create a module to input 5 variables and display their sum.
2. Use the module from step 1 in 3 different programs that lets you input 5 variables and display their sum.
3. From step 1, generate 5 random numbers and display their sum.
4. Write a program to display the current date and time in hours and minutes, in English and Thai.

Chapter 8
String Formatting

Python string formatting is a method that lets programmers make sure the string will display variables as expected, using the following syntax:

Syntax 8-1: String formatting for Strings

```
variable    = String
stringName = "HeaderString{}FooterString"
```

Use String with String format

```
stringName.format(variable)
```

Note :
    {} is replaced String.

Example

```
animal1 = 'lions'
zoo = "There are {} at The Beauty Zoo."
```

```
print(zoo.format(animal1))
```

Results

There are lions at The Beauty Zoo.

If the variable to be displayed in the string has the decimal value to be displayed. The programmer can specify using the following syntax:

Syntax 8- 2: String format for decimal values

variable = *DecimalValue*
stringName = "*HeaderString{:.Nf}FooterString*"

Use String with String format

stringName.format(variable)

Note :
- *{:.Nf} is replaced DecimalValue.*
- N is the number of decimal to be displayed.

Example
```
foodPrice1 = 199.50
zoo = "Beauty Zoo sells animal feed for {:.2f} THB per bag."
print(zoo.format(foodPrice1))
```

Results

Beauty Zoo sells animal feed for 199.50 THB per bag.

For multiple variables to display in a string, use the following syntax:

Syntax 8-3: format to display multiple values inside a string

```
variable₁       = DecimalValue₁
variable₂       = String₁
variable₃       = DecimalValue₂
variable₄       = String₂
stringName = "HeaderString{:.Nf} PartString₁ {}
PartString₂{:.Mf} PartString₃ {}FooterString"
```

Use String with String format

stringName.format(variable₁,variable₂, variable₃,variable₄)

Note :
- {:.Nf} is replaced DecimalValue1.
- N is the number of decimal of *DecimalValue₁* to be displayed.
- M is the number of decimal of *DecimalValue₂* to be displayed.

Example
```
animal1 = 'lion'
foodPrice1 = 199.50
animal2 = 'fish'
foodPrice2 = 19.50
zoo = "Beauty Zoo sells {} feed for {:.2f} THB per bag and {} feed for {:.2f} THB per bag."
print(zoo.format(animal1,foodPrice1,animal2,foodPrice2))
```

Results

Beauty Zoo sells lion feed for 199.50 THB per bag and fish feed for 19.50 THB per bag.

Example
```
animal1 = 'lion'
foodPrice1 = 199.50
```

```
animal2 = 'fish'
foodPrice2 = 19.50
zoo = "Beauty Zoo sells {0} feed for {1:.2f} THB per bag
and {2} feed for {3:.2f} THB per bag. The {0} feeding
time is from 10am to 3pm, while the {2} feeding time is
from 9am to 4pm."
print(zoo.format(animal1,foodPrice1,animal2,foodPrice2))
```

Results

Beauty Zoo sells lion feed for 199.50 THB per bag and fish feed for 19.50 THB per bag. The lion feeding time is from 10am to 3pm, while the fish feeding time is from 9am to 4pm.

Alternatively, you may use the following syntax:

Syntax 8- 4: format with variables inside the string

```
stringName = "HeaderString{variable₁:.Nf}
PartString₁ {variable₂} PartString₂{variable₃:.Mf}
PartString₃ {variable₄}FooterString"
```

Use String with String format

```
stringName.format(variable₁=DecimalValue₁,
                  variable₂= String₁,
                  variable₃=DecimalValue₂,
                  variable₄= String₂)
```

Note :
- {:.Nf} is replaced DecimalValue1.
- N is the number of decimal of $DecimalValue_1$ to be displayed.
- M is the number of decimal of $DecimalValue_2$ to be displayed.

Example

```
zoo = "Beauty Zoo sells {animal1} feed for
{foodprice1:.2f} THB per bag and {animal2} feed for
{foodprice2:.2f} THB per bag. The {animal1} feeding time
is from 10am to 3pm, while the {animal2} feeding time is
from 9am to 4pm."
```

```
print(zoo.format(animal1= 'lion',foodPrice1 =
199.50,animal2 = 'fish', foodPrice2= 19.50))
```

Results

Beauty Zoo sells lion feed for 199.50 THB per bag and fish feed for 19.50 THB per bag. The lion feeding time is from 10am to 3pm, while the fish feeding time is from 9am to 4pm.

Exercises

1. Write a program to display member names in sentences. "Welcome, Member name" greeting them every time the member comes to use the program.
2. Write a program to display product names with prices with decimals and the unit of product in the sentence "Product name price Product price baht per unit" and design a product trading system shown as a class diagram and write the program as designed.

Chapter 9
Object- oriented programming

Object-Oriented Programming, discovered in 1960, is a method of writing code to be consistent with the analysis and design of real-world object-oriented systems by creating abstract **Classes** and creating identifiable **Objects** within those classes. You can then change the state of the class according to the environment with a **State Chart Diagram,** create relationships between classes with a **Class Diagram**, show details of the relationship between classes or objects in **Sequence Diagrams** or **Collaboration**

Diagrams and show work steps in an **Activity Diagram** to visualize how the whole system works before coding a program. System design analysts will make these diagrams to review the understanding of the system and use it as a summary before bringing it to the programmer to write a program, as well as use them to check the programmer's work before delivering it to the user. Since object-oriented programming is also compatible with C++, Java, Smalltalk, Delphi, C#, Perl, Python, Ruby, and PHP, using object-oriented programming in Python will be helpful for coders in making programs consistent with system design analysis using object-oriented principles. More importantly, object-oriented language programmers must be able to understand the diagrams mentioned above. For more information refer to the Advanced Python manual.

Create Class and Object

Class is the classification of things: types of animals, organizational positions, tools, equipment, machinery, furniture etc. When creating classes, create only ones we will use. For example, if we are going to create a system for a zoo, we must create animal-related classes, such as animals, pens, cages, feed, staff, etc. to be used in the system. As programmers, we must understand the diagrams, and if we are acting as both programmers and system analysts, we need to create diagrams to easily communicate to users.By using Unified Modeling Language(UML) class diagrams, it is a standard that ensures every programmer understands how to code object-oriented programs according to the user's needs. Therefore, we should use language in diagrams that is easy to understand. Creating a class consists of three parts,as shown in Figure 9-1.

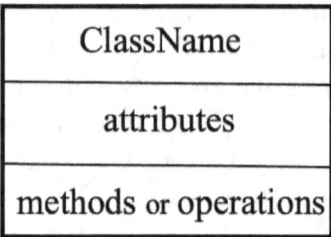

Figure 9-1: UML representation of a class

Class names must be consistent with names used in the real world for ease of understanding between programmers, colleagues in other roles and users involved with this program.

To create class in a program, use the following syntax:

Syntax 9-1: Creating a class in python

```
class ClassName :
    variable₁ = value₁
    variable₂ = value₂
    ...
    variableL = valueL
    # attributes properties
    def __init__(do, attribute₁, attribute₂,..., attributeN):
        do.attribute₁ = attribute₁
        do.attribute₂ = attribute₂
        ...
        do.attributeN = attributeN
    # display attributes properties
    def __str__(do):
        return f"HeaderString {do.attribute₁}partString₁ {do.attribute₂} partString₂...{do.attributeN} FooterString"
```

```
method properties
def method₁(parameter₁.₁,parameter₁.₂,
    ...,parameter₁.P)
  command₁.₁
  command₁.₂
  ...
  command₁.Q
def method₂(parameter₂.₁,parameter₂.₂,
    ...,parameter₂.R)
  command₂.₁
  command₂.₂
  ...
  command₂.S
  ...
def methodV(parameterV.₁,parameterV.₂,
    ...,parameterV.T)
  commandV.₁
  commandV.₂
  ...
  commandV.U
```

Note:
- L is the number of variables of Class
- N is the number of attributes of Class some Class no attribute.
- V is the number of methods of Class some Class no method.

Command of method ranging from 0 and have parameters or no parameter.

To create object in PYTHON program, use the following syntax:

Syntax 9-2: Creating an object in python

```
ObjectName = ClassName(value₁,value₂,...,valueN)
```

Note :
- N is the number of attributes of Class which has a value ranging from 0.
- values are passed in a sequence of attributes in Class when create Object from Class..

Here we will use an example to create an animal class, as shown in Figure 9-2.

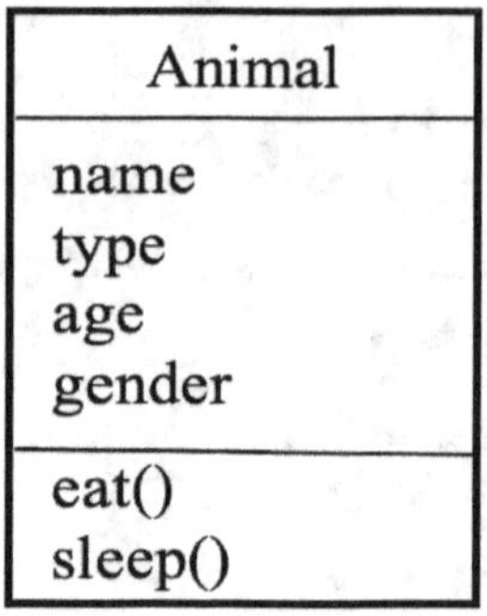

Animal
name type age gender
eat() sleep()

Figure 9-2: UML representation of the "animal" class

To display an object, use the following syntax:

Syntax 9-3: Display an object in python

```
display an Object

print(ObjectName)

use method of Object

ObjectName.method₁(parameter₁.₁,parameter₁.₂,
       ...,parameter₁.L)

ObjectName.method₂(parameter₂.₁,parameter₂.₂,
       ...,parameter₂.M)
...

ObjectName.methodᵥ(parameterᵥ.₁,parameterᵥ.₂,
       ...,parameterᵥ.N)
```

Learn Python with Projects

> **Note:**
> - V is the number of methods of Class some Class no method.
> Command of method ranging from 0 and have parameters or no parameter.

For example, to create the animal class:

```python
class Animal:
  place = 'Beauty Zoo'
  def __init__(do,name,type, age, gender):
    do.name = name
    do.type = type
    do.age = age
    do.gender = gender
  def __str__(do):
    return f"A {do.age} year-old {do.gender} {do.type} named {do.name}."
  def eat(animal):
    print(animal.name+"is feeding.")
  def sleep(animal):
    print(animal.name+"is sleeping.")
A1 = Animal("Sudsuay","lion", "3", "female")
print('At '+A1.place+' are these animals:')
print(A1)
A1.eat()
A1.sleep()
```

When running the program, you will get
At Beauty Zoo are these animals:
A 3 year-old female lion named Sudsuay.
Sudsuay is feeding.
Sudsuay is sleeping.

parent and child

In the case of classes, there are also properties that help make object-oriented programming different from non-object-oriented programming, namely **inheritance**, which requires the creation of a **parent** or **generalization**. For this textbook, we will use the term **parent** class, which is inherited by a

child class (or **specialization.**) This method combines a commonly used program into its parent to keep programs short and easily corrected in the parent class, so all its child classes can be called immediately. Therefore, this is very useful for when designing or drawing class diagrams, as shown in Figure 9-3:

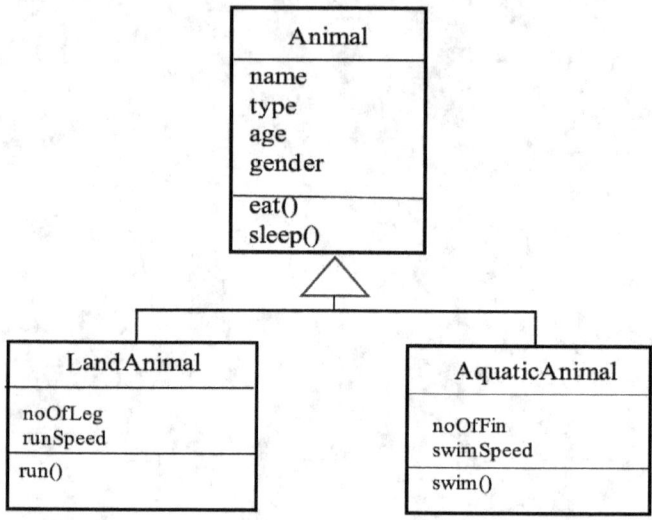

Figure 9-3: UML representation of an inheritance relationship.

This class diagram shows a parent and its children, where the parent is the Animal class. The base of the is divided into 2 child classes: LandAnimal and AquaticAnimal, which contain the same attributes in the Animal class, while different methods and attributes are that the child class, i.e. land animals having number of legs and top running speed, whereas aquatic animals have number of fins and top swimming speed.

To program Parent/Child classes in Python, Using only its parent's attributes and methods, without defining attributes and method for the child class, use the following syntax:

Syntax 9-4: Creating a child class in python

```
class ChildName(ParentName):
    pass
```

Create an and object of child class in python with the following syntax:

Syntax 9-5: Creating an object in a child class in python

$$ChildObjectName = ChildName(value_1, value_2, \ldots, value_N)$$

Note :
- N is the number of attributes of Parent Class which has a value ranging from 0.
- values are passed in a sequence of attributes in Parent Class when create Object from Child Class.

Example
```
class LandAnimal(Animal):
    pass
LA1 = LandAnimal("Sudsuay","lion", "3", "female")
print(LA1)
```
Results
A 3 year-old female lion named Sudsuay.

To add attributes or methods to a Child ,use the following syntax:

Syntax 9-6: Adding attributes or methods to a child class

```
class ChildName(ParentName):
    variable₁ = value₁
    variable₂ = value₂
    ...
    variable_L = value_L
    # attributes properties of Child
    def __init__(do, attribute₁, attribute₂,..., attribute_M)
        do.attribute₁ = attribute₁
        do.attribute₂ = attribute₂
        ...
        do.attribute_M = attribute_M
        # attributes properties of Parent
        ParentName._init_(do, attribute₁.₁, attribute₁.₂,..., attribute₁.N)
    # display attributes properties of Child
    def __str__(do):
        return f"HeaderString {do.attribute₁}partString₁ {do.attribute₂} partString₂...{do.attribute_M} FooterString"
    # method properties of Child
    def method₁(parameter₁.₁,parameter₁.₂,
        ...,parameter₁.P)
        command₁.₁
        command₁.₂
        ...
        command₁.Q
```

```
def method₂(parameter₂.₁,parameter₂.₂,
    ...,parameter₂.R)
  command₂.₁
  command₂.₂
  ...
  command₂.S
...

def methodᵥ(parameterᵥ.₁,parameterᵥ.₂,
    ...,parameterᵥ.T)
  commandᵥ.₁
  commandᵥ.₂
  ...
  commandᵥ.U
```

Note :
- L is the number of variables of Child Class.
- M is the number of attributes of Child Class which has a value ranging from 0.
- N is the number of attributes of Parent Class which has a value ranging from 0.
- P is the number of parameters of Child Class method₁ ranging from 0.
- R is the number of parameters of Child Class method₂ ranging from 0.
- T is the number of parameters of Child Class methodᵥ ranging from 0.
- Q is the number of commands method₁ ranging from 0.
- S is the number of commands method₂ ranging from 0.
- U is the number of commands methodᵥ ranging from 0.

Example

```
class LandAnimal(Animal):
  def __init__(do,name,type, age, gender,noOfLeg,runSpeed):
    do.noOfLeg = noOfLeg
    do.runSpeed = runSpeed
    Animal.__init__(do,name,type, age, gender)
LA1 = LandAAnimal("Sudsuay","lion", "3", "female", "4", "74")
print(LA1)
```

```
    def intro(do):
        print('A land animal '+'with '+LA1.noOfLeg+' legs'+' and a top speed of ' +LA1.runSpeed+' km/h')
LA1 = LandAnimal("Sudsuay","lion","3","female","4","74")
LA1.intro()
```

Results
A 3 year-old female lion named Sudsuay.
A land animal with 4 legs and a top speed of 74 km/h

Overrides

To **Override** an **Attribute** or **Method** of a parent class with one in a child class, you use an **Attribute** or **Method** with the same name as the parent class. For example:

```
class LandAnimal(Animal):
    def __init__(do,name,type, age, gender,noOfLeg,runSpeed):
        Animal.__init__(do,name,type, age, gender)
        do.noOfLeg = noOfLeg
        do.runSpeed = runSpeed
        do.type = 'land animal, the '+type

    def __str__(do):
        return f"A {do.age} year-old {do.gender} {do.type} named {do.name} has    {do.noOfLegs} legs and a top speed of {do.runSpeed} km/h."

LA1 = LandAnimal("Sudsuay","lion","3","female","4","74")
print(LA1)
```

This overrides the attribute of the parent class: **type**.This also overrides the method of the parent class: def __str__(do)

Results
A 3 year-old female land animal, the lion named Sudsuay has 4 legs and a top speed of 74 km/h.

Polymorphism

      Polymorphisms, meaning "many forms," allows coders to program and manage data types and function using a **single interface.** For example, A student's GPA can have multiple statuses, such as "normal" with a GPA of not less than 2.00, "Under probation" with a GPA under 2.00, or "dropped" with a GPA below 1.50. Thus, creating the **student** class that changes according to their context and impacts execution. This in turn lets us **overload** methods, meaning create a method with the same name but behaves differently depending on the input data. An easy example of this in Python are methods that are not class-based for programmers, such as using the '+'.

```
int1 = 22
int2 = 145
float1 = 19.1
str1 = "hello"
str2 = "Python"
print(int1 + int2)
print(type(int1 + int2))
print(float1 + float1)
print(type (float1 + float1))
print(str1 + str2)
print(type(str1 + str2))
```

Results
167
<class 'int'>
38.2
<class 'float'>
helloPython
<class 'str'>

or len()
```
str = 'Fruits starting with M'
fruit = ('Mango','Mangosteen','Melon','Mandarin')
fruit_list = ['Mango','Mangosteen','Melon','Mandarin']
fruit_dict = {'1':'Mango','2':'Mangosteen','3':'Melon','4':'Mandarin'}
print(len(str))
print(len(fruit))
print(len(fruit_list))
print(len(fruit_dict))
```
Results
21
4
4
4

Despite using the same len() method, Different values could be found depending on the type of data inputted.

For example, when animals of different ages receive different types of feed, such as lions over one years old be fed meat instead of milk, do as follows:

```
def eat(animal):
    if animal.age>=1:
        print(animal.name+ 'is over one years old and must be fed meat.')
    else :
        print(animal.name+ "is less than a year old and must be fed milk.')
LA1 = LandAnimal("Sandsuay","lion", 4, "wife", "4", "74")
LA1.eat()
```

Results
Sandsuay is over one years old and must be fed meat.

Example: polymorphism of multiple classes using a method with the same name.

```
class Cat:
  def __hot__(do, name, moveSpeed):
    do.name = name
    do.moveSpeed = moveSpeed

  def move(animal):
    print("The "+animal.name+" runs at a speed of "+animal.moveSpeed)

class Fish:
  def __hot__(do, name, moveSpeed):
    do.name = name
    do.moveSpeed = moveSpeed
  def move(animal):
    print("The "+animal.name+" swims at a speed of "+animal.moveSpeed)

class Bird:
  def __hot__(do, name, moveSpeed):
    do.name = name
    do.moveSpeed = moveSpeed

  def move(animal):
    print("The "+animal.name+" flies at a speed of"+animal.moveSpeed)

tiger1 = Cat("leopard", "60 kilometers per hour")
bird1 = Bird("parrot", "5 kilometers per hour")
fish1 = Fish("Goby", "20 kilometers per hour")

for x in (tiger1, bird1, fish1):
  x.move()
```

Results
The Leopard runs at a speed of 60 kilometers per hour.

The parrot flies at a speed of 5 kilometers per hour.
The goby swims at a speed of 20 kilometers per hour.

Inheriting Multiple Classes

Multi-class inheritance is when multiple parent classes are inherited to a child class, as shown in Figure 9-4:

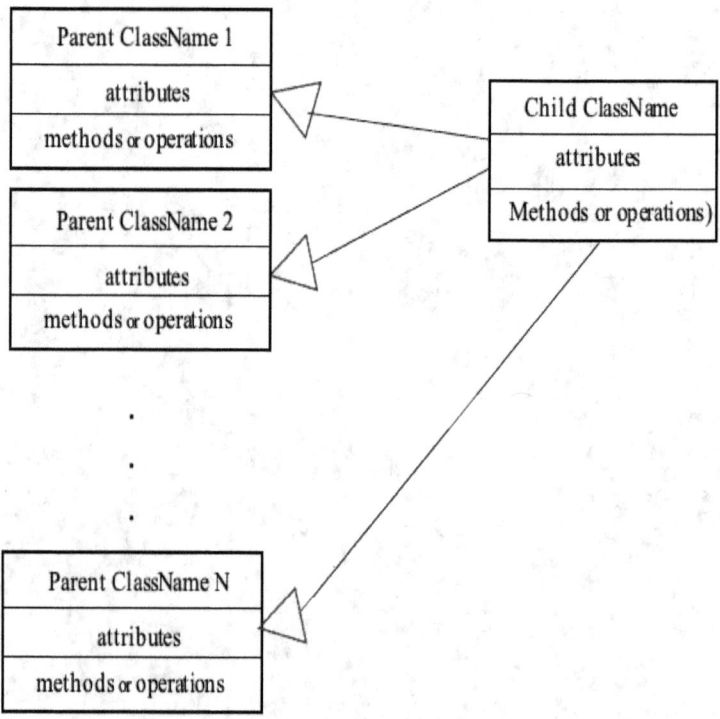

Figure 9-4: UML representation an inheritance relationship with multiple classes.

Example

Diagram of animals in the zoo to show how lions are land animals and mammals.

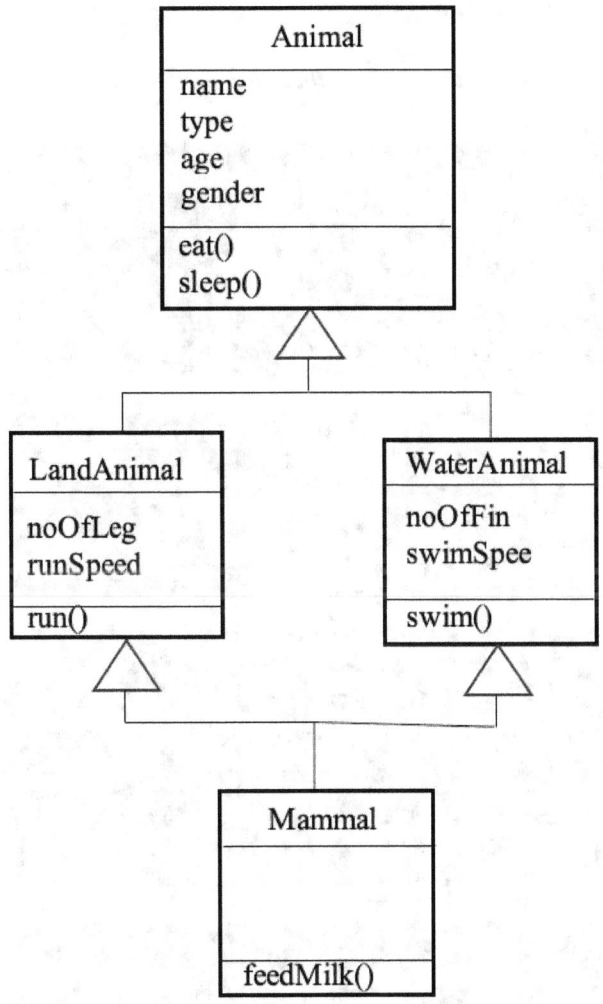

Figure 9-5: Class diagram of animals in the zoo that show an inheritance relationship with multiple classes.

The syntax used to program Python child classes that have multiple parents.

To create a child class that have multiple parents, using the following syntax:

Syntax 9-7: Create a child class that have multiple parent classes in python

```
class ChildName(ParentName₁, ParentName₂, ...,
                ParentNameP):
  variable₁ = value₁
  variable₂ = value₂
  ...
  variableQ = valueQ
  # attributes properties of Child
  def __init__(do, attribute₁, attribute₂,..., attributeR):
    do.attribute₁ = attribute₁
    do.attribute₂ = attribute₂
    ...
    do.attributeR = attributeR
    # attributes properties of Parent
    ParentName₁._init_(do, attribute₁.₁, attribute₁.₂,...,
                      attribute₁.L)
    ParentName₂._init_(do, attribute₂.₁, attribute₂.₂,...,
                      attribute₂.M)
    ...
    ParentNameP._init_(do, attributeP.₁,
                      attributeP.₂,..., attributeP.N)
  # display attributes properties of Child
  def __str__(do):
    return f"HeaderString {do.attribute₁}partString₁
{do.attribute₂} partString₂...{do.attributeR}
FooterString"
```

```
method properties of Child
def method₁(parameter₁.₁,parameter₁.₂,
    ...,parameter₁.ₜ)
  command₁.₁
  command₁.₂
  ...
  command₁.ᵤ
...

def method₂(parameter₂.₁,parameter₂.₂,
    ...,parameter₂.ᵥ)
  command₂.₁
  command₂.₂
  ...
  command₂.w
...

def methodₓ(parameterₓ.₁,parameterₓ.₂,
    ...,parameterₓ.ᵧ)
  commandₓ.₁
  commandₓ.₂
  ...
  commandₓ.z
```
Note :
- Q is the number of variables of Child Class.
- R is the number of attributes of Child Class which has a value ranging from 0.
- L is the number of attributes of ParentName₁ Class which has a value ranging from 0.
- M is the number of attributes of ParentName₂ Class which has a value ranging from 0.
- N is the number of attributes of ParentNameₚ Class which has a value ranging from 0.
- T is the number of parameters of Child Class method₁ ranging from 0.
- V is the number of parameters of Child Class method₂ ranging from 0.
- Y is the number of parameters of Child Class methodᵧ ranging from 0.
- U is the number of commands method₁ ranging from 0.
- W is the number of commands method₂ ranging from 0.
- X is the number of commands methodₓ ranging from 0.

Example program:
```
class Animal:
  place = 'Beauty Zoo'
  def __init__(do,name,type, age, gender):
    do.name = name
    do.type = type
    do.age = age
    do.gender = gender
  def __str__(do):
    return f"A {do.age} year-old {do.gender} {do.type} named {do.name}"

  def eat(animal):
    if animal.age>=1:
      print(animal.name+ ' is over one years old and must be fed meat.')
    else :
      print(animal.name+ ' is less than a year old and must be fed milk.')

  def sleep(animal):
    print(animal.name+" is sleeping.")
A1 = Animal("Rashun","lion", 3, "female")
print('At '+A1.place+' are these animals:')
print(A1)
A1.eat()
A1.sleep()
class LandAnimal(Animal):
  def __init__(do,name,type, age, gender,noOfLeg,runSpeed):
    Animal.__init__(do,name,type, age, gender)
    do.noOfLeg = noOfLeg
    do.runSpeed = runSpeed
    do.type = type+', a land animal'
    do.legFin = 'legs,'
    do.moveMethod = 'and runs with a top speed of'
```

```python
    def __str__(do):
        return f"A {do.age} year-old {do.gender} {do.type} named {do.name} has {do.noOfLeg} {do.legFin} {do.moveMethod} {do.runSpeed} km/h. "
    def run(landAnimal):
        print(landAnimal.name+" is running at the top speed of " +landAnimal.runSpeed+' km/h.')
LA1 = LandAnimal("Sudsuay","lion", 4, "female", "4", "74")
LA1.run()
print(LA1)
class AquaticAnimal(Animal):
    def __init__(do,name,type, age, gender,noOfFin,swimSpeed):
        Animal.__init__(do,name,type, age, gender)
        do.noOfFin = noOfFin
        do.swimSpeed = swimSpeed
        do.type = type+', an aquatic animal'
        do.legFin = 'fins,'
        do.moveMethod = 'and swims with a top speed of'
    def __str__(do):
        return f"A {do.age} year-old {do.gender} {do.type} named {do.name} has {do.noOfFin} {do.legFin} {do.moveMethod} {do.swimSpeed} km/h. "
    def swim(AquaticAnimal):
        print(AquaticAnimal.name+" is swimming at a top speed of " +AquaticAnimal.swimSpeed+' km/h')
AA1 = AquaticAnimal("Bee","goby", 2, "male", "5", "23")

print(AA1)
AA1.swim()

class Mammal(AquaticAnimal,LandAnimal):
    def __init__(do,name,type, age, gender,noOfFin,swimSpeed,noOfLeg,runSpeed):
```

```
    AquaticAnimal.__init__(do,name,type, age,
gender,noOfFin,swimSpeed)
    LandAnimal.__init__(do,name,type, age,
gender,noOfLeg,runSpeed)
    do.type = type+', a mammal'

    def __str__(do):
        return f"A {do.age} year-old {do.gender} {do.type}
named {do.name}."

    def feedMilk(mammal):
        print(mammal.name+" is breastfeeding.")
M1 = Mammal("BB","Dolphin", 2, "female", "5", "0", "0",
"0")
print(M1)
M1.feedMilk()
```

Results
At Beauty Zoo are these animalsL
A 3 year-old female lion named Rashun.
Rashun is over one years old and must be fed meat.
Rashun is sleeping.
Sudsuay is running at the top speed of 74 km/h.
A 4 year-old female lion, a land animal named Sudsuay has 4 legs, and runs with a top speed of 74 km/h.
A 2 year-old male goby, an aquatic animal named Bee has 5 fins, and swims with a top speed of 23 km/h.
Bee is swimming at a top speed of 23 km/h.
A 2 year-old female Dolphin, a mammal named BB.
BB is breastfeeding.

Association

Association is when a class is related to another class, such as the driver class being associated with a car class. To create associations, use the following Diagram:

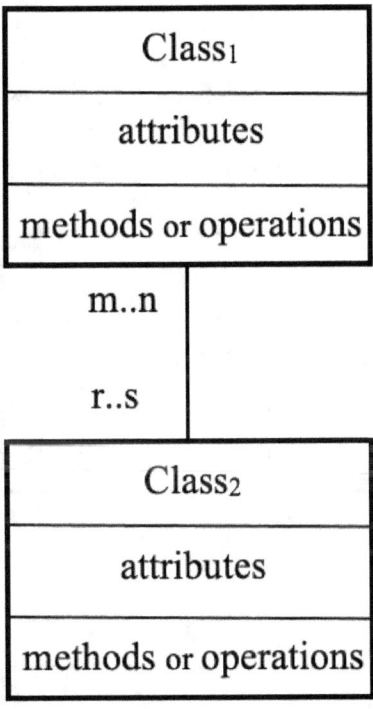

Figure 9-6: UML representation of an association relationship.

To create an association between $class_1$ and $class_2$ with method in python, using following syntax:

Syntax 9-8: Create an association between class₁ and class₂ with method in python

Aggregation

Aggregation is when a class has other classes join in, and will remain even if the joined classes no longer exist. For example, the "Company" class has aggregated "department" classes inside. Diagram as shown:

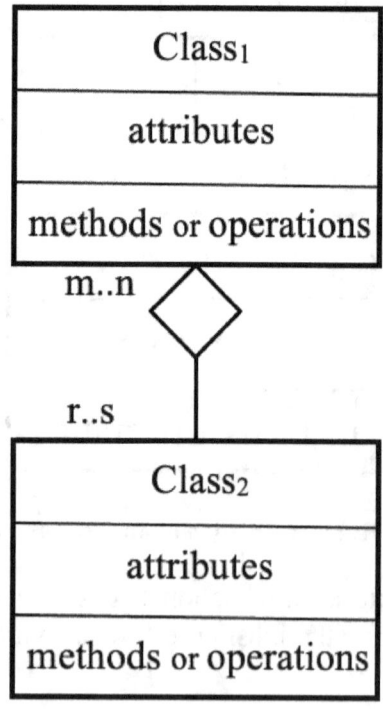

Figure 9-7: UML representation an aggregation relationship.

Note: m is the minimum and n is the maximum number of attributes in class 1, which is the aggregate class, within class 2. (This could be more than class, depending on the aggregate class.) r is the minimum and s is the maximum number of attributes in class 2, which is the subclass, within class 1.

Composition

Compositions are classes composed by the classes, such as the 'Cars' class is composed of wheels, doors, roofs, seats, etc., i.e. its components. diagram as shown:

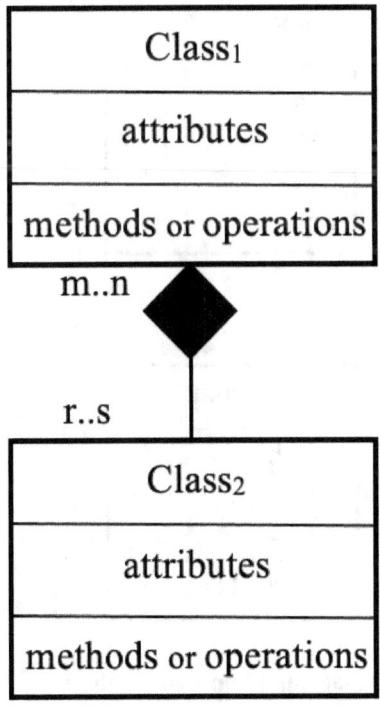

Figure 9- 8: UML representation a composition relationship.

Examples
1. **Association:** **Animals** have **habitats** of various **sizes** and in different **locations** within the zoo. Each animal can only belong in 1 enclosure.
2. **Aggregation**: in the **zoo** class, there are **habitats**, one **ticket office**, one **staff office**, and one **Gift Shop**.
3. **Composition:** A Land mammal is composed of body parts, such as a **head**, a **body** and **legs**

Example Diagram of a class Association

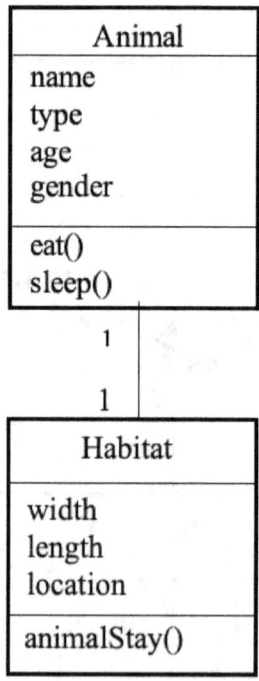

Figure 9-9: Class diagram of animals in the zoo with an association relationship.

Example Program

```
class Animal:
  place = 'Beauty Zoo'
  def __init__(do,name,type, age, gender):
    do.name = name
    do.type = type
    do.age = age
    do.gender = gender
  def __str__(do):
    return f"A {do.age} year-old {do.gender} {do.type} named {do.name}."

  def eat(animal):
    if animal.age>=1:
      print(animal.name+ ' is over one years old and must be fed meat.')
    else :
      print(animal.name+ ' is less than a year old and must be fed milk.')

  def sleep(animal):
    print(animal.name+" is sleeping.")

class Habitat():
  def __init__(do, location, width, length):
    do.location = location
    do.width = width
    do.length = length
  def __str__(do):
    return f"{'Located '+do.location+', the enclosure is '+str(do.width)+' meters wide and '+str(do.length)+' meters long.'}"

  def animalStay(do, animal):
```

```
    print(animal+' is located '+do.location+'. The
enclosure has an area of '+str(do.width * do.length)+'
meters squared.')


Habitat1 = Habitat("across the pool", 2, 6)
print(Habitat1)
A1 = Animal("Rashun","Lion", 3, "Female")
print(A1)
Habitat1.animalStay(A1.name)
```

Results
Located across the pool, the enclosure is 2 meters wide and 6 meters long.
A 3 year-old Female Lion named Rashun.
Rashun is located across the pool. The enclosure has an area of 12 meter squared.

Example
diagram of a class Aggregation

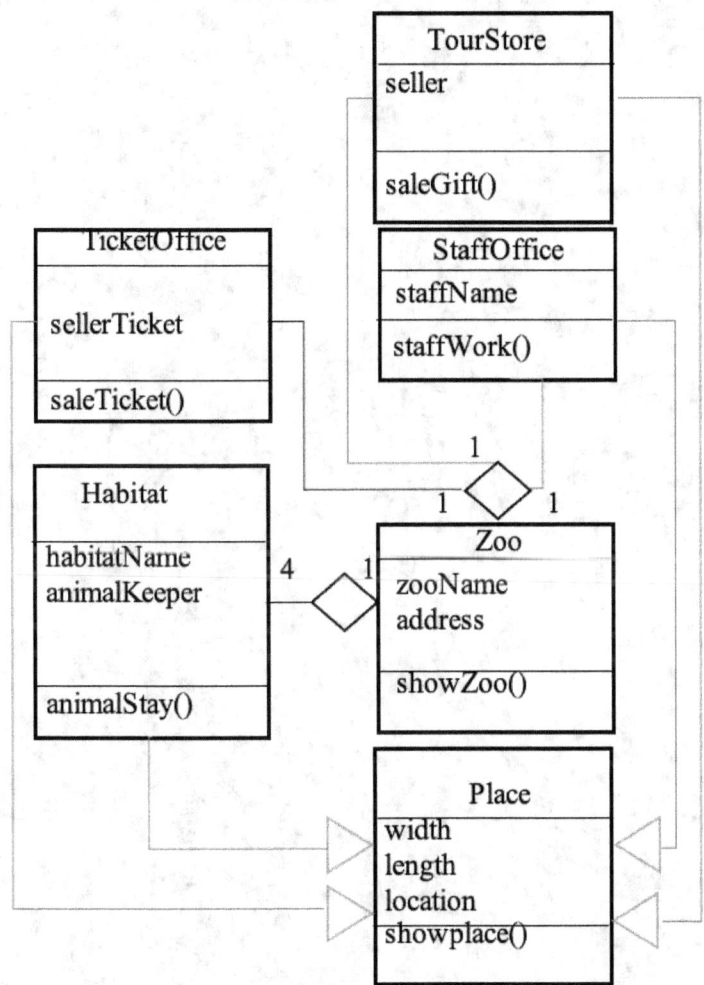

Figure 9-10: Class diagram of animals in the zoo with an aggregation relationship.

Example program

```
class Habitat():
    def __init__(do, location, width, length):
        do.location = location
        do.width = width
        do.length = length
    def __str__(do):
        return f"{'Located '+do.location+', the enclosure is '+str(do.width)+' meters wide and '+str(do.length)+' meters long.'}"

    def animalStay(do, animal):
        print(animal+' is located '+do.location+'. The enclosure has an area of '+str(do.width * do.length)+' meters squared.')

class TicketOffice():
    def __init__(do,location, width, length, sellerTicket):
        do.location = location
        do.width = width
        do.length = length
        do.sellerTicket = sellerTicket

    def __str__(do):
        return f"{'Ticket Office, staffed by '+do.sellerTicket}"

class StaffOffice():
    def __init__(do,location, width, length, staffName):
        do.location = location
        do.width = width
        do.length = length
        do.staffName = staffName
```

```python
    def __str__(do):
        return f"{'Staffed by'+do.staffName}"

class TourStore():
    def __init__(do,location, width, length, seller):
        do.location = location
        do.width = width
        do.length = length
        do.seller = seller

    def __str__(do):
        return f"{'Staffed by'+do.seller}"

class Zoo(object):
    def __init__(do, name, address, Habitat1,Habitat2,Habitat3,Habitat4,TicketOffice,StaffOffice,TourStore):
        do.name = name
        do.address = address
        do.Habitat1 = Habitat1
        do.Habitat2 = Habitat2
        do.Habitat3 = Habitat3
        do.Habitat4 = Habitat4
        do.TicketOffice=TicketOffice
        do.StaffOffice=StaffOffice
        do.TourStore=TourStore
    def __str__(do):
        return f"{do.name+' is located at '+do.address+'. Habitat 1 is located '+do.Habitat1.location+'. Habitat 2 is located '+do.Habitat2.location+'. Habitat 3 is located '+do.Habitat3.location+'. The Aquarium is located '+do.Habitat4.location+'. The ticket office is staffed by '+do.TicketOffice.sellerTicket+'. The staff office is staffed by '+do.StaffOffice.staffName+'. The gift shop is staffed by '+do.TourStore.seller}"
```

```
H1 = Habitat("across the pool", 2, 6)
H2 = Habitat("right of the entrance", 5, 6)
H3 = Habitat("right of the entrance", 5, 6)
H4 = Habitat("at the end of the pool", 2, 3)

print(H1)
T1 = TicketOffice("at the entrance", 2, 6,"Smiley Mcwelcome")
S1 = StaffOffice("end of zoo ", 2, 6,"Manny Jerial")
TS1 = TourStore("near exit door ", 3, 4,"Kassho Credit")
Z1 = Zoo("Beauty Zoo", "999, Bangkok, Thailand",H1,H2,H3,H4,T1,S1,TS1)
print(Z1)
```

Results

Beauty Zoo is located at 999, Bangkok, Thailand. Habitat 1 is located across the pool. Habitat 2 is located right of the entrance. Habitat 3 is located right of the entrance. The Aquarium is located at the end of the pool. The ticket office is staffed by Smiley Mcwelcome. The staff office is staffed by Manny Jerial. The gift shop is staffed by Kassho Credit.

Example diagram of a composition

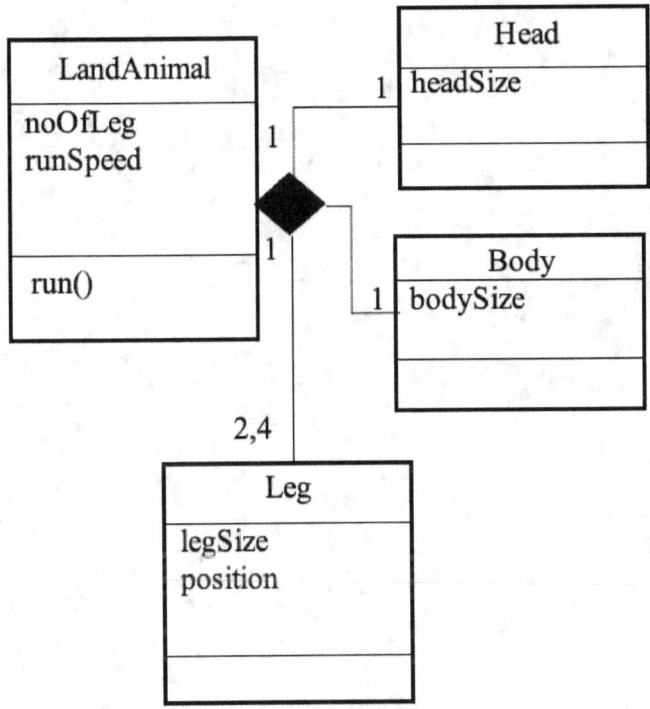

Figure 9-11: Class diagram of animals in the zoo with a composition relationship.

Example program

```
class Head:
    def __init__(do, headSize):
        do.headSize = headSize
    def __str__(do):
        return f"{str(do.headSize)}"
```

```python
class Body:
    def __init__(do, bodySize):
        do.bodySize = bodySize
    def __str__(do):
        return f"{str(do.bodySize)}"

class Leg:
    def __init__(do, legSize, position):
        do.legSize = legSize
        do.position = position
    def __str__(do):
        return f"{do.position+' '+str(do.legSize)+' cm. '}"

class LandAnimal:
    def __init__(do,headSize,bodySize,leg1Size,position1,leg2Size,position2,leg3Size,position3,leg4Size,position4):

        do.headSize = Head(headSize)
        do.bodySize = Body(bodySize)
        do.leg1Size = Leg(leg1Size,position1)
        do.leg2Size = Leg(leg2Size,position2)
        do.leg3Size = Leg(leg3Size,position3)
        do.leg4Size = Leg(leg4Size,position4)

    def __str__(do):
        return f"{'Head Length: '+str(do.headSize)+' cm. '+'Body Length: ' +str(do.bodySize)+' cm. ' +str(do.leg1Size)+str(do.leg2Size)+str(do.leg3Size)+str(do.leg4Size)}"

A1 = LandAnimal(80,120,60,'Front Left:',60,'Front Right:',60,'Back Left:',60,'Back Right:')
print(A1)
```

```
print('The head is '+str(Head(A1.headSize))+' cm long.')
print('The body is '+str(Body(A1.bodySize))+' cm long.')
A2 = LandAnimal(5,8,3,'Front Left:',3,'Front Right:',0,'',0,'')
print(A2)
print('The head is '+str(Head(A2.headSize))+' cm long.')
print('The body is '+str(Body(A2.bodySize))+' cm long.')
```

Results
Head Length: 80 cm. Body Length: 120 cm. Front Left: 60 cm. Front Right: 60 cm. Back Left: 60 cm. Back Right: 60 cm.
The head is 80 cm long.
The body is 120 cm long.
Head Length: 5 cm. Body Length: 8 cm. Front Left: 3 cm. Front Right: 3 cm. 0 cm. 0 cm.
The head is 5 cm long.
The body is 8 cm long.

Exercises
1. From exercise 1 in Chapter 8, add an association as part of its design.
2. From exercise 1 in Chapter 8, add an aggregation as part of its design.
3. From exercise 1 in Chapter 8, add a composition as part of its design.

Chapter 10
Try... Exception

When a program is being used, there's always a chance of malfunction, either from users, the hardware, network, equipment or power. This affects the operation of the program, so errors must be pre-written as follows:

> try: A set of instructions used to find errors, and if found, to perform any action.
> except : A set of instructions that, if an error is encountered, make an exception and do nothing.
> else : A command that executes when no errors are found.
> finally : Command when the error check has been completed.

Example

```
while True:
    try:
        x = int(input("Please enter a number: "))
    except ValueError:
        print("Sorry, that is not a number. Please enter again...")
    else :
        print("We've got the numbers.")
    finally :
        print("Thank you very much.")
```

Result in the case where numbers are not entered

Please enter numbers: !

Sorry, that is not a number. Please enter again...

Thank you very much

Result in case of entering numbers

Please enter number: 1

We've got the numbers.

Thank you very much.

Note: The 'finally' command is executed every time.

Exercises

1. From exercise 1 in Chapter 8, create an **exception** for 3 user errors.

Chapter 11
File Management with...as and JSON

File management includes
1. Open
2. Create
3. Edit/Write
4. Delete

Open File

To open a file, use the **open()** function with two parameters: the name of the file you want to open and the mode, as follows:

Mode 1: "r"– **reads** the specified value in the file instead of opening it. If that file doesn't exist, it will show an error.

Example
Create a txt file.

Type 'Test file command' and save the file name as 'test.txt' in the same folder where the program is stored.

```
f = open("test.txt")

print(f.read())
```

Results
Test file command

If the file is not found
```
f = open("test2.txt")

print(f.read())
```

Results
FileNotFoundError: [Errno 2] No such file or directory: 'test2.txt'

Create

Mode 2: "a"- **Appends** (creates) a file.

Example

Create test2.txt file.
```
f = open("test2.txt","a")
```

A new file, test2.txt, is created.

If this file already exists, no error will be displayed.

Write File

Mode 3: "w"- **Writes** into a file.

Example

Write the file Sawasdee.txt
```
Sawasdee= open("Sawasdee.txt", "w")
Sawasdee.write("Hello, this is Thailand.\n")
Sawasdee.write("A country with delicious food,\n")
Sawasdee.write("everyone has a smile.\n")
Sawasdee.write("A beautiful, safe place.\n")
```

with...as

with...as is a command that is similar to defining a variable with a different way to code, but yields the same results.

Example 1

In case the file you want to open is in the folder '/ExamplePythonCode/FileForPythonTest/'
```
f = open("/ExamplePythonCode/FileForPythonTest/Open.txt", "r")
print(f.read())
```
The command used to open the open.txt file is long since it is located in a very deep folder. Therefore, to make the programmer's work easier, it can be done by specifying it as a variable, f, which the programmer can write using with...as.

Example 2
```
with open("/ExamplePythonCode/FileForPythonTest/Open.txt", "r") as The dead one:
    print(The dead one.read())
```

Both examples have the same effect, meaning the files can be opened in the same way.

If the programmer wants to use a command to read each line of a file, write the command as follows:

```
with open("Sawasdee2.txt") as Sawasdee3:
    for line in Sawasdee3:
        print(line)
```

Or it could be written like this:

```
Sawasdee= open("Sawasdee.txt")
with Sawasdee:
    for line in Sawasdee:
        print(line)
```

Results
Hello, this is Thailand.

A country with delicious food,

everyone has a smile.

A beautiful, safe place.

Create File

Mode 4: "x"- Creating a file, but if an **extra** file with the same name already exists, an error will be displayed.

Example

```
f = open("Sawasdee.txt", "x")
```
Results
have file

> ≡ Sawasdee.txt

```
f = open("Sawasdee.txt", "x")
```
Results
FileExistsError: [Errno 17] File exists: 'Sawasdee.txt'
If not there will be a file created.

Delete File
If you want to delete a file, **import os** and use the **remove** command as in the example.

```
import os
os.remove("S.txt")
```

If the file to delete is not found, the following will be displayed:

FileNotFoundError: [Errno 2] No such file or directory: 'S.txt'
```
import os
os.remove("Hello3.txt")
```

The file named Hello3.txt will be deleted.
To create an exception, use the following:

```
import os
if os.path.exists("Hello3.txt"):
  os.remove("Hello3.txt")
else:
  print("File hello3.txt not found")
```

Results
The file Hello3.txt was not found.

Delete Folder

if we want to delete a folder, use the following:
```
import os
os.is rm("myfolder")
```
Results
delete folder myfolder

If this folder is not found

Results
FileNotFoundError: [Errno 2] No such file or directory: 'myfolder'

If the folder is found, it will be deleted.

JSON

JSON, short for JavaScript Object Notation, is a standard format for representing structured data based on the JavaScript Object syntax, typically used for sending data in web applications. (e.g. sending some data from a server to a client so that it can be displayed on a web page or vice versa.) Python itself has commands that can be used with JSON files, but you must import JSON first, where specific data type in Python can be converted to JSON as shown in the table.

Table 11- 1:Python to JSON conversion table

Python	JSON
dict	Object
list	Array
tuple	Array
str	String
int	Number
float	Number
True	true
False	false
None	null

loads

Using the **loads** command to convert the **person** value in Python to json, namely **person2**, then **print** to display the **person2** values, and to display only the **Marriage** value of **person2['Marriage']**

Example:
```
import json

person = '{"name": "Somsak", "Marriage": true,"age":87,"Country":"Thai"}'

person2 = json.loads(person)

print( person2)

print(person2['Marriage'])
```
Results
{'name': 'Somsak', 'Marriage': True, 'age': 87, 'Country': 'Thai'}
True

You can also use commands to use the values in the json file, for example:

fileperson.json
```
{"name": "Somsak", "Marriage": true,"age":87,"Country":"Thai"
}
```

open

Open a json file and read the value, then create a variable that loads the value, named **data**.

Example:
```
with open('person.json', 'r') as f:
  data = json.load(f)

print(data)
```

Results
{'name': 'Somsak', 'Marriage': True, 'age': 87, 'Country': 'Thai'}

convert Python to JSON
You can convert values from Python to JSON using the **dumps** command and improve readability using the **indent**, **separators** and **sort_keys** commands as in the example.

```python
import json
print(json.dumps({"name": "Nest", "age": 30}))
print(json.dumps(["orange", "pineapple"]))
print(json.dumps(("orange", "pineapple")))
print(json.dumps("orange"))
print(json.dumps(241))
print(json.dumps(50.23))
print(json.dumps(True))
print(json.dumps(False))
print(json.dumps(None))
person = {"name": "Somsak",
"marriage": True,"age": 87,"country":"Thai",
"children": ("Odd","Nee","Also","Jar","Small"),
  "pets": None,
  "cars": [
    {"model": "Benz S-Class", "price": 3.5},
    {"model": "BMW 500", "price": 2.5}
  ]
}
# Convert person to JSON:
person_json = json.dumps(person)
print(person_json)
# Make it easier to read by using the paragraph indent :
print(json.dumps(person, indent=4))
# By using separators with specified values:
print(json.dumps(person, indent=4, separators=(".", " = ")))
```

```python
# Sorting
print(json.dumps(person, indent=4, sort_keys=True))
```

Results
{"name": "Manee", "age": 30}
["orange", "pineapple"]
["orange", "pineapple"]
"orange"
241
50.23
true
false
null
{"name": "Somsak", "marriage": true, "age": 87, "country": "Thai", "children": ["Odd", "Nee", "Pun", "Jar", "Yar"], "pets": null, "cars": [{"model": "Benz S-Class", "price": 3.5}, {"model": "BMW 500", "price": 2.5}]}

```
{
    "name": "Somsak",
    "marriage": true,
    "age": 87,
    "country": "Thai",
    "children": [
        "Odd",
        "Nee",
        "Also",
        "Jar",
        "Small"
    ],
    "pets": null,
    "cars": [
        {
            "model": "Benz S-Class",
            "price": 3.5
```

```
      },
      {
        "model": "BMW 500",
        "price": 2.5
      }
    ]
  }
{
  "name" = "Somsak".
  "marriage" = true.
  "age" = 87.
  "country" = "Thai".
  "children" = [
    "Odd".
    "Nee".
    "Also".
    "Jar".
    "Small"
  ].
  "pets" = null.
  "cars" = [
    {
      "model" = "Benz S-Class".
      "price" = 3.5
    }.
    {
      "model" = "BMW 500".
      "price" = 2.5
    }
  ]
}
{
  "age": 87,
  "cars": [
    {
```

Exercises

1. Write a program to create, open, and edit a file to introduce yourself.
2. Create a json file introducing yourself and write a program to display the json file.

Part II
Software Development Projects

Congratulations! You now have enough knowledge about Python to create a project from Part I.

In Part II, readers will be introduced to four types of projects developed with Python so that readers can practice and adapt them for their own work. A brief description of the four types of projects is as follows.

Project 1 Game

In this project, readers will use the **Pygame** package to develop a 2D game that lets players shoot alien ships to explode. Make it in time before the alien ship drops down to the player's place. and must dodge alien bombs as they drop, and readers will be able to use the examples the author created to make changes to the program to make it more understandable at the end of the project. Readers will learn skills that will help you develop your own 2D games in Pygame.

As for Python, there are many game program developers who use it to develop famous games such as Pacman, Snake, Tic-tac-toe, etc., which readers can use to modify it in developing their own games as well.

Project 2 Web Application

In this project, reader will be able to use the **Django** package to easily develop a Web Application. Python, itself has a database that can be used without having to install any database. In this section, readers will be able to learn how to develop programs that can update, add, edit, and delete data.

Project 3 Data Analysis

In this project, readers will learn how to use beautiful and functional data visualization using **matplotlib** and **pygal** in a way that can be used for data analysis which is very useful in research. Various business jobs You can also create map presentations.

Project 4 Artificial Intelligence (AI)

In this project, readers will learn about Artificial Intelligence using **matplotlib, scipy, scikit-learn, numpy** package and Python development tools. The following Artificial Intelligence tools are available:

Mathematical Tools :
  Statistics
  - Mean
  - Median
  - Mode
  - Standard Deviation
  - Percentiles
  Creating data for testing
  Data Analysis

- Scatter Plot Analysis
- Linear Regression Analysis
- Polynomial Regression Analysis
- Multiple Regression Analysis
- Categorical Data Analysis

Data Mining
- Decision Tree
- Hierarchical Clustering
- K-Means
- Association Rules

Teaching and Testing Tools.

Project I
Game

Our first software development project is a simple game as a basis to be modified according to the programmer's needs to make programming more fun.

free games
For Python, there are **free games** that can be converted into games for programmers. For further study, follow the link

https://pypi.org/project/freegames/

Learn Python with Projects

To install freegames, go to terminal and use pip to install as follows:

VaritSris>python3 -m pip install freegames

When the installation is complete, the following is shown: Successfully installed freegames-2.5.3

To get help information, use the command

VaritSris> python3 -m freegames --help
usage: freegames [-h] {list,play,show,copy} ...

Free Python Games

positional arguments:
  {list,play,show,copy}
                        sub-command help
    list   list games
    play   play free Python games
    show   show game source code
    copy   copy game source code

optional arguments:
  -h, --help   show this help message and exit

Copyright 2023 Grant Jenks

To see which games can be played and edited:

VaritSris>python3 -m freegames list
on
avoid
bagels
bounce
cannon

connect
crypto
fidget
flappy
guess
illusion
life
madlibs
maze
memory
minesweeper
pacman
paint
pong
rps
simonsays
snake
tictactoe
tiles
tron
typing

Which are popular games with simple rules that players and programmers can understand.
Try using the snake program and use this command.

VaritSris>python3 -m freegames.snake

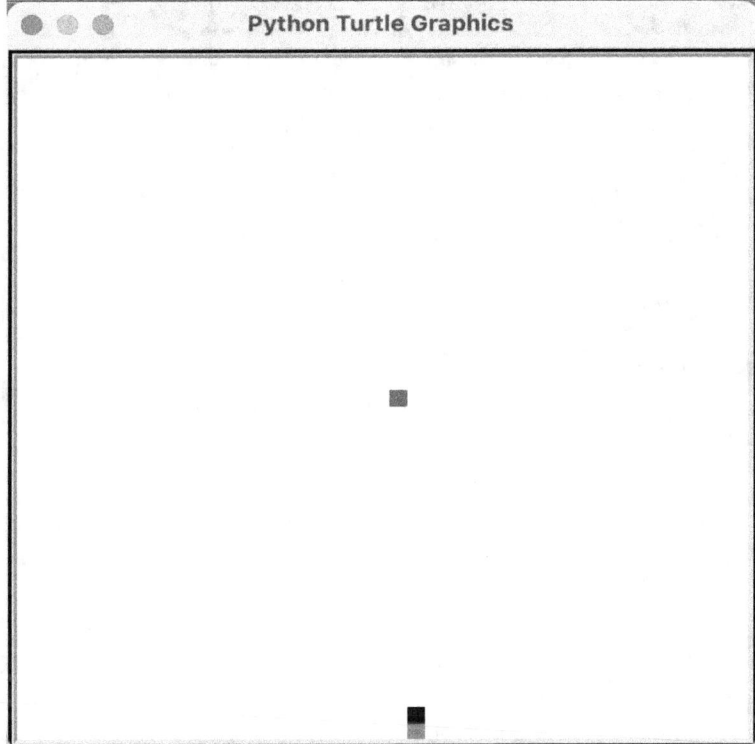

Figure Project I- 1: freegame.snake

If the programmer wants to develop it, do the following:

python -m freegames copy snake

python3 -m idlelib.idle snake.py

A programming window will appear.

```
"""Snake, classic arcade game.

Exercises

1. How do you make the snake faster or slower?
2. How can you make the snake go around the edges?
3. How would you move the food?
4. Change the snake to respond to mouse clicks.
"""

from random import randrange
from turtle import *

from freegames import square, vector

food = vector(0, 0)
snake = [vector(10, 0)]
aim = vector(0, -10)

def change(x, y):
    """Change snake direction."""
    aim.x = x
    aim.y = y

def inside(head):
    """Return True if head inside boundaries."""
    return -200 < head.x < 190 and -200 < head.y < 190

def move():
    """Move snake forward one segment."""
    head = snake[-1].copy()
    head.move(aim)

    if not inside(head) or head in snake:
        square(head.x, head.y, 9, 'red')
        update()
        return
```

Figure Project I- 2 : snake.py for developer

Pygame

To develop games, use **Pygame**, which has modules such as graphics management, animations, sound effects and drawing tools to make game development convenient and fast. Start by installing Pygame:

Installing Pygame

Pygame can be installed on UNIX (Debian/Ubuntu/Fedora/Red Hat/OpenSUSE), Mac, Windows, Raspberry PI by following the installation link:

https://www.pygame.org/wiki/GettingStarted

You must create a virtual environment so that when installing the pygame package and the game programs you want to develop, since at time of writing, pygame itself was developed under stable Python version 3.9.

In this case, use Python version 3.9 and name the virtual environment Here the name is ExPygame. Go to the terminal and use the command

VaritSris> pyenv activate PyGame
(PyGame) VaritSris> python3 -m pip install -U pygame==2.5.0

Results of installation
Successfully installed pygame-2.5.0

Check if something has been installed with pip.

(ExPygame) VaritSris>pip list

Package	Version
----------	-------
pip	22.0.4
pygame	2.5.0
setuptools	58.1.0

Using the Example program to create a new game

To use an example program of pygame to create a new game, we will be using the **aliens** game. To install aliens, use the following command:

(ExPygame) VaritSris>python3 -m pygame.examples.aliens

Results
pygame 2.5.0 (SDL 2.28.0, Python 3.9.16)
Hello from the pygame community.
https://www.pygame.org/contribute.html

When finished installing, you will see the game as shown in the picture.

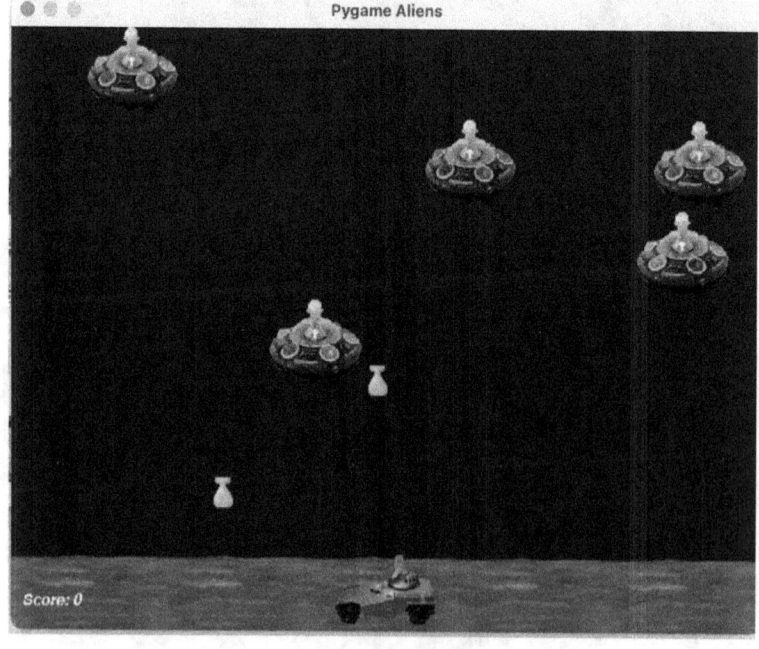

Figure Project I- 3:Pygame Aliens

Try playing. You move the car around by clicking on the left and right arrows and use the spacebar to shoot at the flying aliens while dodging falling bombs. When an alien is hit, the score increases and the aliens will explode, but if you fail to dodge a bomb or an alien, you will explode and the game is over.

We will create folder Game and subfolder under Game folder is data to store image files (png), animations (gif), sound, and fonts (Font) stored shown as follows.

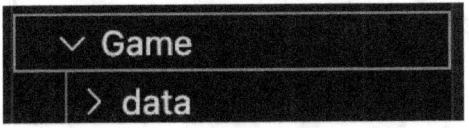

Our example is the "Poison rain removal" game. The player will be a car shooting the poison rain, turning it into clean rain. Each time you hit the poison rain you will score 1 point and if you are hit by the poison rain it will explode and you will lose. The files prepared and changed from the original files are as follows.

Table Project I- 1: Assets of aliens game files to be replaced

Assets of Aliens game files to be replaced	
Original Aliens Files	Poison Rain Files
alien1.gif	poisonRain1.gif
alien2.gif	poisonRain2.gif
alien3.gif	poisonRain3.gif
background.gif	greenGround.gif
shot.gif	bullet.gif

Assets of Aliens game files to be replaced	
Original Aliens Files	Poison Rain Files
bomb.gif	redRain.gif
player1.gif	GreenCar.gif
explosion1.gif	cleanWater.gif
Added for when poison rain falls to the ground.	badWater.gif

Assets can be downloaded at

https://www.variitsris.org/learning-python/

or Scan QR Code

Then, create a poisonRainRemoval.py with the program code as follows.

```
"""
Shows a mini game where you have to Poison rain removal.

What does it show you about pygame?

* pg.sprite, the difference between Sprite and Group.
* dirty rectangle optimization for processing for speed.
* music with pg.mixer.music, including fadeout
* sound effects with pg.Sound
* event processing, keyboard handling, QUIT handling.
* a main loop frame limited with a game clock from pg.time.Clock
* fullscreen switching.


Controls
--------

* Left and right arrows to move.
* Space bar to shoot
* f key to toggle between fullscreen.

"""

import random
import os
from typing import List

# import basic pygame modules
import pygame as pg

# See if we can load more than standard BMP
if not pg.image.get_extended():
    raise SystemExit("Sorry, extended image module required")
```

```python
# game constants
MAX_SHOTS = 2  # most player bullets onscreen
POISONRAIN_ODDS = 22  # chances a new POISONRAIN appears
BOMB_ODDS = 60  # chances a new bomb will drop
POISONRAIN_RELOAD = 12  # frames between new POISONRAINs
SCREENRECT = pg.Rect(0, 0, 640, 480)
SCORE = 0

main_dir = os.path.split(os.path.abspath(__file__))[0]

def load_image(file):
    """loads an image, prepares it for play"""
    file = os.path.join(main_dir, "data", file)
    try:
        surface = pg.image.load(file)
    except pg.error:
        raise SystemExit(f'Could not load image "{file}" {pg.get_error()}')
    return surface.convert()

def load_sound(file):
    """because pygame can be be compiled without mixer."""
    if not pg.mixer:
        return None
    file = os.path.join(main_dir, "data", file)
    try:
        sound = pg.mixer.Sound(file)
        return sound
    except pg.error:
        print(f"Warning, unable to load, {file}")
    return None

# Each type of game object gets an init and an update function.
# The update function is called once per frame, and it is when each object should
# change its current position and state.
#
```

```python
# The Player object actually gets a "move" function instead of update,
# Since it is passed extra information about the keyboard.

class Player(pg.sprite.Sprite):
    """Representing the player as a moon buggy type car."""

    speed = 10
    bounce = 24
    gun_offset = -11
    images: List[pg.Surface] = []

    def __init__(self, *groups):
        pg.sprite.Sprite.__init__(self, *groups)
        self.image = self.images[0]
        self.rect = self.image.get_rect(midbottom=SCREENRECT.midbottom)
        self.reloading = 0
        self.origtop = self.rect.top
        self.facing = -1

    def move(self, direction):
        if direction:
            self.facing = direction
        self.rect.move_ip(direction * self.speed, 0)
        self.rect = self.rect.clamp(SCREENRECT)
        if direction < 0:
            self.image = self.images[0]
        elif direction > 0:
            self.image = self.images[1]
        self.rect.top = self.origtop - (self.rect.left // self.bounce % 2)

    def gunpos(self):
        pos = self.facing * self.gun_offset + self.rect.centerx
        return pos, self.rect.top

class PoisonRain(pg.sprite.Sprite):
    """An poison rain fall. That slowly moves down the screen."""
```

```python
    speed = 13
    animcycle = 12
    images: List[pg.Surface] = []

    def __init__(self, *groups):
        pg.sprite.Sprite.__init__(self, *groups)
        self.image = self.images[0]
        self.rect = self.image.get_rect()
        self.facing = random.choice((-1, 1)) * PoisonRain.speed
        self.frame = 0
        if self.facing < 0:
            self.rect.right = SCREENRECT.right

    def update(self):
        self.rect.move_ip(self.facing, 0)
        if not SCREENRECT.contains(self.rect):
            self.facing = -self.facing
            self.rect.top = self.rect.bottom + 1
            self.rect = self.rect.clamp(SCREENRECT)
        self.frame = self.frame + 1
        self.image = self.images[self.frame // self.animcycle % 3]

class Explosion(pg.sprite.Sprite):
    """An explosion. Hopefully the PoisonRain and not the player!"""

    defaultlife = 12
    animcycle = 3
    images: List[pg.Surface] = []

    def __init__(self, actor, *groups):
        pg.sprite.Sprite.__init__(self, *groups)
        self.image = self.images[0]
        self.rect = self.image.get_rect(center=actor.rect.center)
        self.life = self.defaultlife
```

```python
    def update(self):
        """"called every time around the game loop.

        Show the explosion surface for 'defaultlife'.
        Every game tick(update), we decrease the 'life'.

        Also we animate the explosion.
        """
        self.life = self.life - 1
        self.image = self.images[self.life // self.animcycle % 2]
        if self.life <= 0:
            self.kill()
class ExplosionG(pg.sprite.Sprite):
    """"An explosion. Hopefully the PoisonRain and not the player!"""

    defaultlife = 12
    animcycle = 3
    images: List[pg.Surface] = []

    def __init__(self, actor, *groups):
        pg.sprite.Sprite.__init__(self, *groups)
        self.image = self.images[0]
        self.rect = self.image.get_rect(center=actor.rect.center)
        self.life = self.defaultlife

    def update(self):
        """"called every time around the game loop.

        Show the explosion surface for 'defaultlife'.
        Every game tick(update), we decrease the 'life'.

        Also we animate the explosion.
        """
        self.life = self.life - 1
        self.image = self.images[self.life // self.animcycle % 2]
        if self.life <= 0:
```

```python
            self.kill()

class Shot(pg.sprite.Sprite):
    """a bullet the Player sprite fires."""

    speed = -11
    images: List[pg.Surface] = []

    def __init__(self, pos, *groups):
        pg.sprite.Sprite.__init__(self, *groups)
        self.image = self.images[0]
        self.rect = self.image.get_rect(midbottom=pos)

    def update(self):
        """called every time around the game loop.

        Every tick we move the shot upwards.
        """
        self.rect.move_ip(0, self.speed)
        if self.rect.top <= 0:
            self.kill()

class Bomb(pg.sprite.Sprite):
    """A bomb the poison_rains drop."""

    speed = 9
    images: List[pg.Surface] = []

    def __init__(self, poison_rain, explosion_group, *groups):
        pg.sprite.Sprite.__init__(self, *groups)
        self.image = self.images[0]
        self.rect = self.image.get_rect(midbottom=poison_rain.rect.move(0,
5).midbottom)
        self.explosion_group = explosion_group

    def update(self):
```

```python
    """called every time around the game loop.

    Every frame we move the sprite 'rect' down.
    When it reaches the bottom we:

    - make an explosion.
    - remove the Bomb.
    """
    self.rect.move_ip(0, self.speed)
    if self.rect.bottom >= 470:
        ExplosionG(self, self.explosion_group)
        self.kill()

class Score(pg.sprite.Sprite):
    """to keep track of the score."""

    def __init__(self, *groups):
        pg.sprite.Sprite.__init__(self, *groups)
        fontSri = os.path.join(main_dir, "data", "SrinhichaarnunN.ttf")
        self.font = pg.font.Font(fontSri, 20)
        # self.font.set_italic(1)
        self.color = "white"
        self.lastscore = -1
        self.update()
        self.rect = self.image.get_rect().move(10, 450)

    def update(self):
        """We only update the score in update() when it has changed."""
        if SCORE != self.lastscore:
            self.lastscore = SCORE
            msg = "Score : %d" % SCORE

            self.image = self.font.render(msg, 0, self.color)

def main(winstyle=0):
    # Initialize pygame
```

```python
if pg.get_sdl_version()[0] == 2:
    pg.mixer.pre_init(44100, 32, 2, 1024)
pg.init()
if pg.mixer and not pg.mixer.get_init():
    print("Warning, no sound")
    pg.mixer = None


fullscreen = False
# Set the display mode
winstyle = 0  # |FULLSCREEN
bestdepth = pg.display.mode_ok(SCREENRECT.size, winstyle, 32)
screen = pg.display.set_mode(SCREENRECT.size, winstyle, bestdepth)

# Load images, assign to sprite classes
# (do this before the classes are used, after screen setup)
img = load_image("GreenCar.gif")
Player.images = [img, pg.transform.flip(img, 1, 0)]
img = load_image("cleanWater.gif")
Explosion.images = [img, pg.transform.flip(img, 1, 1)]
# Add wastewater when poison rain falls to the ground.
img = load_image("badWater.gif")
ExplosionG.images = [img, pg.transform.flip(img, 1, 1)]
PoisonRain.images = [load_image(im) for im in ("poisonRain1.gif",
"poisonRain2.gif", "poisonRain3.gif")]
Bomb.images = [load_image("redRain.gif")]
Shot.images = [load_image("bullet.gif")]

# Decorate the game window
icon = pg.transform.scale(PoisonRain.images[0], (32, 32))
pg.display.set_icon(icon)
pg.display.set_caption("Pygame PoisonRains")
pg.mouse.set_visible(0)

# Create the background, tile the bgd image
bgdtile = load_image("greenGround.gif")
background = pg.Surface(SCREENRECT.size)
```

```python
    for x in range(0, SCREENRECT.width, bgdtile.get_width()):
        background.blit(bgdtile, (x, 0))
    screen.blit(background, (0, 0))
    pg.display.flip()

    # Load the sound effects
    boom_sound = load_sound("boom.wav")
    shoot_sound = load_sound("car_door.wav")
    if pg.mixer:
        music = os.path.join(main_dir, "data", "house_lo.wav")
        pg.mixer.music.load(music)
        pg.mixer.music.play(-1)

    # Initialize Game Groups
    poison_rains = pg.sprite.Group()
    shots = pg.sprite.Group()
    bombs = pg.sprite.Group()
    all = pg.sprite.RenderUpdates()
    lastpoison_rain = pg.sprite.GroupSingle()

    # Create Some Starting Values
    global score
    poison_rainreload = POISONRAIN_RELOAD
    clock = pg.time.Clock()

    # initialize our starting sprites
    global SCORE
    player = Player(all)
    PoisonRain(
        poison_rains, all, lastpoison_rain
    ) # note, this 'lives' because it goes into a sprite group
    if pg.font:
        all.add(Score(all))

    # Run our main loop whilst the player is alive.
    while player.alive():
```

```python
# get input
for event in pg.event.get():
    if event.type == pg.QUIT:
        return
    if event.type == pg.KEYDOWN and event.key == pg.K_ESCAPE:
        return
    elif event.type == pg.KEYDOWN:
        if event.key == pg.K_f:
            if not fullscreen:
                print("Changing to FULLSCREEN")
                screen_backup = screen.copy()
                screen = pg.display.set_mode(
                    SCREENRECT.size, winstyle | pg.FULLSCREEN, bestdepth
                )
                screen.blit(screen_backup, (0, 0))
            else:
                print("Changing to windowed mode")
                screen_backup = screen.copy()
                screen = pg.display.set_mode(
                    SCREENRECT.size, winstyle, bestdepth
                )
                screen.blit(screen_backup, (0, 0))
            pg.display.flip()
            fullscreen = not fullscreen

keystate = pg.key.get_pressed()

# clear/erase the last drawn sprites
all.clear(screen, background)

# update all the sprites
all.update()

# handle player input
direction = keystate[pg.K_RIGHT] - keystate[pg.K_LEFT]
player.move(direction)
```

```python
firing = keystate[pg.K_SPACE]
if not player.reloading and firing and len(shots) < MAX_SHOTS:
    Shot(player.gunpos(), shots, all)
    if pg.mixer and shoot_sound is not None:
        shoot_sound.play()
player.reloading = firing

# Create new poison_rain
if poison_rainreload:
    poison_rainreload = poison_rainreload - 1
elif not int(random.random() * POISONRAIN_ODDS):
    PoisonRain(poison_rains, all, lastpoison_rain)
    poison_rainreload = POISONRAIN_RELOAD

# Drop bombs
if lastpoison_rain and not int(random.random() * BOMB_ODDS):
    Bomb(lastpoison_rain.sprite, all, bombs, all)

# Detect collisions between poison_rains and players.
for poison_rain in pg.sprite.spritecollide(player, poison_rains, 1):
    if pg.mixer and boom_sound is not None:
        boom_sound.play()
    Explosion(poison_rain, all)
    Explosion(player, all)
    SCORE = SCORE + 1
    player.kill()

# See if shots hit the poison_rains.
for poison_rain in pg.sprite.groupcollide(poison_rains, shots, 1, 1).keys():
    if pg.mixer and boom_sound is not None:
        boom_sound.play()
    Explosion(poison_rain, all)
    SCORE = SCORE + 1

# See if poison_rain bombs hit the player.
for bomb in pg.sprite.spritecollide(player, bombs, 1):
```

```
        if pg.mixer and boom_sound is not None:
            boom_sound.play()
        Explosion(player, all)
        Explosion(bomb, all)
        player.kill()

    # draw the scene
    dirty = all.draw(screen)
    pg.display.update(dirty)

    # cap the framerate at 40fps. Also called 40HZ or 40 times per second.
    clock.tick(40)

if pg.mixer:
    pg.mixer.music.fadeout(1000)
pg.time.wait(1000)

# call the "main" function if running this script
if __name__ == "__main__":
    main()
    pg.quit()
```

run poisonRainRemoval.py with command:

(PyGame) VariitSris> python poisonRainRemoval.py
Result

Learn Python with Projects

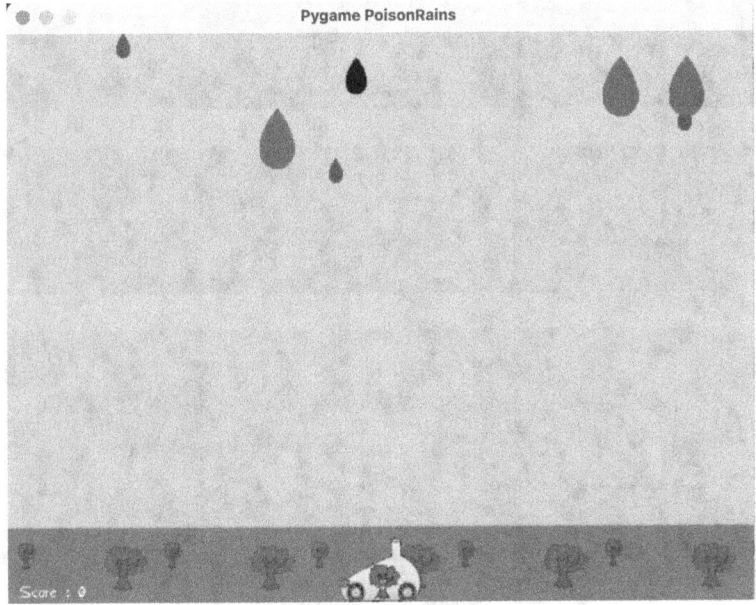

Figure Project I-4: Pygame PoisonRains

Display the background as the desired image.

With the original program, to display the background as the desired image (in this case, image 1.png) store the image in a folder that you created yourself with the screen size of height x width (400 pixels x 400 pixels).

```
import pygame
pygame.init()
white = (255, 255, 255)
# assigning values to height and width variable
height = 400
width = 400
# creating the display surface object
# of specific dimension..e(X, Y).
display_surface = pygame.display.set_mode((height, width))
```

```python
# set the pygame window name
pygame.display.set_caption('Image')

# creating a surface object, image is drawn on it.
image = pygame.image.load(r'
/Users/Python/ExamplePythonCode/Game/data/1.png'
)

# infinite loop
while True:
    display_surface.fill(white)
    display_surface.blit(image, (0, 0))

    for event in pygame.event.get():
        if event.type == pygame.QUIT:
            pygame.quit()
            # quit the program.
            quit()
        # Draws the surface object to the screen.
        pygame.display.update()
```

Results

Figure Project I- 5: Replaced background Image

Drawing Geometric Shapes

```python
import pygame

pygame.init()
screen = pygame.display.set_mode((500, 500))
pygame.display.set_caption(u'Display drawing geometric shapes ')
done = False
changeColor = True
x = 5
y = 5

while not done:
    for event in pygame.event.get():
        if event.type == pygame.QUIT:
            done = True

        #red color
        color = (253, 2, 40)
        color2 = (253, 247, 2)
        color3 = (255, 255, 255)
        color4 = (2, 6, 253)
        color5 = (23, 115, 44)
#Draw a square. If width == 0, a square will be created
with the color filling the square area.
        pygame.draw.rect(screen, color, pygame.Rect(30,30,30,30),0)
    #Draw a rectangle. If width > 0, a rectangle will be
created with a rectangular box sized according to the width
value.
        pygame.draw.rect(screen, color, pygame.Rect(60, 60, 30, 30),10)
    #Draw a rectangle If width > 0, no rectangle will be
created.
```

```
    pygame.draw.rect(screen, color, pygame.Rect(90, 90, 30, 30),-2)
    #Draw a polygon. Enter 5 points. You can enter width like drawing a rectangle.
    pygame.draw.polygon(screen, color2, ((170,40),(40,180),(180,200),(200,225),(225,170)))
    #Draw a sphere. Enter the position. Enter the size. You can enter the width as well as drawing a rectangle.
    pygame.draw.circle(screen, color3, (300,300), 60)
    #Draw a straight line. Enter the starting and ending position of the line. You can enter the width just like drawing a rectangle.
    pygame.draw.line(screen, color4, (300,50), (450,250), 4)
    #Draw a straight line. Enter start and end positions. You can enter width just like drawing a rectangle.
    pygame.draw.ellipse(screen, color5, (30, 320, 130, 80))
    pygame.display.flip()
```

Results as shown

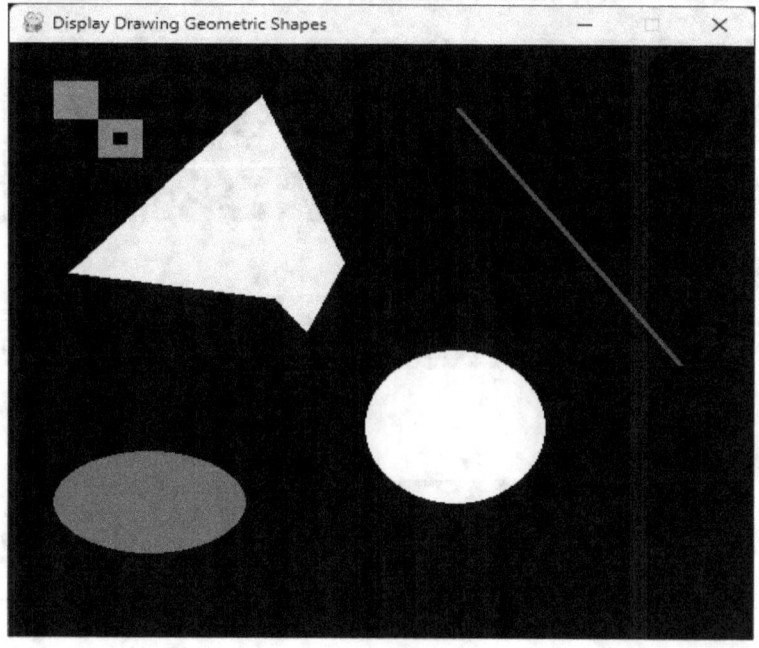

Figure Project I- 6: Drawing geometric shapes

Drawing a Rectangle

Drawing and moving a rectangle can be done in many ways. Use the following configuration:
1. x,y
2. top, left, right, bottom
3. topleft, bottomleft, topright, bottomright
4. midtop, midleft, midbottom, midright
5. center, centerx, centery
6. size, width, height
7. w,h

pygame defines the rectangle as follows:

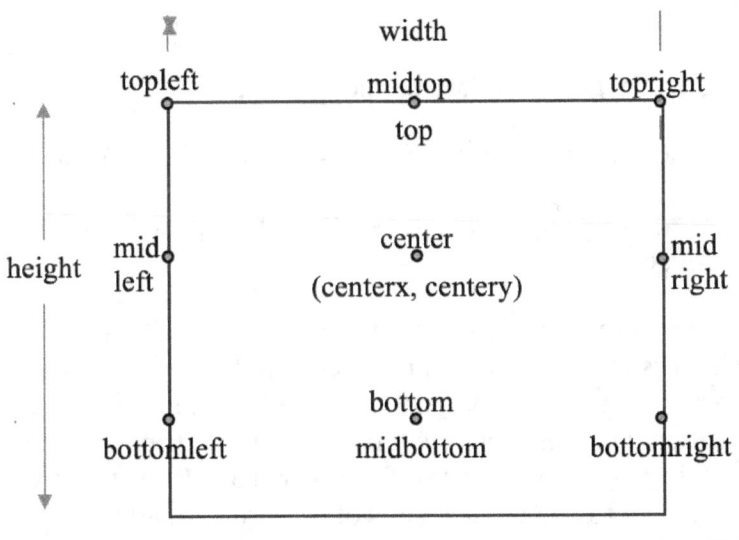

Figure Project I- 7: Pygame defines rectangles

Example Program

```
import pygame
```

```
pygame.init()
screen = pygame.display.set_mode((400, 300))
done = False

while not done:
    for event in pygame.event.get():
        if event.type == pygame.QUIT:
            done = True
    pygame.draw.rect(screen, (254, 247, 2),
pygame.Rect(30, 30, 60, 60))

    pygame.display.flip()
```

The command

screen = pygame.display.set_mode((400, 300))

sets the display screen to (height) 400 px by (width) 300 px

pygame.draw.rect(screen, (254, 247, 2), pygame.Rect(30, 30, 60, 60))

Creates a rectangle with RGB colors values of 254, 247, 2 which is yellow. Programmers can find the desired color from https://htmlcolorcodes.com/ and display it at the position counting from the top right corner of the screen as 0,0. By program the upper right corner at 30,30 and the lower left corner as 60,60, the results of this program are:

Figure Project I- 8: a drawn rectangle

Programming Keyboard Controls

An example of a program for keyboard control checking key presses and releases.

```
import pygame
pygame.init()
# Show caption in window
pygame.display.set_caption(u'Show key presses and releases.')
# Create a window size 400x400 px
pygame.display.set_mode((400, 400))

while True:
    # Wait for key press event
    event = pygame.event.wait()
    # Click to close window
```

```python
        if event.type == pygame.QUIT:
            break
        # Check which keys were pressed or released at the console
        if event.type in (pygame.KEYDOWN, pygame.KEYUP):
            # Show key
            key_name = pygame.key.name(event.key)
            # Show keys in uppercase letters
            key_name = key_name.upper()
            # If the key is pressed
            if event.type == pygame.KEYDOWN:
                # Display the pressed key on the console.
                print(u'Key pressed: "{}"'.format(key_name))
            # If the key is released
            elif event.type == pygame.KEYUP:
                # Display the released key on the console.
                print(u'Key released: "{}"'.format(key_name))
```

Results show on screen

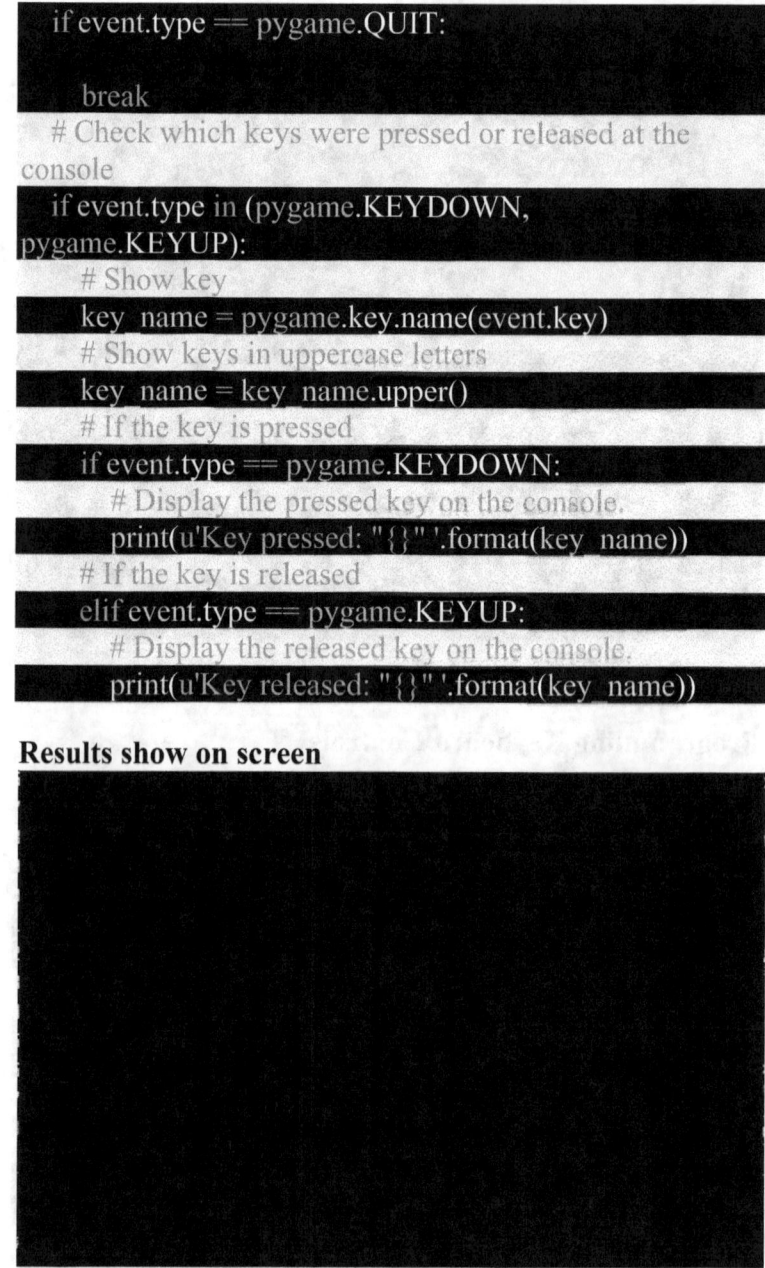

Figure Project I- 9:Initial keyboard controls screen

Terminal display results as you press and release keys.
Key pressed: "UP"
Key released: "UP"
Key pressed: "RIGHT"
Key released: "RIGHT"
Key pressed: "LEFT"
Key released: "LEFT"
Key pressed: ""
Key released: ""
Key pressed: ""
Key released: ""
Key pressed: "LEFT META"
Key released: "LEFT META"
Key pressed: "LEFT CTRL"
Key released: "LEFT CTRL"
Key pressed: "LEFT SHIFT"
Key released: "LEFT SHIFT"
Key pressed: "1"
Key released: "1"
Key pressed: "2"
Key released: "2"
Key pressed: ""
Key released: ""
Key pressed: "CAPS LOCK"
Key released: "CAPS LOCK"
Key pressed: "Q"
Key released: "Q"
Key pressed: "W"
Key released: "W"
Key pressed: "X"
Key released: "X"
Key pressed: "LEFT SHIFT"
Key pressed: "LEFT ALT"
Key released: "LEFT SHIFT"
Key released: "LEFT ALT"

To program to create a square when using the keys to draw colored lines using directional buttons, do the following:

```python
import pygame

pygame.init()
screen = pygame.display.set_mode((800, 600))
pygame.display.set_caption(u'Show key presses, lines drawn and color changes.')
done = False
changeColor = True
x = 5
y = 5

while not done:
    for event in pygame.event.get():
        if event.type == pygame.QUIT:
            done = True
            #Press SPACE to change colors.
        if event.type == pygame.KEYDOWN and event.key == pygame.K_SPACE:
            changeColor = not changeColor
    #Set each press to increase and decrease the x,y position values by 0.5. If you press and hold, it will increase and decrease the x,y position values indefinitely.
    pressed = pygame.key.get_pressed()
    if pressed[pygame.K_UP]: y -= 0.5
    if pressed[pygame.K_DOWN]: y += 0.5
    if pressed[pygame.K_LEFT]: x -= 0.5
    if pressed[pygame.K_RIGHT]: x += 0.5
    #change to yellow
    if changeColor:
        color = (254, 247, 2)
    else:
    #change to red
        color = (253, 2, 40)
    #Draw a 5x5 px rectangle in changing positions.
```

Learn Python with Projects

```
pygame.draw.rect(screen, color, pygame.Rect(x, y, 5, 5))

pygame.display.flip()
```
Results as Shown

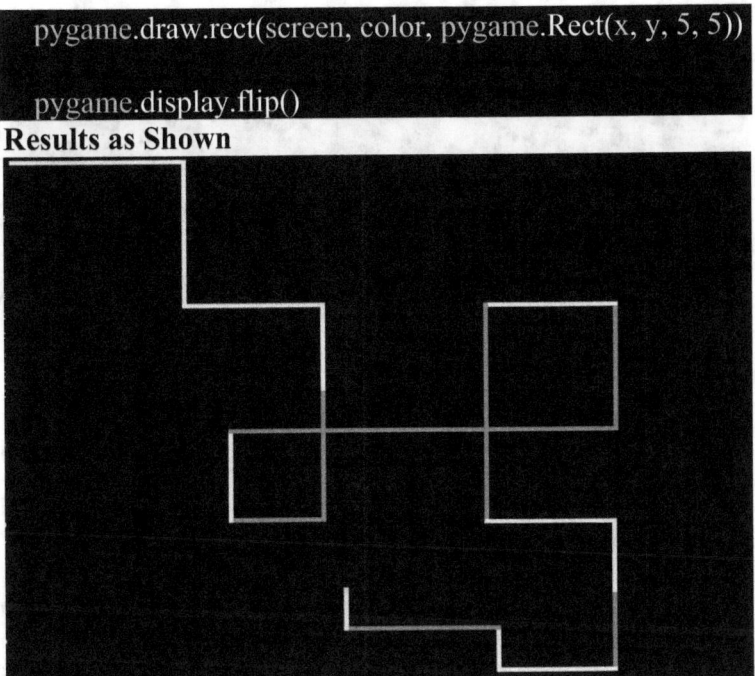

Figure Project I- 10:Lines drawn with keyboard controls

Programming Mouse Controls

In this example, we will demonstrate mouse controls by displaying coordinates of x and y in the console whenever a mouse is clicked in the game area.

```
import pygame, sys

pygame.init()
screen = pygame.display.set_mode((640, 480))
pygame.display.set_caption("MouseControlGame")
while True:
    for event in pygame.event.get():
        if event.type == pygame.QUIT:
```

```
        pygame.quit()
        sys.exit()
    if event.type == pygame.MOUSEBUTTONDOWN:
    # Use pygame.mouse.get_pos() to get the x and y
positions when clicking in the area.
        pos=pygame.mouse.get_pos()
        btn=pygame.mouse
        print ("x = {}, y = {}".format(pos[0], pos[1]))
```

Results

Figure Project I- 11:Mouse Control Game

Terminal display results:
pygame 2.5.0 (SDL 2.28.0, Python 3.9.16)
Hello from the pygame community.
https://www.pygame.org/contribute.html
x = 252, y = 190
x = 252, y = 189
x = 320, y = 182
x = 167, y = 244
x = 362, y = 136

The next example program also displays red and white for right and left clicks respectively, in addition to the x and y coordinates.

```
import pygame
```

```python
pygame.init()
screen = pygame.display.set_mode((640, 480))
pygame.display.set_caption("MouseControlGamePress")
running = True
while running:
    for event in pygame.event.get():
        if event.type == pygame.QUIT:
            running = False
    buttons = pygame.mouse.get_pressed()

    if buttons[0]:
        print("Left click")
        #Show left mouse click location
        Mouse = pygame.mouse.get_pos()
        X = (Mouse[0]//10)*10
        Y = (Mouse[1]//10)*10
        print('X,Y values = '+str(X)+','+str(Y))
        #Create a white square
        pygame.draw.rect(screen,(255,255,255),(X,Y,10,10))
    if buttons[2]:
        print("Right click")
        #Show right mouse click location
        Mouse = pygame.mouse.get_pos()
        X = (Mouse[0]//10)*10
        Y = (Mouse[1]//10)*10
        print('X,Y values = '+str(X)+','+str(Y))
        #Create a red square
        pygame.draw.rect(screen,(254,18,1),(X,Y,10,10))
    pygame.display.update()
```

Results

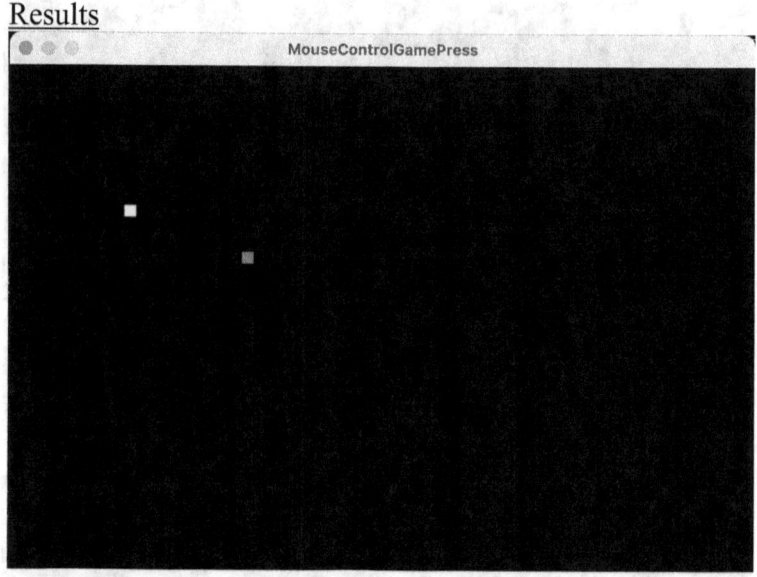

Figure Project I- 12:Mouse Control Game Press

Left click
X,Y values = 100,120
Left click
X,Y values = 100,120
Left click
X,Y values = 100,120
Right click
X,Y values = 200,160
Right click
X,Y values = 200,160
Right click
X,Y values = 200,160
Right click
X,Y values = 200,160
Right click
X,Y values = 200,160

Learn Python with Projects

For additional commands, see:

https://www.pygame.org/docs/ref/mouse.html

Project II
Web Application

Developing a web application using Python requires the use of a Python **framework**. To make development easier, **Django** will be used, which has **components** with ready-to-use features such as a login system, connecting to databases and CRUD operations. (Create, Read, Update, Delete) Here, we will use the database packaged with Django, namely **SQLite**, which is compatible with these databases:

- PostgreSQL
- MariaDB
- MySQL
- Oracle
- MongoDB

To access virtual environment
See, virtual environment, Chapter 1.
VaritSris> pyenv activate PyWebApp

Result
(PyWebApp) VaritSris>

Check python version

(PyWebApp) VaritSris> python --version

Python 3.9.16

Check Django suitable version

The installation method is as per the link:

https://docs.djangoproject.com/en/4.2/faq/install/

Which shows the Django versions that are suitable for different Python versions as shown in the table.

Table Project II- 1: Django vs python versions

Django version	Python versions
3.2	3.6, 3.7, 3.8, 3.9, 3.10 (added in 3.2.9)
4.0	3.8, 3.9, 3.10
4.1	3.8, 3.9, 3.10, 3.11 (added in 4.1.3)
4.2	3.8, 3.9, 3.10, 3.11 , 3.12 (added in 4.2.8)

install django

Then install the Django program as follows.

(PyWebApp) VaritSris> pip install Django

When the installation is complete, check the following:

(PyWebApp) VaritSris> django-admin --version

4.2.13

create web project

Create a web project named **Population** as follows.

(PyWebApp) VaritSris>django-admin startproject Population

When creating the Population project, you will get the Population folder and in the folder there will be the following files.

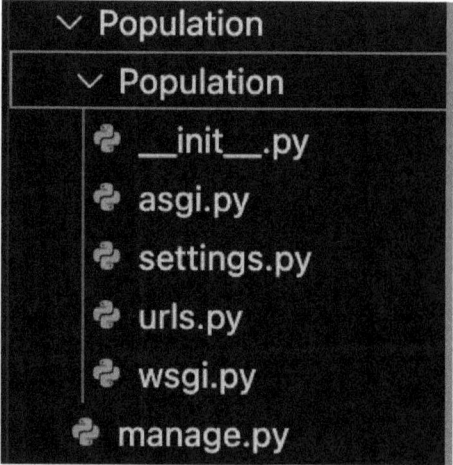

Figure Project II- 1: Created ExampleWebPython folder

runserver

In the Population folder, use the command run server.

(PyWebApp) VaritSris>python manage.py runserver

The results are shown as follows.
Watching for file changes with StatReloader
Performing system checks...

System check identified no issues (0 silenced).

You have 18 unapplied migration(s). Your project may not work properly until you apply the migrations for app(s): admin, auth, contenttypes, sessions.
Run 'python manage.py migrate' to apply them.
May 13, 2024 - 09:02:45
Django version 4.2.13, using settings 'Population.settings'
Starting development server at http://127.0.0.1:8000/
Quit the server with CONTROL-C.

This is a virtual machine running as a server. You can go to http://127.0.0.1:8000/ on a web browser to display the results as follows:

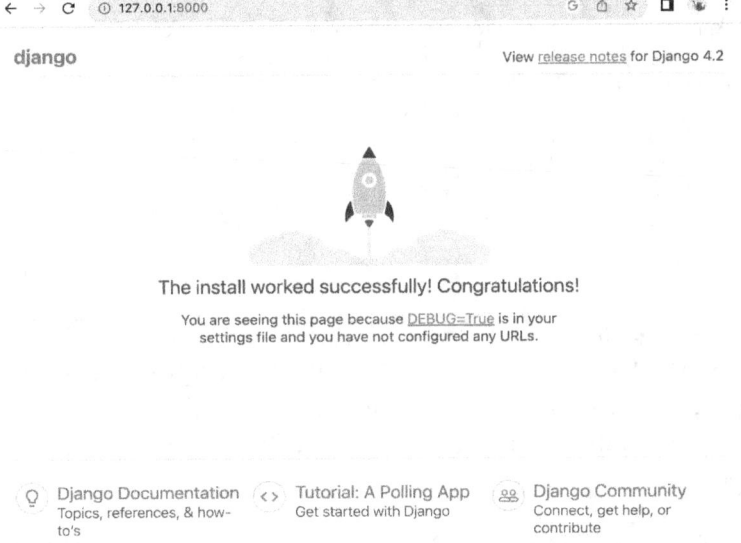

Figure Project II- 2: Django Server running on a virtual machine

Exit running the program on the server using CONTROL-C

Migrate

Run 'python manage.py migrate' to apply them.

(PyWebApp) VariitSris>python manage.py migrate
Result
Operations to perform:
  Apply all migrations: admin, auth, contenttypes, sessions
Running migrations:
  Applying contenttypes.0001_initial... OK
  Applying auth.0001_initial... OK
  Applying admin.0001_initial... OK
  Applying admin.0002_logentry_remove_auto_add... OK
  Applying admin.0003_logentry_add_action_flag_choices... OK
  Applying contenttypes.0002_remove_content_type_name... OK
  Applying auth.0002_alter_permission_name_max_length... OK
  Applying auth.0003_alter_user_email_max_length... OK
  Applying auth.0004_alter_user_username_opts... OK
  Applying auth.0005_alter_user_last_login_null... OK
  Applying auth.0006_require_contenttypes_0002... OK
  Applying auth.0007_alter_validators_add_error_messages... OK
  Applying auth.0008_alter_user_username_max_length... OK
  Applying auth.0009_alter_user_last_name_max_length... OK
  Applying auth.0010_alter_group_name_max_length... OK
  Applying auth.0011_update_proxy_permissions... OK
  Applying auth.0012_alter_user_first_name_max_length... OK
  Applying sessions.0001_initial... OK

Start Application

Then create a new folder. Once in the **Population** folder (you can use the pwd command to check where the folder is), use this command to create the web application **population**.

(PyWebApp) VaritSris>python manage.py startapp country

The **country** folder will be found.

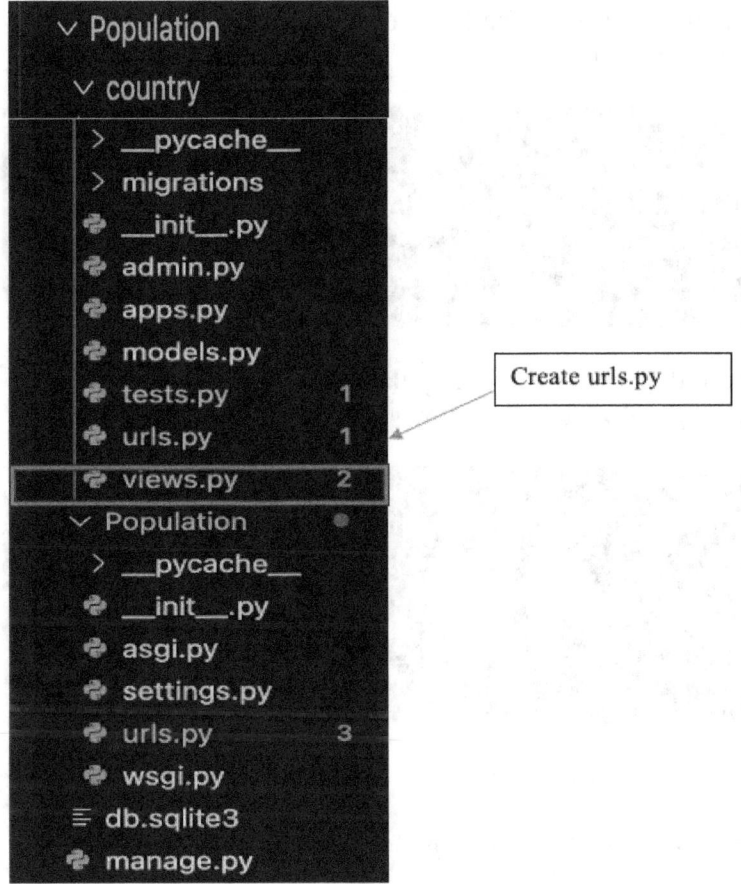

Figure Project II- 3: Members folder found in ThaiFruits

Edit the views.py file in Population/country/views.py folder as follows:

```
from django.shortcuts import render

from django.http import HttpResponse

def country(request):
    return HttpResponse("Hi, World Population")
```

Create an urls.py file located in Population/country/urls.py folder as follows:

```python
from django.urls import path
from . import views

urlpatterns = [
    path('country/', views.country, name='country'),
]
```

Edit the urls.py file in Population/Population/urls.py folder by adding **include** as follows:

```python
from django.contrib import admin
from django.urls import include, path

urlpatterns = [
    path('', include('country.urls')),
    path('admin/', admin.site.urls),
]
```

Go to Population folder and run the server as follows:

(PyWebApp) VaritSris>python manage.py runserver

Results
Watching for file changes with StatReloader
Performing system checks...

System check identified no issues (0 silenced).

You have 18 unapplied migration(s). Your project may not work properly until you apply the migrations for app(s): admin, auth, contenttypes, sessions.
Run 'python manage.py migrate' to apply them.
September 06, 2023 - 07:35:41
Django version 4.2.5, using settings 'Population.settings'
Starting development server at http://127.0.0.1:8000/
Quit the server with CONTROL-C.

Create HTML

Create a templates folder inside the country folder:

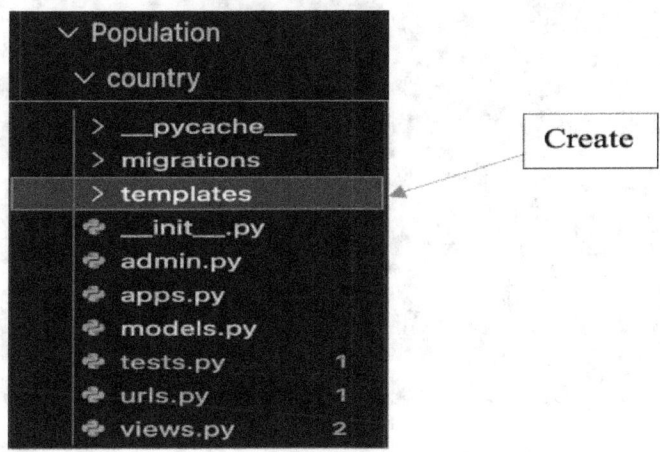

Create populationHome.html in the templates folder

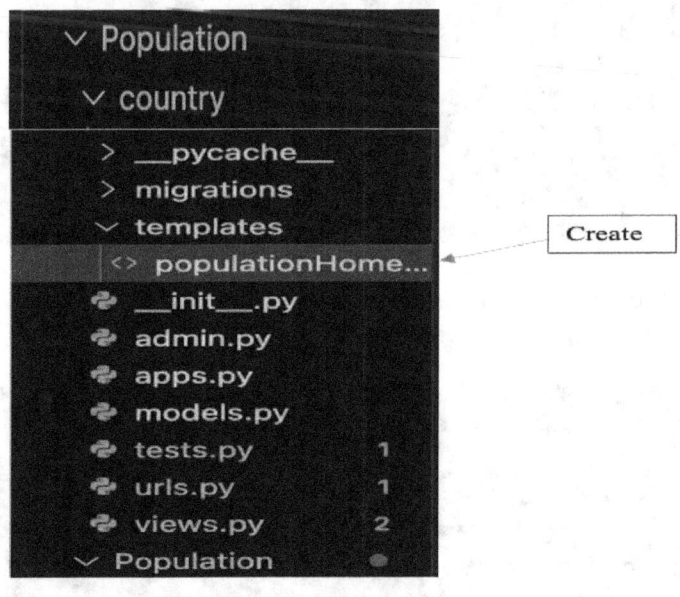

with the following command:

```html
<!DOCTYPE html>
<html>

<body>

  <h1>Hi.</h1>
  <p>Welcome to CRUD Population data Application.</p>

</body>

</html>
```

Edit Population/country/views.py to display populationHome.html on your browser as follows:

```python
from django.http import HttpResponse
from django.template import loader

def country(request):
  template = loader.get_template('populationHome.html')
  return HttpResponse(template.render())
```

Make the created application visible by adding country to the Population/Population/setting.py file as follows:

```
"""
Django settings for Population project.

Generated by 'django-admin startproject' using Django 4.2.13.

For more information on this file, see
```

```
https://docs.djangoproject.com/en/4.2/topics/settings/

For the full list of settings and their values, see
https://docs.djangoproject.com/en/4.2/ref/settings/
"""

from pathlib import Path

# Build paths inside the project like this: BASE_DIR /
'subdir'.
BASE_DIR = Path(__file__).resolve().parent.parent


# Quick-start development settings - unsuitable for
production
# See
https://docs.djangoproject.com/en/4.2/howto/deployment/c
hecklist/

# SECURITY WARNING: keep the secret key used in
production secret!
SECRET_KEY = 'django-insecure-
eeyti8_egjfack^oayn2_ai#qpl5q#6d#cyo6jf0ujv$rk801$'

# SECURITY WARNING: don't run with debug turned on
in production!
DEBUG = True

ALLOWED_HOSTS = []


# Application definition

INSTALLED_APPS = [
    'django.contrib.admin',
    'django.contrib.auth',
```

```
    'django.contrib.contenttypes',
    'django.contrib.sessions',
    'django.contrib.messages',
    'django.contrib.staticfiles',
# Add Application country
    'country'
]

MIDDLEWARE = [
    'django.middleware.security.SecurityMiddleware',

'django.contrib.sessions.middleware.SessionMiddleware',
    'django.middleware.common.CommonMiddleware',
    'django.middleware.csrf.CsrfViewMiddleware',

'django.contrib.auth.middleware.AuthenticationMiddleware',

'django.contrib.messages.middleware.MessageMiddleware',

'django.middleware.clickjacking.XFrameOptionsMiddleware',
]

ROOT_URLCONF = 'Population.urls'

TEMPLATES = [
    {
        'BACKEND':
'django.template.backends.django.DjangoTemplates',
        'DIRS': [],
        'APP_DIRS': True,
        'OPTIONS': {
            'context_processors': [
                'django.template.context_processors.debug',
                'django.template.context_processors.request',
```

```
                'django.contrib.auth.context_processors.auth',
                'django.contrib.messages.context_processors.messages',
            ],
        },
    },
]

WSGI_APPLICATION = 'Population.wsgi.application'


# Database
# https://docs.djangoproject.com/en/4.2/ref/settings/#databases

DATABASES = {
    'default': {
        'ENGINE': 'django.db.backends.sqlite3',
        'NAME': BASE_DIR / 'db.sqlite3',
    }
}


# Password validation
# https://docs.djangoproject.com/en/4.2/ref/settings/#auth-password-validators

AUTH_PASSWORD_VALIDATORS = [
    {
        'NAME': 'django.contrib.auth.password_validation.UserAttributeSimilarityValidator',
    },
    {
```

```python
        'NAME':
'django.contrib.auth.password_validation.MinimumLength
Validator',
    },
    {
        'NAME':
'django.contrib.auth.password_validation.CommonPasswor
dValidator',
    },
    {
        'NAME':
'django.contrib.auth.password_validation.NumericPasswor
dValidator',
    },
]


# Internationalization
# https://docs.djangoproject.com/en/4.2/topics/i18n/

LANGUAGE_CODE = 'en-us'

TIME_ZONE = 'UTC'

USE_I18N = True

USE_TZ = True


# Static files (CSS, JavaScript, Images)
# https://docs.djangoproject.com/en/4.2/howto/static-files/

STATIC_URL = 'static/'

# Default primary key field type
```

```
#
https://docs.djangoproject.com/en/4.2/ref/settings/#default-
auto-field

DEFAULT_AUTO_FIELD =
'django.db.models.BigAutoField'
```

CONTROL-C

Migrate the database to the Population folder with command
(PyWebApp) VaritSris>python manage.py migrate

Results

Operations to perform:
  Apply all migrations: admin, auth, contenttypes, sessions
Running migrations:
  No migrations to apply.

Run the server again.
(PyWebApp) VaritSris>python manage.py runserver
The result when running 127.0.0.1:8000/country/ on a browser is:

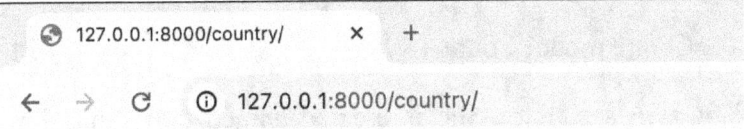

Hi.World

Welcome to CRUD Population data Application.

Figure Project II- 4: 127.0.0.1:8000/country/

According to the populationHome.html

Use SQLite database

To apply the SQLite database with the file name db.sqlite3 that comes with Django, edit the models in the folder Population/country/models.py

```
from django.db import models

class Country(models.Model):
    Name = models.CharField(max_length=255)
    Population = models.IntegerField()
```

Then go to the Population folder to create the desired database as follows:

(PyWebApp) VaritSris>python manage.py makemigrations country

Results

Migrations for 'country':

  country/migrations/0001_initial.py

    - Create model Country

You will see that a file is created named 0001_initial.py, which shows the details of the newly created table as follows:

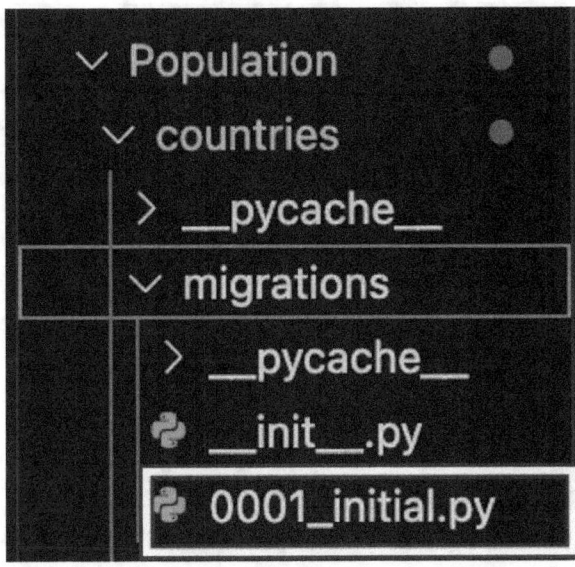

```
# Generated by Django 4.2.13 on 2024-05-13 13:38

from django.db import migrations, models


class Migration(migrations.Migration):

    initial = True

    dependencies = [
    ]

    operations = [
        migrations.CreateModel(
            name='Country',
            fields=[
                ('id', models.BigAutoField(auto_created=True, primary_key=True, serialize=False, verbose_name='ID')),
```

```
            ('Name', models.CharField(max_length=255)),
            ('Population', models.IntegerField()),
        ],
    ),
]
```

You will find that a **field id** is created by adding a value every time there is a record entry and will find that there is no Country table until you use the command at Population folder.

(PyWebApp) VaritSris>python manage.py migrate

Result

Operations to perform:

  Apply all migrations: admin, auth, contenttypes, country, sessions

Running migrations:

  Applying country.0001_initial... OK

To view the command to create a table in SQL language, you can do so by using the following command:

(PyWebApp) VaritSris> python manage.py sqlmigrate country 0001

BEGIN;

--

-- Create model Country

--

CREATE TABLE "country_country" ("id" integer NOT NULL PRIMARY KEY AUTOINCREMENT, "Name" varchar(255) NOT NULL, "Population" integer NOT NULL);

COMMIT;

Python has a shell to write commands, which could be accessed with

(PyWebApp) VaritSris>python manage.py shell

Python 3.9.16 (main, May 8 2024, 16:13:04)

[Clang 14.0.0 (clang-1400.0.29.202)] on darwin

Type "help", "copyright", "credits" or "license" for more information.

(InteractiveConsole)

>>>

Write the commands after the >>> to add country population.

To refer to the database and table to add information, use command:

>>> from country.models import Country

To check if there are any items in the Country table:

\>\>\> Country.objects.all()

Result is now empty.

<QuerySet []>

\>\>\> country = Country(Name='China', Population=1409670000)

To save entries into the Fruit Table:

\>\>\> country.save()

To show the number of items in the Fruit Table:

\>\>\> Country.objects.all()

<QuerySet [<Country: Country object (1)>]>

To display values in Country Table:

\>\>\> Country.objects.all().values()

<QuerySet [{'id': 1, 'Name': 'China', 'Population': 1409670000}]>

record multiple entries

To record multiple entries using the shell, do the following:

\>\>\> country1 = Country(Name='India', Population=1400744000)

\>\>\> country2 = Country(Name='USA', Population=335893238)

\>\>\> country3 = Country(Name='Indonesia', Population=279118866)

```
>>> country4 = Country(Name='Pakistan', Population=
241499431)

>>> country5 = Country(Name='Nigeria', Population=
223800000)

>>> country6 = Country(Name='Brazil', Population=
203080756)

>>> country7 = Country(Name='Bangladesh', Population=
169828911)

>>> country8 = Country(Name='Russia', Population=
146150789)

>>> country9 = Country(Name='Mexico', Population=
129625968)

>>> country10 = Country(Name='Japan', Population=
124000000)
```

>To save Country Data 1 to 10 in the countryList variable:

```
>>> countryList = [country1, country2, country3, country4,
country5, country6, country7, country8, country9,
country10]
```

Loop All Items:

```
>>> for c in countryList: c.save()

...

>>> Country.objects.all().values()
<QuerySet [{'id': 1, 'Name': 'China', 'Population':
1409670000}, {'id': 2, 'Name': 'India', 'Population':
1400744000}, {'id': 3, 'Name': 'USA', 'Population':
```

335893238}, {'id': 4, 'Name': 'Indonesia', 'Population': 279118866}, {'id': 5, 'Name': 'Pakistan', 'Population': 241499431}, {'id': 6, 'Name': 'Nigeria', 'Population': 223800000}, {'id': 7, 'Name': 'Brazil', 'Population': 203080756}, {'id': 8, 'Name': 'Bangladesh', 'Population': 169828911}, {'id': 9, 'Name': 'Russia', 'Population': 146150789}, {'id': 10, 'Name': 'Mexico', 'Population': 129625968}, {'id': 11, 'Name': 'Japan', 'Population': 124000000}]>

edit data

In this case, items 1 and 2 are duplicates, so one must be called to correct by referring to the order in which they want to be solved. Specifically, the first item in an array sequence is numbered 0.

To change the first country:

```
>>> from country.models import Country
>>> c = Country.objects.all()[0]
>>> c.Name
'China'
>>> c.Name = 'Chaina'
>>> c.save()
>>> Country.objects.all().values()
<QuerySet [{'id': 1, 'Name': 'Chaina', 'Population': 1409670000}, {'id': 2, 'Name': 'India', 'Population': 1400744000}, {'id': 3, 'Name': 'USA', 'Population': 335893238}, {'id': 4, 'Name': 'Indonesia', 'Population': 279118866}, {'id': 5, 'Name': 'Pakistan', 'Population': 241499431}, {'id': 6, 'Name': 'Nigeria', 'Population': 223800000}, {'id': 7, 'Name': 'Brazil', 'Population': 203080756}, {'id': 8, 'Name': 'Bangladesh', 'Population': 169828911}, {'id': 9, 'Name': 'Russia', 'Population': 146150789}, {'id': 10, 'Name': 'Mexico', 'Population': 129625968}, {'id': 11, 'Name': 'Japan', 'Population': 124000000}]>
```

change back
```
>>> c = Country.objects.all()[0]
>>> c.Name
'Chaina'
>>> c.Name = 'China'
>>> c.save()
```

To delete an item, specify the order of the you want to delete, then use the following command:

```
>>> from country.models import Country
>>> c = Country.objects.all()[10]
>>> c.Name
'Japan'
>>> c.delete()
(1, {'country.Country': 1})
```

To edit a model or table structure, go to models.py created in the Population/country/ folder. If you want to add continent as new field, you must specify null=true to allow null as values (since databases require that all fields contain a value).

```
from django.db import models

class Country(models.Model):
    Name = models.CharField(max_length=255)
    Population = models.IntegerField()
    #Add field you must specify null=true to allow null as values,Because there are already data items in the table.
    Continent = models.CharField(max_length=255,null=True)
```

Once added or modified, perform the command in the terminal as follows:

```
(PyWebApp) VaritSris>python manage.py makemigrations country
```
Results
Migrations for 'country':
  country/migrations/0002_country_continent.py
    - Add field Continent to country

Followed by the command.

```
(PyWebApp) VaritSris>python manage.py migrate
```

Results

Operations to perform:
  Apply all migrations: admin, auth, contenttypes, country, sessions
Running migrations:
  Applying country.0002_country_continent... OK

Then fill in the additional fields.
To exit the shell, type Ctrl+Z.
To bring the data from the Fruit Table database to the Web: Edit populationHome.html in the templates folder by adding Django tags {% %} and {{ }}, which are explained in the Django syntax section at the end of this chapter.

```
<!DOCTYPE html>
<html>

<body>

    <h1>Hi.World</h1>
```

```html
<p>Welcome to CRUD Population data Application.</p>
  <ul>
    {% for c in countryList %}
    <li>{{ c.Name }} {{ c.Population }}</li>
    {% endfor %}
  </ul>


</body>

</html>
```

and edit at Population/country/views.py as follows:

```python
from django.http import HttpResponse
from django.template import loader
from .models import Country


def country(request):
  countryList = Country.objects.all().values()
  template = loader.get_template('populationHome.html')
  context = {
   'countryList': countryList,
  }
  return HttpResponse(template.render(context, request))

def continent(request, id):
  countryList = Country.objects.get(id=id)
  template = loader.get_template('continent.html')
  context = {
   'countryList': countryList,
  }
```

```
return HttpResponse(template.render(context, request))
```

Then run the server at Population folder as follows:
(PyWebApp) VaritSris>python manage.py runserver

Results

Hi.World

Welcome to CRUD Population data Application.

- Chaina 1409670000
- India 1400744000
- USA 335893238
- Indonesia 279118866
- Pakistan 241499431
- Nigeria 223800000
- Brazil 203080756
- Bangladesh 169828911
- Russia 146150789
- Mexico 129625968

Figure Project II- 5:country page

Add CSS to populationHome.html to make the display more beautiful, as shown in the program as follows.

```
<!DOCTYPE html>
<html>
  <head>
    <style>
      table {
        font-family: arial, sans-serif;
        border-collapse: collapse;
        width: 100%;
      }

      td, th {
        border: 1px solid #dddddd;
```

```html
            text-align: left;
            padding: 8px;
        }

        tr:nth-child(even) {
            background-color: #dddddd;
        }
        </style>
<body>

    <h1>Hi.World</h1>
    <p>Welcome to CRUD Population data Application.</p>
    <table>
        <tr>
           <th>Country</th>
           <th>Population</th>

        </tr>
        {% for c in countryList %}
        <tr>
           <td>{{ c.Name }}</td>
           <td>{{ c.Population }}</td>

        </tr>
        {% endfor %}
    </table>



</body>

</html>
```

Result

Hi.World

Welcome to CRUD Population data Application.

Country	Population
Chaina	1409670000
India	1400744000
USA	335893238
Indonesia	279118866
Pakistan	241499431
Nigeria	223800000
Brazil	203080756
Bangladesh	169828911
Russia	146150789
Mexico	129625968

Figure Project II- 6: country page after use CSS

Display as Links

To display a link to a web page, such as having the first page list country items but not display the continent, first edit the continent as mentioned above, and then do the following

1. Go to the Templates folder, create continent.html as follows:

```html
<!DOCTYPE html>
<html>

<body>

    <h1>{{ countryList.Name }} {{ countryList.Population }}</h1>

    <p>Continent: {{ countryList.Continent }}</p>

    <p>Back to <a href="/country">Country</a></p>
```

</body>

2. Add links to populationHome.html in the templates folder.

```html
<!DOCTYPE html>
<html>
  <head>
    <style>
      table {
        font-family: arial, sans-serif;
        border-collapse: collapse;
        width: 100%;
      }

      td, th {
        border: 1px solid #dddddd;
        text-align: left;
        padding: 8px;
      }

      tr:nth-child(even) {
        background-color: #dddddd;
      }
    </style>
<body>

    <h1>Hi,World.</h1>
    <p>Welcome to CRUD Population data Application.</p>
    <table>
      <tr>
        <th>Country</th>
        <th>Population</th>
```

```html
    </tr>
    {% for c in countryList %}
    <tr>
      <td><a href="continent/{{ c.id }}">{{ c.Name }}</a></td>
      <td>{{ c.Population }}</td>

    </tr>
    {% endfor %}
   </table>
</body>
</html>
```

3. Edit Population/country/views.py to add def continent() to load the continent.html file as follows:

```python
from django.http import HttpResponse
from django.template import loader
from .models import Country


def country(request):
  countryList = Country.objects.all().values()
  template = loader.get_template('populationHome.html')
  context = {
   'countryList': countryList,
  }
  return HttpResponse(template.render(context, request))

def continent(request, id):
  countryList = Country.objects.get(id=id)
  template = loader.get_template('continent.html')
  context = {
   'countryList': countryList,
  }
```

```
return HttpResponse(template.render(context, request))
```

4. Edit Population/country/urls.py to add **continent** in **urlpatterns:**

```
from django.urls import path
from . import views

urlpatterns = [
    path('country/', views.country, name='country'),
    path('country/continent/<int:id>', views.continent, name='continent'),
]
```

Then run the server at Population folder as follows:

(PyWebApp) VaritSris>python manage.py runserver

If you encounter this error:

Watching for file changes with StatReloader
Performing system checks...

System check identified no issues (0 silenced).
Error: That port is already in use.

Use this command:

(PyWebApp) VaritSris>sudo lsof -t -i tcp:8000 | xargs kill -9
Then execute the command:
(PyWebApp) VaritSris>python manage.py runserver
or use another port (8080)
(PyWebApp) VaritSris>python manage.py runserver 8080

Results

Hi.World

Welcome to CRUD Population data Application.

Country	Population
China	1409670000
India	1400744000
USA	335893238
Indonesia	279118866
Pakistan	241499431
Nigeria	223800000
Brazil	203080756
Bangladesh	169828911
Russia	146150789
Mexico	129625968

Figure Project II- 7: country page with link

List countries will appear as link, that when clicked, displays the continent.

Clicking on China brings you to this page:

China 1409670000

Continent: None

Back to Country

Figure Project II- 8:after click link China

Clicking Country brings you back to the main menu.

Create, Read, Update, Delete : CRUD

Fundamentally, Database Management must provide functionality to create, read, update and delete data items in the database in development. Python has provided an example of Web Applications database management. With a browser, go to http://127.0.0.1:8080/admin/ The result is shown as follows:

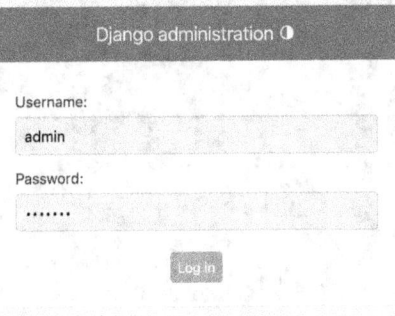

Figure Project II- 9: Django administration login page

The program displaying this is Population/Population/urls.py

```
"""
URL configuration for Population project.

The `urlpatterns` list routes URLs to views. For more information please see:
    https://docs.djangoproject.com/en/4.2/topics/http/urls/
Examples:
Function views
    1. Add an import:  from my_app import views
    2. Add a URL to urlpatterns:  path('', views.home, name='home')
Class-based views
    1. Add an import:  from other_app.views import Home
    2. Add a URL to urlpatterns:  path('', Home.as_view(), name='home')
Including another URLconf
    1. Import the include() function: from django.urls import include, path
    2. Add a URL to urlpatterns:  path('blog/', include('blog.urls'))
"""
from django.contrib import admin
from django.urls import include, path

urlpatterns = [
    path('', include('country.urls')),
    path('admin/', admin.site.urls),
]
```

Here's an example of how to use it in a program:
1. Create a superuser to access Django's admin database management system using the command:
   (PyWebApp) VaritSris>python manage.py createsuperuser
   Username (leave blank to use 'admin'): admin
   Email address: variitsris@variitsris.org
   Password:
   Password (again):
   Superuser created successfully.
2. After Log in, it will appear as follows:

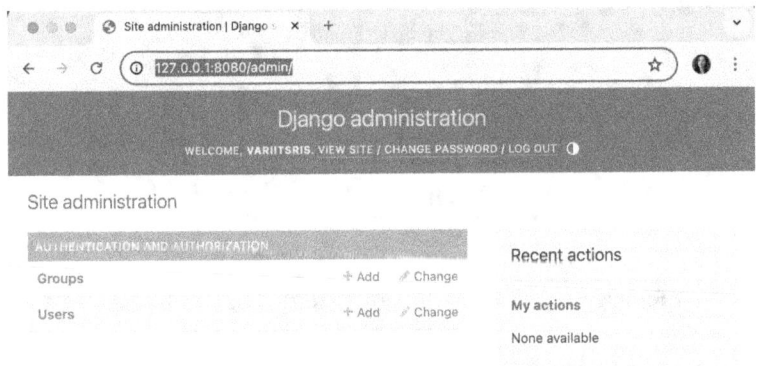

Figure Project II- 10: After login success

3. Add a Programmer's Application, **Country**, to the admin page by adding to Population/country/admin.py file as follows:

```
from django.contrib import admin
from .models import Country

# Register your models here.
admin.site.register(Country)
```

Refresh by clicking ⟳ to find **Country** has been added and is changeable, as follows:

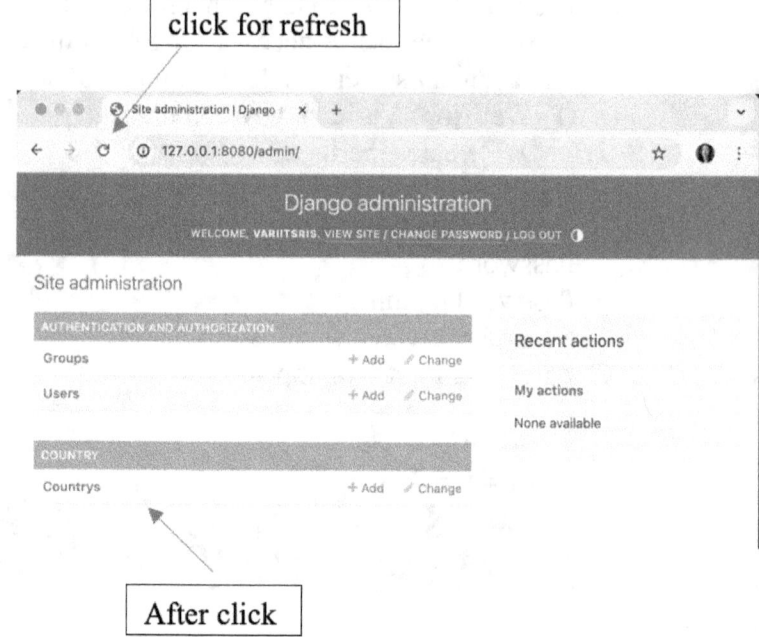

Figure Project II- 11: Country added to admin page

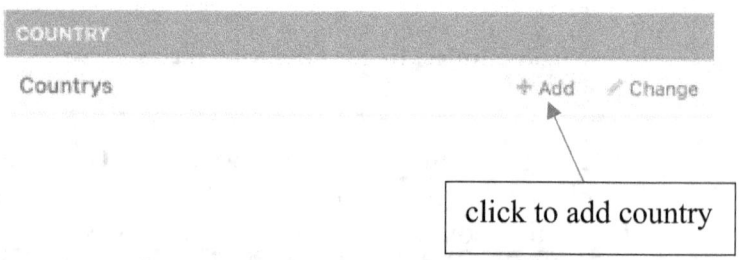

Figure Project II- 12: click to add country

Clicking + Add to add new country.

Learn Python with Projects

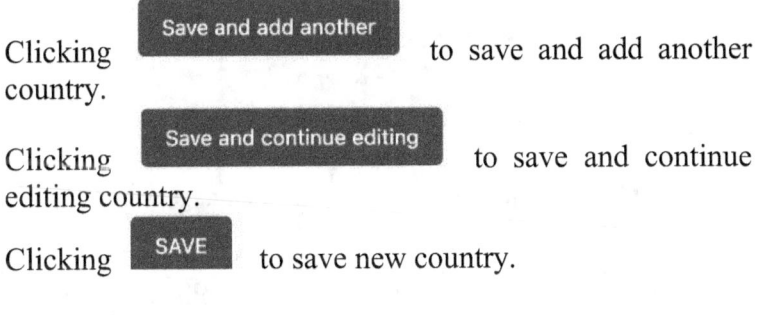

Figure Project II- 13:add country page

Clicking **Save and add another** to save and add another country.

Clicking **Save and continue editing** to save and continue editing country.

Clicking **SAVE** to save new country.

Clicking **Countrys** will switch to a page that lists the data available in the **Country** model.

Learn Python with Projects

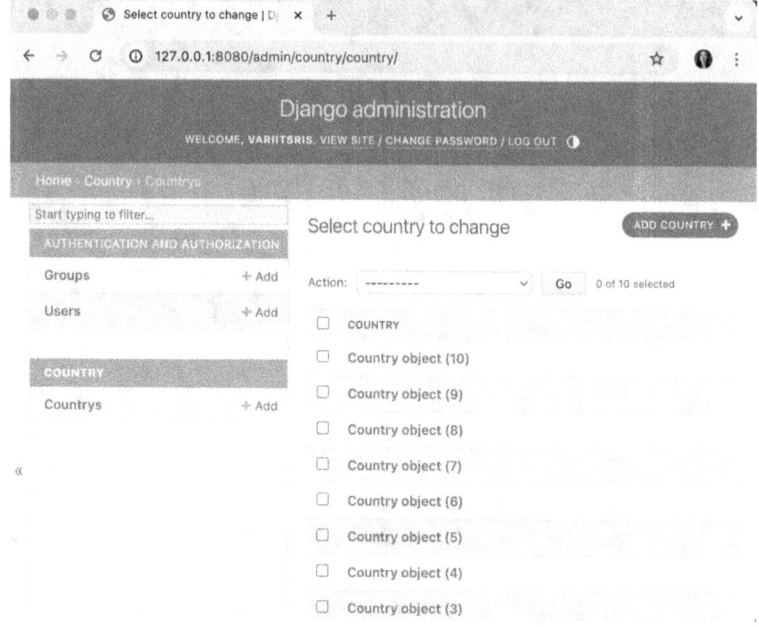

Figure Project II- 14:country data management

Clicking Country object (10) goes to to the following page:

Change country

Country object (10)

Name: Mexico

Population: 1296₂

Continent:

[SAVE] [Save and add another] [Save and continue editing]

[Delete]

Figure Project II- 15: after click country for edit or delete

to be able to edit or delete items.

To **customize the look** of the admin management system
1. Edit the **admin titles** as desired by going to the urls.py in the Population/urls.py folder, as follows:

```
from django.contrib import admin
from django.urls import include, path

urlpatterns = [
    path('', include('country.urls')),
    path('admin/', admin.site.urls),
]
admin.site.site_header = 'Thai Fruit (ผลไม้ไทย) ADMIN'
# default: "Django Administration"
admin.site.index_title = 'Thai Fruit index admin '
# default: "Site administration".
```

admin.site.site_title = 'Thai Fruit (ผลไม้ไทย) Site'
# default: "Django site admin"
Results

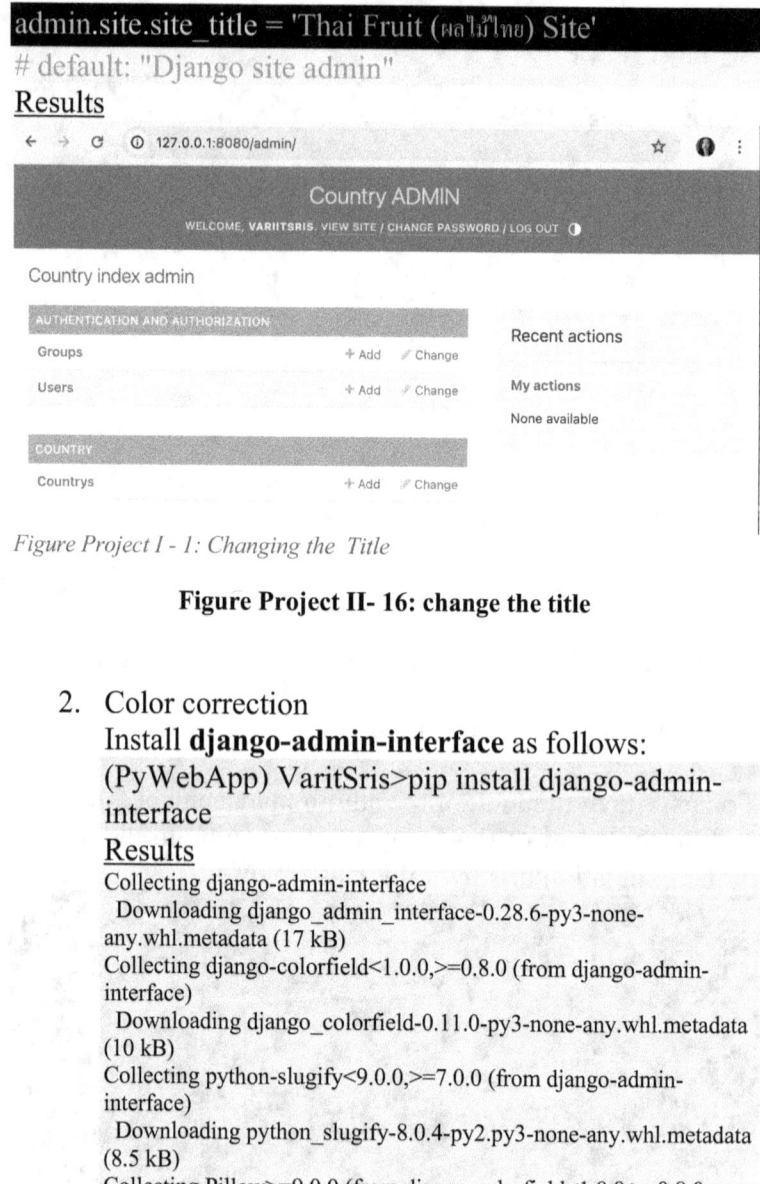

Figure Project I - 1: Changing the Title

Figure Project II- 16: change the title

2. Color correction
Install **django-admin-interface** as follows:
(PyWebApp) VaritSris>pip install django-admin-interface
Results
Collecting django-admin-interface
  Downloading django_admin_interface-0.28.6-py3-none-any.whl.metadata (17 kB)
Collecting django-colorfield<1.0.0,>=0.8.0 (from django-admin-interface)
  Downloading django_colorfield-0.11.0-py3-none-any.whl.metadata (10 kB)
Collecting python-slugify<9.0.0,>=7.0.0 (from django-admin-interface)
  Downloading python_slugify-8.0.4-py2.py3-none-any.whl.metadata (8.5 kB)
Collecting Pillow>=9.0.0 (from django-colorfield<1.0.0,>=0.8.0->django-admin-interface)
  Downloading pillow-10.3.0-cp39-cp39-macosx_10_10_x86_64.whl.metadata (9.2 kB)

Learn Python with Projects

```
Collecting text-unidecode>=1.3 (from python-slugify<9.0.0,>=7.0.0-
>django-admin-interface)
  Downloading text_unidecode-1.3-py2.py3-none-any.whl.metadata
(2.4 kB)
Downloading django_admin_interface-0.28.6-py3-none-any.whl (250
kB)
   ──────────────────────────── 250.6/250.6 kB 4.4 MB/s eta 0:00:00
Downloading django_colorfield-0.11.0-py3-none-any.whl (53 kB)
   ──────────────────────────── 53.2/53.2 kB 1.7 MB/s eta 0:00:00
Downloading python_slugify-8.0.4-py2.py3-none-any.whl (10 kB)
Downloading pillow-10.3.0-cp39-cp39-macosx_10_10_x86_64.whl
(3.5 MB)
   ──────────────────────────── 3.5/3.5 MB 9.3 MB/s eta 0:00:00
Downloading text_unidecode-1.3-py2.py3-none-any.whl (78 kB)
   ──────────────────────────── 78.2/78.2 kB 2.4 MB/s eta 0:00:00
Installing collected packages: text-unidecode, python-slugify, Pillow,
django-colorfield, django-admin-interface
Successfully installed Pillow-10.3.0 django-admin-interface-0.28.6
django-colorfield-0.11.0 python-slugify-8.0.4 text-unidecode-1.3
```

Then go to Population/Population/setting.py to run django-admin-interface as follows:

```python
from pathlib import Path

# Build paths inside the project like this: BASE_DIR /
'subdir'.
BASE_DIR = Path(__file__).resolve().parent.parent


# Quick-start development settings - unsuitable for
production
# See
https://docs.djangoproject.com/en/4.2/howto/deployment/c
hecklist/
```

```python
# SECURITY WARNING: keep the secret key used in production secret!
SECRET_KEY = 'django-insecure--g#t(p%hknluf24cu=)7skc-%6dyz6n0so-_qj+b@1#hdlm*vp'

# SECURITY WARNING: don't run with debug turned on in production!
DEBUG = True

ALLOWED_HOSTS = []

# Application definition

INSTALLED_APPS = [
    #add admin_interface and colorfield before django.contrib.admin To be able to edit the colors of the admin management system.
    "admin_interface",
    "colorfield",

    'django.contrib.admin',
    'django.contrib.auth',
    'django.contrib.contenttypes',
    'django.contrib.sessions',
    'django.contrib.messages',
    'django.contrib.staticfiles',
    #Add Application
    'country'

]
#Add X_FRAME_OPTIONS and SILENCED_SYSTEM_CHECKS To be able to edit the colors of the admin management system.
X_FRAME_OPTIONS = "SAMEORIGIN"
```

```
SILENCED_SYSTEM_CHECKS = ["security.W019"]
MIDDLEWARE = [
  'django.middleware.security.SecurityMiddleware',

'django.contrib.sessions.middleware.SessionMiddleware',
  'django.middleware.common.CommonMiddleware',
  'django.middleware.csrf.CsrfViewMiddleware',

'django.contrib.auth.middleware.AuthenticationMiddleware
',

'django.contrib.messages.middleware.MessageMiddleware',

'django.middleware.clickjacking.XFrameOptionsMiddlewa
re',
]

ROOT_URLCONF = 'Population.urls'

TEMPLATES = [
    {
     'BACKEND':
'django.template.backends.django.DjangoTemplates',
     'DIRS': [],
     'APP_DIRS': True,
     'OPTIONS': {
        'context_processors': [
           'django.template.context_processors.debug',
           'django.template.context_processors.request',
           'django.contrib.auth.context_processors.auth',

'django.contrib.messages.context_processors.messages',
        ],
     },
    },
]
```

```python
WSGI_APPLICATION = 'Population.wsgi.application'

# Database
# https://docs.djangoproject.com/en/4.2/ref/settings/#databases

DATABASES = {
    'default': {
        'ENGINE': 'django.db.backends.sqlite3',
        'NAME': BASE_DIR / 'db.sqlite3',
    }
}

# Password validation
# https://docs.djangoproject.com/en/4.2/ref/settings/#auth-password-validators

AUTH_PASSWORD_VALIDATORS = [
    {
        'NAME': 'django.contrib.auth.password_validation.UserAttributeSimilarityValidator',
    },
    {
        'NAME': 'django.contrib.auth.password_validation.MinimumLengthValidator',
    },
    {
        'NAME': 'django.contrib.auth.password_validation.CommonPasswordValidator',
```

```python
    },
    {
        'NAME':
'django.contrib.auth.password_validation.NumericPasswor
dValidator',
    },
]
```

```python
# Internationalization
# https://docs.djangoproject.com/en/4.2/topics/i18n/
```

```python
LANGUAGE_CODE = 'en-us'
```

```python
TIME_ZONE = 'UTC'
```

```python
USE_I18N = True
```

```python
USE_TZ = True
```

```python
# Static files (CSS, JavaScript, Images)
# https://docs.djangoproject.com/en/4.2/howto/static-files/
```

```python
STATIC_URL = 'static/'
```

```python
# Default primary key field type
# https://docs.djangoproject.com/en/4.2/ref/settings/#default-auto-field
```

```python
DEFAULT_AUTO_FIELD =
'django.db.models.BigAutoField'
```

Then migrate:

(PyWebApp) VaritSris>python manage.py migrate

Results

Operations to perform:
  Apply all migrations: admin, admin_interface, auth, contenttypes, country, sessions
Running migrations:
  Applying admin_interface.0001_initial... OK
  Applying admin_interface.0002_add_related_modal... OK
  Applying admin_interface.0003_add_logo_color... OK
  Applying admin_interface.0004_rename_title_color... OK
  Applying admin_interface.0005_add_recent_actions_visible... OK
  Applying admin_interface.0006_bytes_to_str... OK
  Applying admin_interface.0007_add_favicon... OK
  Applying admin_interface.0008_change_related_modal_background_opacity_type... OK
  Applying admin_interface.0009_add_enviroment... OK
  Applying admin_interface.0010_add_localization... OK
  Applying admin_interface.0011_add_environment_options... OK
  Applying admin_interface.0012_update_verbose_names... OK
  Applying admin_interface.0013_add_related_modal_close_button... OK
  Applying admin_interface.0014_name_unique... OK
  Applying admin_interface.0015_add_language_chooser_active... OK
  Applying admin_interface.0016_add_language_chooser_display... OK
  Applying admin_interface.0017_change_list_filter_dropdown... OK
  Applying admin_interface.0018_theme_list_filter_sticky... OK
  Applying admin_interface.0019_add_form_sticky... OK
  Applying admin_interface.0020_module_selected_colors... OK
  Applying admin_interface.0021_file_extension_validator... OK
  Applying admin_interface.0022_add_logo_max_width_and_height... OK
  Applying admin_interface.0023_theme_foldable_apps... OK
  Applying admin_interface.0024_remove_theme_css... OK
  Applying admin_interface.0025_theme_language_chooser_control... OK
  Applying admin_interface.0026_theme_list_filter_highlight... OK
  Applying admin_interface.0027_theme_list_filter_removal_links... OK
  Applying admin_interface.0028_theme_show_fieldsets_as_tabs_and_more... OK
  Applying admin_interface.0029_theme_css_generic_link_active_color... OK
  Applying admin_interface.0030_theme_collapsible_stacked_inlines_and_more... OK

(PyWebApp) VaritSris>python manage.py collectstatic --clear

Results

You have requested to collect static files at the destination location as specified in your settings.

Learn Python with Projects

This will DELETE ALL FILES in this location!
Are you sure you want to do this?

Type 'yes' to continue, or 'no' to cancel: yes
Traceback (most recent call last):
  File "/Users/Python/ExamplePythonCode/Population/manage.py", line 22, in <module>
    main()
  File "/Users/Python/ExamplePythonCode/Population/manage.py", line 18, in main
    execute_from_command_line(sys.argv)
  File "/Users/nee/.pyenv/versions/PyWebApp/lib/python3.9/site-packages/django/core/management/__init__.py", line 442, in execute_from_command_line
    utility.execute()
  File "/Users/nee/.pyenv/versions/PyWebApp/lib/python3.9/site-packages/django/core/management/__init__.py", line 436, in execute
    self.fetch_command(subcommand).run_from_argv(self.argv)
  File "/Users/nee/.pyenv/versions/PyWebApp/lib/python3.9/site-packages/django/core/management/base.py", line 412, in run_from_argv
    self.execute(*args, **cmd_options)
  File "/Users/nee/.pyenv/versions/PyWebApp/lib/python3.9/site-packages/django/core/management/base.py", line 458, in execute
    output = self.handle(*args, **options)
  File "/Users/nee/.pyenv/versions/PyWebApp/lib/python3.9/site-packages/django/contrib/staticfiles/management/commands/collectstatic.py", line 209, in handle
    collected = self.collect()
  File "/Users/nee/.pyenv/versions/PyWebApp/lib/python3.9/site-packages/django/contrib/staticfiles/management/commands/collectstatic.py", line 117, in collect
    self.clear_dir("")
  File "/Users/nee/.pyenv/versions/PyWebApp/lib/python3.9/site-packages/django/contrib/staticfiles/management/commands/collectstatic.py", line 251, in clear_dir
    if not self.storage.exists(path):
  File "/Users/nee/.pyenv/versions/PyWebApp/lib/python3.9/site-packages/django/core/files/storage/filesystem.py", line 165, in exists
    return os.path.lexists(self.path(name))
  File "/Users/nee/.pyenv/versions/PyWebApp/lib/python3.9/site-packages/django/contrib/staticfiles/storage.py", line 39, in path
    raise ImproperlyConfigured(
django.core.exceptions.ImproperlyConfigured: You're using the staticfiles app without having set the STATIC_ROOT setting to a filesystem path.

Learn Python with Projects

You will be asked to answer <u>yes</u> to create and edit the same file you created earlier.
Once installed, run the server again as follows:
(PyWebApp) VaritSris>python manage.py runserver
Then go to the browser running 127.0.0.1:8000/admin/ and you will find the link used to modify the admin management screen as follows:

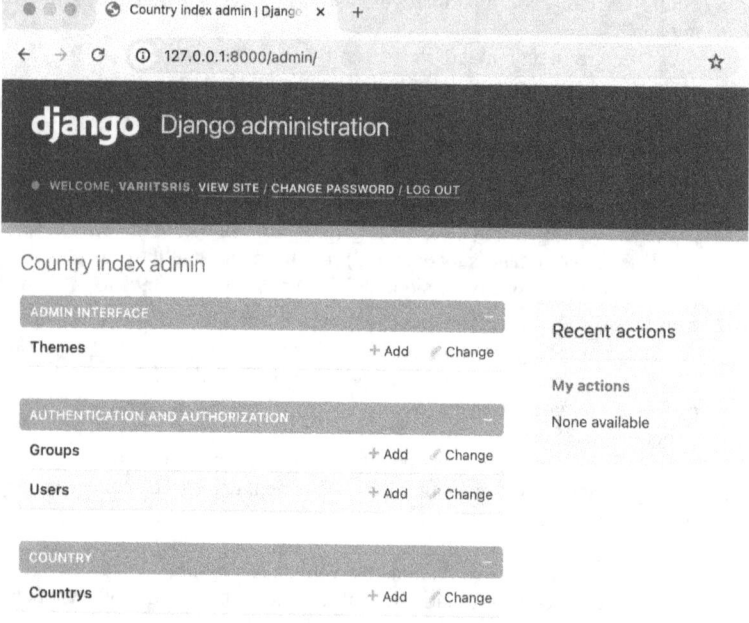

Figure Project II- 17: ADMIN INTERFACE has shown

Click **themes** to edit the desired theme as follows:

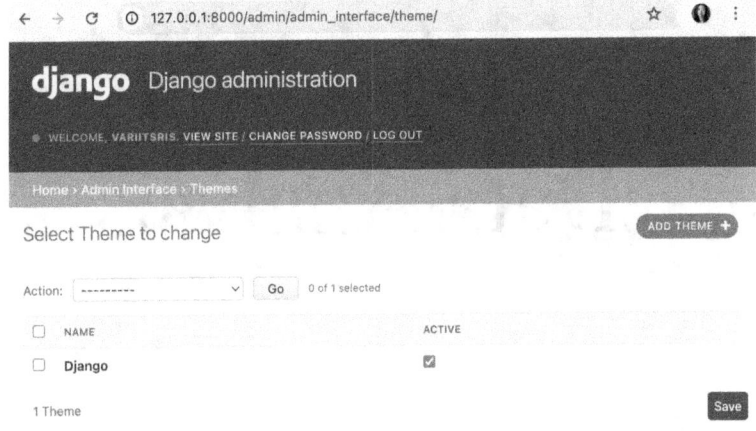

Figure Project II- 18:Select Theme to change page

You can make a backup and then use the checkmark to choose the admin management system to modify.

Learn Python with Projects

Project III
Data Analysis

Python can be used to display data for Business Analysis, Business Intelligence, Science and Research, Statistics, Mathematics, Artificial Intelligence and Data Mining, since it has libraries with modules to support these functions such as matplotlib, pandas, numpy, Seaborn, Shapefile, Basemap, Geopandas, etc. In project 3, we will use Python to display information that allows programmers to apply it in these various tasks.

matplotlib
To install the matplotlib library, go to:

https://matplotlib.org/stable/users/installing/index.html

matplotlib policy:

Learn Python with Projects

https://matplotlib.org/stable/devel/min_dep_policy.html

To access virtual environment
See, virtual environment, Chapter 1.
VaritSris> pyenv activate PyDataAnalysis

With pip installed:
(PyDataAnalysis) VariitSris> python -m pip install -U matplotlib
Collecting matplotlib
  Downloading matplotlib-3.8.4-cp39-cp39-macosx_10_12_x86_64.whl (7.6 MB)
──────────────────────────────── 7.6/7.6 MB 5.6 MB/s eta 0:00:00
Collecting numpy>=1.21
  Using cached numpy-1.26.4-cp39-cp39-macosx_10_9_x86_64.whl (20.6 MB)
Collecting pillow>=8
  Downloading pillow-10.3.0-cp39-cp39-macosx_10_10_x86_64.whl (3.5 MB)
──────────────────────────────── 3.5/3.5 MB 5.7 MB/s eta 0:00:00
Collecting cycler>=0.10
  Using cached cycler-0.12.1-py3-none-any.whl (8.3 kB)
Collecting fonttools>=4.22.0
  Downloading fonttools-4.51.0-cp39-cp39-macosx_10_9_x86_64.whl (2.3 MB)
──────────────────────────────── 2.3/2.3 MB 5.8 MB/s eta 0:00:00
Collecting importlib-resources>=3.2.0
  Downloading importlib_resources-6.4.0-py3-none-any.whl (38 kB)
Collecting contourpy>=1.0.1
  Downloading contourpy-1.2.1-cp39-cp39-macosx_10_9_x86_64.whl (260 kB)
──────────────────────────────── 261.0/261.0 KB 4.0 MB/s eta 0:00:00
Collecting pyparsing>=2.3.1
  Using cached pyparsing-3.1.2-py3-none-any.whl (103 kB)
Collecting packaging>=20.0
  Downloading packaging-24.0-py3-none-any.whl (53 kB)
──────────────────────────────── 53.5/53.5 KB 1.4 MB/s eta 0:00:00
Collecting python-dateutil>=2.7
  Using cached python_dateutil-2.9.0.post0-py2.py3-none-any.whl (229 kB)
Collecting kiwisolver>=1.3.1
  Using cached kiwisolver-1.4.5-cp39-cp39-macosx_10_9_x86_64.whl (68 kB)
Collecting zipp>=3.1.0

Downloading zipp-3.18.1-py3-none-any.whl (8.2 kB)
Collecting six>=1.5
  Downloading six-1.16.0-py2.py3-none-any.whl (11 kB)
Installing collected packages: zipp, six, pyparsing, pillow, packaging, numpy, kiwisolver, fonttools, cycler, python-dateutil, importlib-resources, contourpy, matplotlib
Successfully installed contourpy-1.2.1 cycler-0.12.1 fonttools-4.51.0 importlib-resources-6.4.0 kiwisolver-1.4.5 matplotlib-3.8.4 numpy-1.26.4 packaging-24.0 pillow-10.3.0 pyparsing-3.1.2 python-dateutil-2.9.0.post0 six-1.16.0 zipp-3.18.1

Example Program: Line Graph
```
import matplotlib.pyplot as lineplt
Firstline = [2, 6, 3, 16, 25]
lineplt.plot(Firstline)
lineplt.show()
```

(PyDataAnalysis) VariitSris> python lineGraph.py
  As a result, you will find an icon:

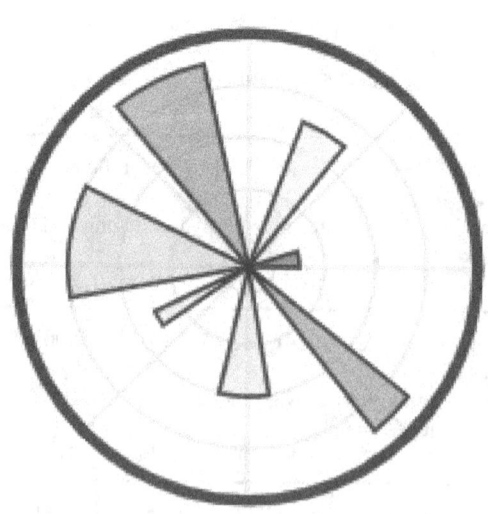

and graphs:

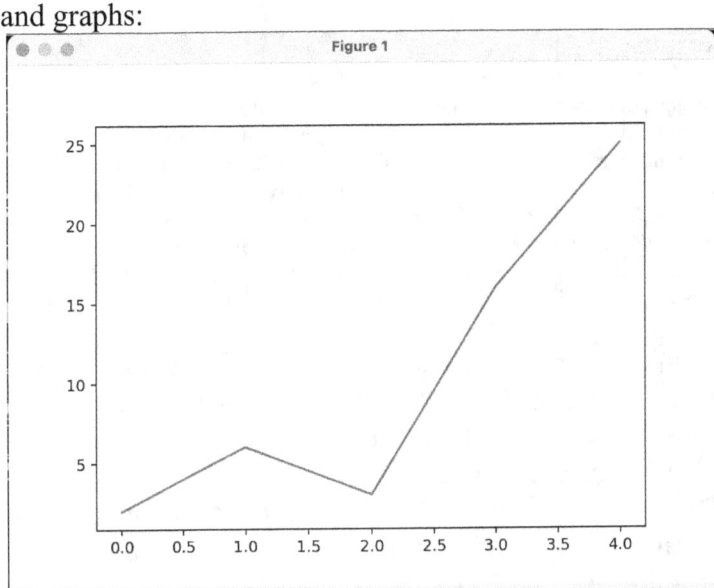

Figure Project III- 1::Line Graph example

Clicking 💾 saves the graph image.
To find out what type of graphs matplotlib can make, go to:

https://matplotlib.org/stable/gallery/index

For displaying Thai characters, you must use fonts that support Thai.
If you want to check which fonts can be used, use the following command:

```
from matplotlib import font_manager
print("Display fonts that could be used in matplotlib:")
print(*font_manager.findSystemFonts(fontpaths=None, fontext='ttf'), end= "\n")
```

VaritSris>python findFontsMat.py

Results
Display fonts that could be used in matplotlib:
/System/Library/Fonts/Supplemental/Arial Bold.ttf
/System/Library/Fonts/Supplemental/NotoSansImperialAramaic-Regular.ttf
/System/Library/Fonts/Supplemental/NotoSansOldNorthArabian-Regular.ttf
/System/Library/AssetsV2/com_apple_MobileAsset_Font7/6207b1b7f2281b63327c7286feb841d5ca37f8e6.asset/AssetData/K2D.ttc
/System/Library/Fonts/Supplemental/Bodoni 72 Smallcaps Book.ttf
/System/Library/Fonts/Supplemental/NotoSansOldItalic-Regular.ttf
/System/Library/Fonts/Supplemental/Georgia Bold.ttf

To use custom fonts, The font must be found and stored in the reference folder. For example, the font **SrinhichaarnunN.ttf** is stored in /Users/admin/Library/Fonts/
Then write an additional command to refer to the desired storage location and font file name, using **import pathlib** as follows:

```
import matplotlib as mpLib
import matplotlib.pyplot as lineplt
import matplotlib.font_manager as font_manager
from pathlib import Path
Firstline = [2, 6, 3, 16, 25]
lineplt.rcParams["font.family"] = "TH Sarabun New"
fontSri = Path(mpLib.get_data_path(),
"/Users/admin/Library/Fonts/SrinhichaarnunN.ttf")
# Increase the thickness of the linewidth curve
lineplt.plot(Firstline,linewidth=5)
# Define the title using the given font, fontSri.
lineplt.title("Exampleกราฟเส้นTEst",
fontsize=24,font=fontSri)
# Define sentence displayed at the X axis
lineplt.xlabel("ค่า X", fontsize=14)
# Define sentences displayed at the Y axis
lineplt.ylabel("ค่า Y", fontsize=14)
```

lineplt.show()
Results

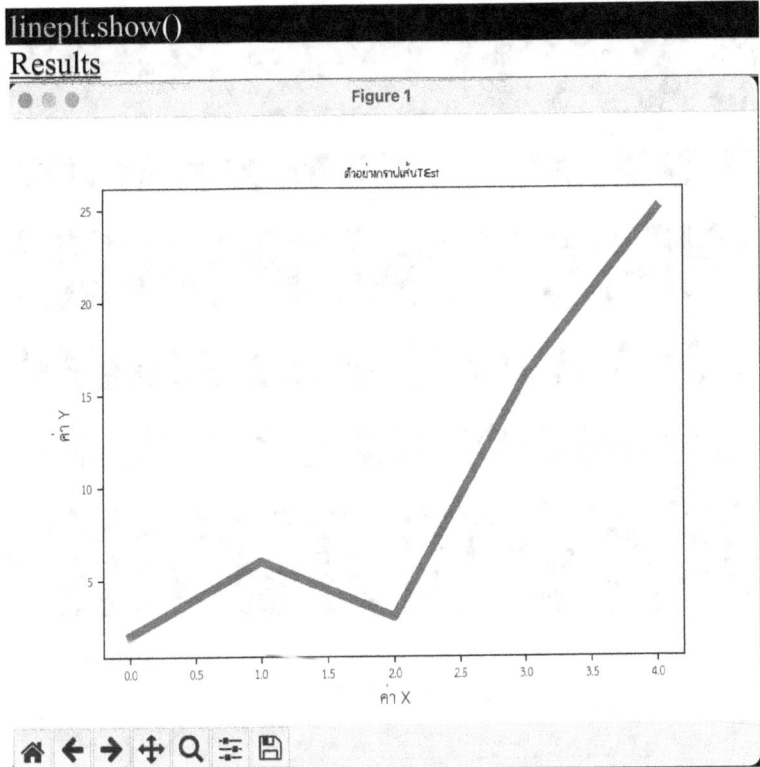

Figure Project III- 2:Line graph with custom font

Where TH Sarabun New is used, except for the title which uses SrinhichaarnunN.ttf

To show markers, add:
```
lineplt.plot(Firstline, 'r+', markersize=12,linestyle='dashed',markerfacecolor='blue')
```

Example
```
import matplotlib as mpLib
import matplotlib.pyplot as lineplt
import matplotlib.font_manager as font_manager
from pathlib import Path
Firstline = [2, 6, 3, 16, 25]
```

```
lineplt.rcParams["font.family"] = "TH Sarabun New"
fontSri = Path(mpLib.get_data_path(),
"/Users/admin/Library/Fonts/SrinhichaarnunN.ttf")
# Increase the thickness of the linewidth curve
linePlt.plot(Firstline,linewidth=5)
# Define the title using the given font, fontSri.
linePlt.title("Exampleกราฟเส้นTEst",
fontsize=24,font=fontSri)
# Define sentence displayed at the X axis
linePlt.xlabel("ค่า X", fontsize=14)
# Define sentences displayed at the Y axis
linePlt.ylabel("ค่า Y", fontsize=14)
# Line formatting and markers
lineplt.plot(Firstline, 'r+',
markersize=12,linestyle='dashed',markerfacecolor='blue')
lineplt.show()
```

Results

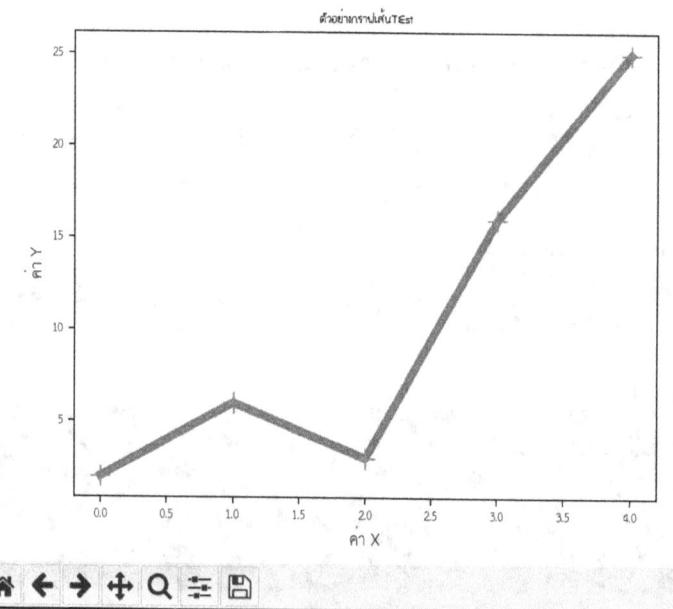

Figure Project III- 3:Line graph with added markers

For more information, please refer to the link.

https://matplotlib.org/2.1.1/api/_as_gen/matplotlib.pyplot.plot.html

To show a grid:
```
import matplotlib as mpLib
import matplotlib.pyplot as linePlt
import matplotlib.font_manager as font_manager
from pathlib import Path
Firstline = [2, 6, 3, 16, 25]
linePlt.rcParams["font.family"] = "TH Sarabun New"
fontSri = Path(mpLib.get_data_path(),
"/Users/admin/Library/Fonts/SrinhichaarnunN.ttf")
# Increase the thickness of the linewidth curve
linePlt.plot(Firstline,linewidth=5)
# Define the title using the given font, fontSri.
linePlt.title("Exampleกราฟเส้นTEst",
fontsize=24,font=fontSri)
# Define sentence displayed at the X axis
linePlt.xlabel("ค่า X", fontsize=14)
# Define sentences displayed at the Y axis
linePlt.ylabel("ค่า Y", fontsize=14)
# Line formatting and markers
linePlt.plot(Firstline, 'r+',
markersize=12,linestyle='dashed',markerfacecolor='blue')
linePlt.grid()
linePlt.show()
```

Results

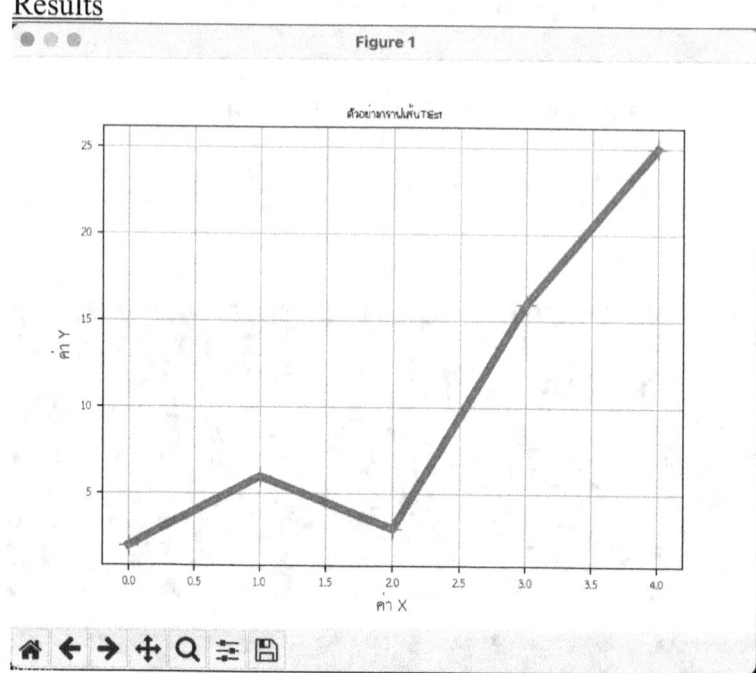

Figure Project III- 4 : Line graph with grid

Example Program: Histogram

```
import numpy as np
import matplotlib.pyplot as histPlt

x = [20,30,30,34,11,12,50,30,25,35,35,49,20,30,30,34,31,32,40,30,25,35,40,41,35,
49,20,30,30,34,21,22,30,30,25,35,35,24,32,33,38,45,44,43,13,18,15]
count = [int(i) for i in x]

# Create a graph image by defining the size
fig, grade = histPlt.subplots(figsize=(10,5))

# Set font size
count_size = 9
```

```python
label_size = 10
# Determine the number of bins and the range of values
num_bins = np.arange(0, max(count) + 1, 1)
n, bins, patches = grade.hist(count, bins=num_bins)

# Display the number on the bars
for i in range(len(num_bins) - 1):
    if n[i] > 0:
        grade.text(bins[i]+0.4 , n[i]+0.2 , str(int(n[i])), fontsize=count_size, ha='center')

grade.set_xlabel('Score', fontsize=label_size)
grade.set_ylabel('Number of Students', fontsize=label_size)
# Define graph range
grade.set_xticks(np.arange(0, 51, 1))

fig.tight_layout()
# Save archive as file
fig.savefig('gradePython.png')
# Display
histPlt.show()
```

Results

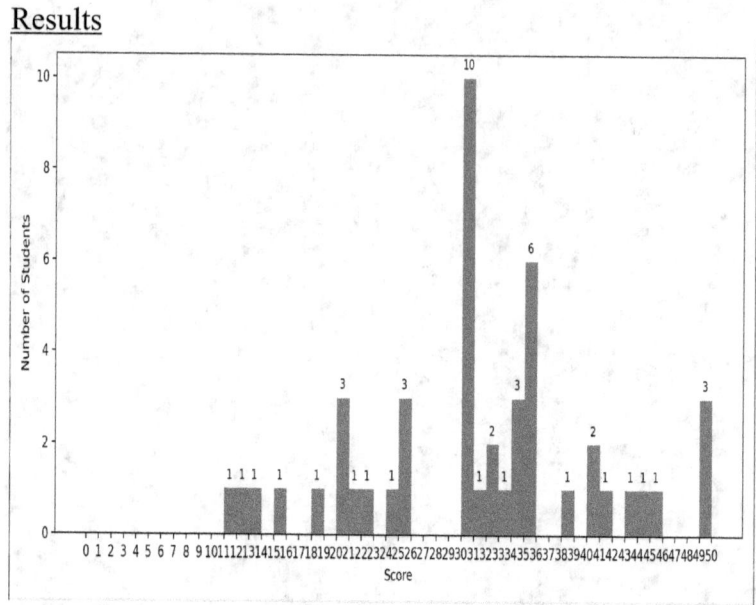

Figure Project III- 5:Histogram

Opening Score.png

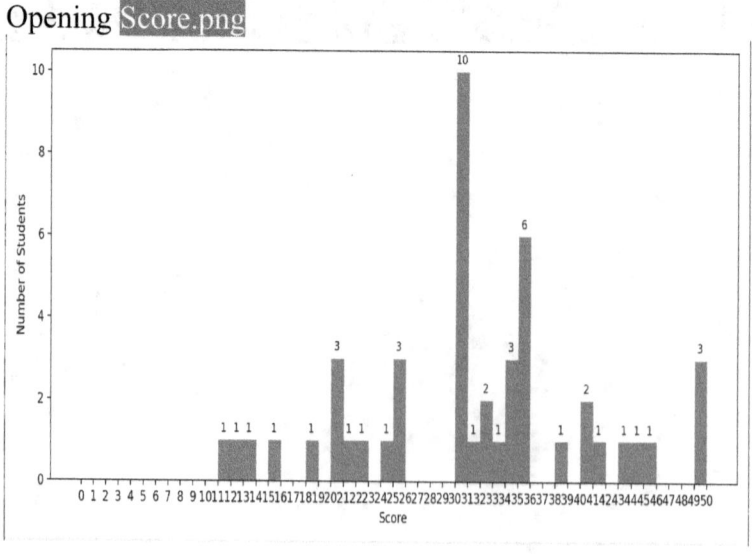

Figure Project III- 6:PNG image of histogram

Example Program: Pie Chart

```python
import matplotlib.pyplot as piePlt
import numpy as np

revenueOfFood = np.array([102, 21, 32, 98, 86])

piePlt.pie(revenueOfFood)
#Define label
revenueOfFoodLabels = ["ThaiFood", "USFood",
"ChinaFood", "IndiaFood", "EuroFood"]
#Define Legend, Title and Location
piePlt.legend(["ThaiFood", "USFood", "ChinaFood",
"IndiaFood", "EuroFood"],title = "Revenue Of
Food",loc='right',bbox_to_anchor=(1.3, 0.9))
pieColors = ["#4CAF50", "Magenta", "b", "y",'r']
piePlt.pie(revenueOfFood, labels = revenueOfFoodLabels,
colors = pieColors)
piePlt.show()
```

Results

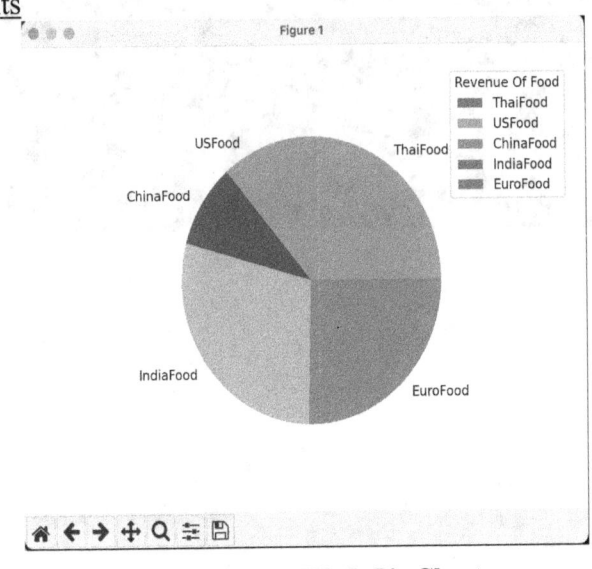

Figure Project III- 7: Pie Chart

Example Program: Bar Chart
```
import matplotlib as mpLib
import matplotlib.pyplot as barPlt
import matplotlib.font_manager as font_manager
from pathlib import Path
#Use subplots to display graphs as subgraphs
fig, fruitAx = barPlt.subplots()
#Define label (fruit names)
fruits = ['Durian','Coconut','Papaya','Lemon','Orange' ]
#Define Data
counts = [23, 21, 28, 25, 34]
#Set the color of each bar (for each fruit)
bar_labels = ['Durian','Coconut','Papaya','Lemon','Orange']
bar_colors = ['tab:green', 'tab:blue', 'tab:red', 'tab:pink', 'tab:orange']
fruitAx.bar(fruits, counts, label=bar_labels, color=bar_colors)
#Define y-axis (Income from selling fruits)
fruitAx.set_ylabel('Income from selling fruits')
#Define Title (Income from selling fruits by type)
fruitAx.set_title('Income from selling fruits by type')
#Define Legend (fruit vs. bar color)
fruitAx.legend(title='color of fruit')

barPlt.show()
```

Results

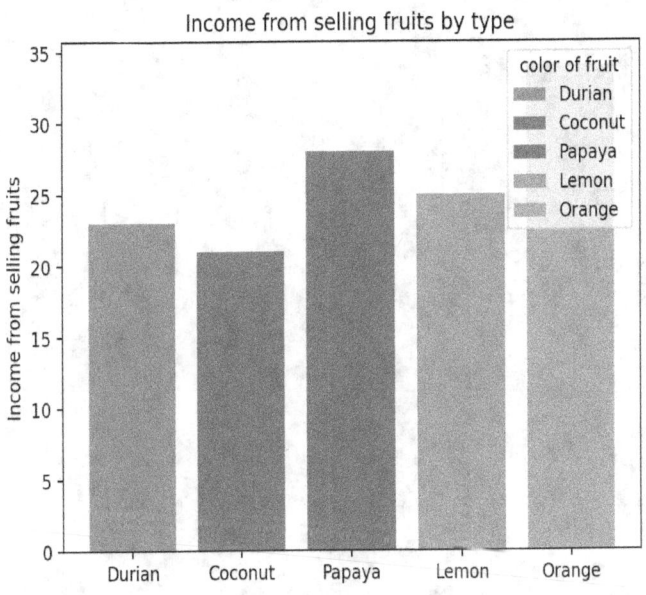

Figure Project III- 8: Bar Chart

For a comparative bar graph, do as follows.

```
import matplotlib as mpLib
import matplotlib.pyplot as barPlt
import numpy as np
import matplotlib.font_manager as font_manager
from pathlib import Path
#Define label (fruit names)

fruits = ('Durian', 'Orange', 'Mango', 'WaterMelon')
#Define Data
noFruitsYear = {
    '2023': (18, 18, 14, 23),
    '2024': (38, 48, 47, 53),
```

```
'2025': (189, 195, 217, 120),
}

#Define Label Locations
labelFruit = np.arange(len(fruits))
#Define The width of each bar graph
width = 0.25
multiplier = 0
#Define subgraph display. To require multiple bars to be displayed next to each other, layout='constrained' is required.
fig, fruitsAx = barPlt.subplots(layout='constrained')
#Set multiple subgraphs to be displayed side by side
# attribute is the label shown in the graph description.
for attribute, measurement in noFruitsYear.items():
    offset = width * multiplier
# Display the value on each bar
    rects = fruitsAx.bar(labelFruit + offset, measurement, width, label=attribute)
    fruitsAx.bar_label(rects, padding=1)
    multiplier += 1

# Define Title, Label and Legend position.
#  Y axis is '1,000 tons', Title is 'Total Fruits Exported"
fruitsAx.set_ylabel('1,000 Ton')
fruitsAx.set_title('Number of fruits exported')

fruitsAx.set_xticks(labelFruit + width, fruits)

fruitsAx.legend(loc='upper left', ncols=3)
fruitsAx.set_ylim(0, 250)

barPlt.show()
```

Results

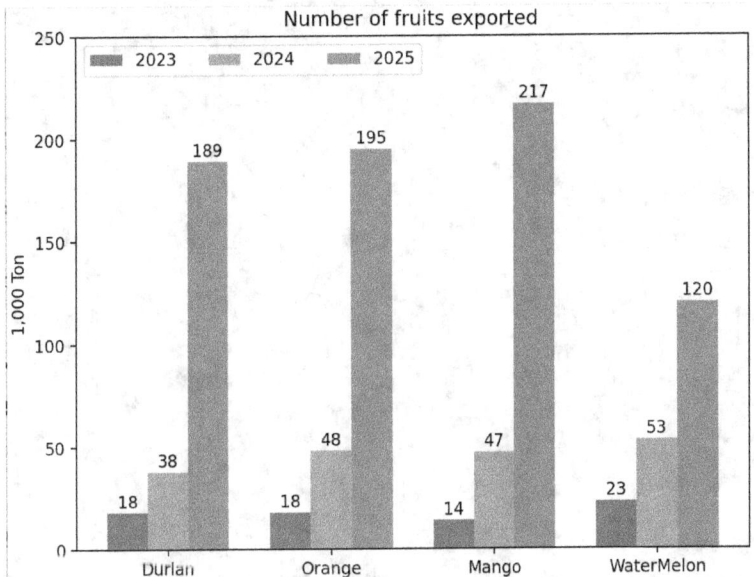

Figure Project III- 9:Comparative bar graph

When you want to create a Dashboard, if the data is connected to a database, when the data in that database is updated, the graph will be adjusted accordingly, for ease of data management. To demonstrate we will use the subplot command.

> **subplot(p,q,r)** where p is the number of rows, q is the number of columns and r is the position of the graph.

Example
```
import matplotlib as mpLib
import matplotlib.pyplot as DashPlt
```

```python
import matplotlib.font_manager as font_manager
from pathlib import Path
#Plot 1 are the numbers displayed in the columns and rows of graph 1.
x = [0, 2, 6, 7, 9]
y = [2, 6, 8, 10, 12]

#Here, 1 row and 2 columns are defined, and the graph is in position 1.
DashPlt.subplot(1, 2, 1)

DashPlt.plot(x,y,'r+',
markersize=12,linestyle='dashed',markerfacecolor='blue',linewidth=5)

DashPlt.title("Line1", fontsize=24)
# Define words displayed at the X axis
DashPlt.xlabel("X", fontsize=14)
# Define words displayed at the Y axis
DashPlt.ylabel("Y", fontsize=14)
DashPlt.grid()

#Plot 2 are the numbers displayed in the columns and rows of graph 2.
x2 =[0, 1, 2, 3, 4]
y2 = [1, 2, 3, 4, 8]

#Here, 1 row and 2 columns are defined, and the graph is in position 2.
DashPlt.subplot(1, 2, 2)
DashPlt.plot(x2,y2,'b+',
markersize=12,markerfacecolor='blue',linestyle='dotted',linewidth=5)

DashPlt.title("Line2", fontsize=24)
# Define words displayed at the X axis
```

```
DashPlt.xlabel("X2", fontsize=14)
# Define words displayed at the Y axis
DashPlt.ylabel("Y2", fontsize=14)

DashPlt.show()
```

Results

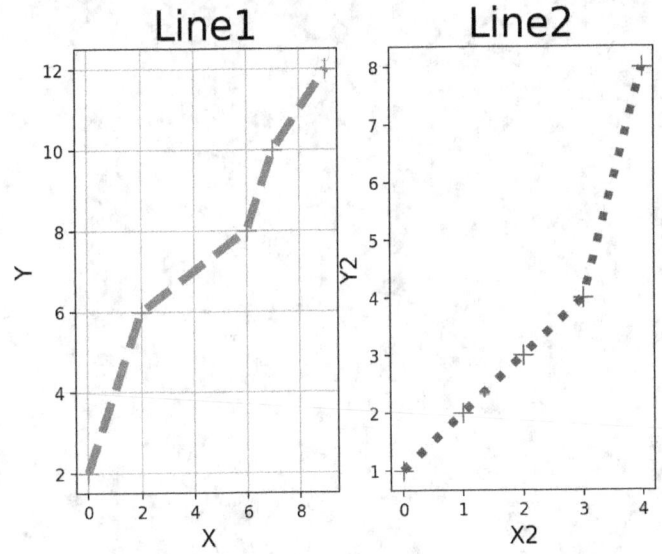

Figure Project III- 10 : Using subplot to create a dashboard

Example 2

```
import matplotlib.pyplot as dashPlt
import numpy as np
#Plot 1 are the numbers displayed in the columns and rows of graph 1.
x = np.array([9, 5, 4, 7, 5, 8])
y = np.array([9, 1, 2, 8, 3, 2])
#Here, 2 rows and 3 columns are defined, and the graph is in position 1.
dashPlt.subplot(2, 3, 1)
dashPlt.bar(x,y)

#Plot 2 are the numbers displayed in the columns and rows of graph 2.
```

```python
x = [0, 1, 2, 3,34,2,3,5,6,32,11,21,53]
y = [10, 21, 32, 23,44,22,31,15,32,43,11,11,23]
#Here, 2 rows and 3 columns are defined, and the graph is in position 2.
dashPlt.subplot(2, 3, 2)
dashPlt.scatter(x,y)


#Plot 3 are the numbers displayed in the columns and rows of graph 3.
x = np.array([0, 1, 2, 3])
y = np.array([3, 8, 1, 10])
#Here, 2 rows and 3 columns are defined, and the graph is in position 3.
dashPlt.subplot(2, 3, 3)
dashPlt.plot(x,y)


#Plot 4 are the numbers displayed in the columns and rows of graph 4.
x = np.array([0, 1, 2, 3])
y = np.array([5, 6, 2, 7])
#Here, 2 rows and 3 columns are defined, and the graph is in position 4.
dashPlt.subplot(2, 3, 4)
dashPlt.plot(x,y)


#Plot 5 are the numbers displayed in the columns and rows of graph 5.
x = np.array([0, 1, 2, 3, 0, 1, 2, 3])
y = np.array([3, 8, 3, 8, 1, 10, 4, 5])
#Here, 2 rows and 3 columns are defined, and the graph is in position 5.
dashPlt.subplot(2, 3, 5)
dashPlt.bar(x,y)

#Plot 6 are the numbers displayed in the columns and rows of graph 6.
x = np.array([0, 1, 2, 4, 3, 5, 3])
#Here, 2 rows and 3 columns are defined, and the graph is in position 6.
dashPlt.subplot(2, 3, 6)
dashPlt.pie(x)


dashPlt.show()
```

Results

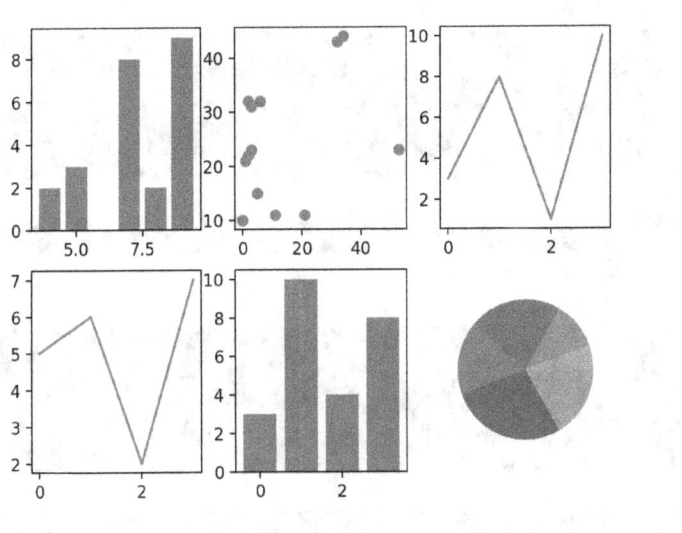

Figure Project III- 11: Using subplot to create a dashboard 2

In case of using data from a CSV file, that data may be stored in Excel and then displayed according to the program .

Example data in Excel

    Durian   34
    Mango   32
    Melon   12
    Orange   23
    Coconut   73
    Banana   15

file is saved as NoOfFruit.csv

Example Program: Retrieving Data from a CSV File

```
import matplotlib.pyplot as csvPlt
```

```python
import csv
# Define variables of data values from the CSV file, where
row 1 is Fruits.
# The 2nd row is noFruits.
fruits = []
noFruits = []

with open('NoOfFruit.csv','r') as csvfile:
    # Define plots variable to read CSV files
    plots = csv.reader(csvfile, delimiter = ',')
    #Get data values from CSV file, where row 1 is fruits
    and row 2 is noFruits one by one until complete.
    for row in plots:
        fruits.append(row[0])
        noFruits.append(int(row[1]))

# Display data as bar graph
csvPlt.bar(fruits, noFruits, color = 'g', width = 0.72, label = "Ton")
csvPlt.xlabel('Fruit')
csvPlt.ylabel('Number(Ton)')
csvPlt.title('No Of Fruits')
csvPlt.legend()
csvPlt.show()
```

Results

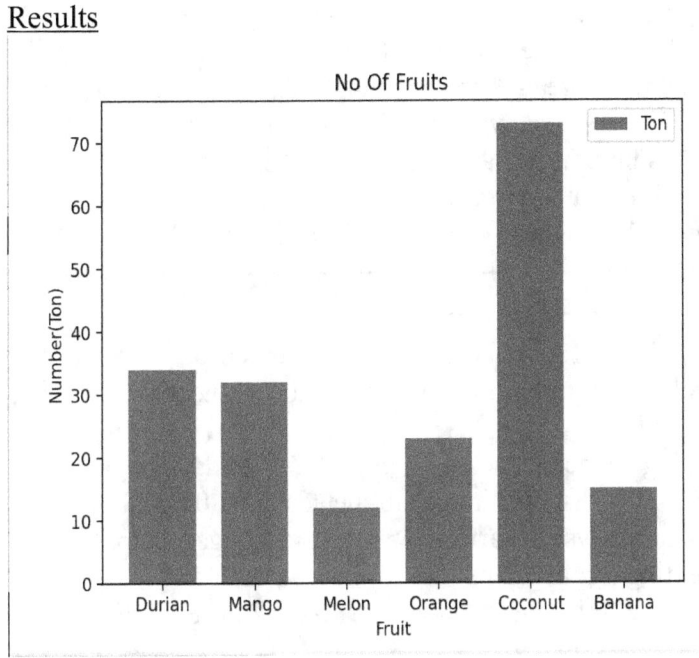

Figure Project III- 12: graph from a CSV file

Map graphing

Map graphing can be done with **pygal** and **pygal_maps_world** installed.

Firstly, create a virtual environment specific to the pygal, since at the time of writing, it can only be used with python Version 3.6, 3.7, 3.8 and 3.9. To learn more, visit

https://www.pygal.org

(PyDataAnalysis) VariitSris>pip install pygal
Collecting pygal
  Downloading pygal-3.0.4-py2.py3-none-any.whl.metadata
      (3.6 kB)
Collecting importlib-metadata (from pygal)

Downloading importlib_metadata-7.1.0-py3-none-any.whl.metadata (4.7 kB)
Requirement already satisfied: zipp>=0.5 in /Users/nee/.pyenv/versions/3.9.16/envs/PyDataAnalysis/lib/python3.9/site-packages (from importlib-metadata->pygal) (3.18.1)
Downloading pygal-3.0.4-py2.py3-none-any.whl (130 kB)

130.4/130.4 kB 2.5 MB/s eta 0:00:00
Downloading importlib_metadata-7.1.0-py3-none-any.whl (24 kB)
Installing collected packages: importlib-metadata, pygal
Successfully installed importlib-metadata-7.1.0 pygal-3.0.4
(PyDataAnalysis) VariitSris>pip install pygal_maps_world
Collecting pygal_maps_world
  Downloading pygal_maps_world-1.0.2.tar.gz (270 kB)

270.8/270.8 kB 607.6 kB/s eta 0:00:00
  Installing build dependencies ... done
  Getting requirements to build wheel ... done
  Installing backend dependencies ... done
  Preparing metadata (pyproject.toml) ... done
Requirement already satisfied: pygal>=1.9.9 in /Users/nee/.pyenv/versions/3.9.16/envs/PyDataAnalysis/lib/python3.9/site-packages (from pygal_maps_world) (3.0.4)
Requirement already satisfied: importlib-metadata in /Users/nee/.pyenv/versions/3.9.16/envs/PyDataAnalysis/lib/python3.9/site-packages (from pygal>=1.9.9->pygal_maps_world) (7.1.0)
Requirement already satisfied: zipp>=0.5 in /Users/nee/.pyenv/versions/3.9.16/envs/PyDataAnalysis/lib/python3.9/site-packages (from importlib-

```
        metadata->pygal>=1.9.9->pygal_maps_world)
        (3.18.1)
Building wheels for collected packages: pygal_maps_world
  Building wheel for pygal_maps_world (pyproject.toml) ...
        done
  Created wheel for pygal_maps_world:
        filename=pygal_maps_world-1.0.2-py3-none-
        any.whl size=278544
        sha256=7b6579f107755c3ae8b43a5367af93fd4be0
        8600438734aaee35822c52204051
  Stored in directory:
        /Users/nee/Library/Caches/pip/wheels/f8/ff/bd/a3cb
        8647e19834039de7bfd2f9304e06d3314f87c135cb8
        b1a
Successfully built pygal_maps_world
Installing collected packages: pygal_maps_world
Successfully installed pygal_maps_world-1.0.2
```

To check what packages have been installed:

```
(PyDataAnalysis) VariitSris>pip list
Package                Version
----------------       -------
pip                    24.0
pygal                  3.0.4
pygal-maps-world       1.0.2
pygame                 2.5.0
setuptools             58.1.0
```

When complete you can try the packages with the following sample program:

```
import pygal.maps.world

# Create a world map object
exportFruit = pygal.maps.world.World()

# Set the title of the map
exportFruit.title = 'No of Fruit in Country 2025'
```

```python
# Add data to the map
exportFruit.add('FruitCountry',
 [('af', 14),
  ('bd', 1),
  ('by', 3),
  ('cn', 2240),
  ('gm', 9),
  ('in', 1),
  ('ir', 314),
  ('iq', 129),
  ('jp', 7),
  ('kp', 6),
  ('pk', 1),
  ('ps', 6),
  ('sa', 79),
  ('so', 6),
  ('sd', 5),
  ('tw', 6),
  ('ae', 1),
  ('us', 43),
  ('ye', 28), ('th', 1334)])  # Canada, USA, Mexico
exportFruit.render()
# Render the map to an SVG file
exportFruit.render_to_file('exportFruit.svg')
```

Results
open exportFruit.svg with browser.

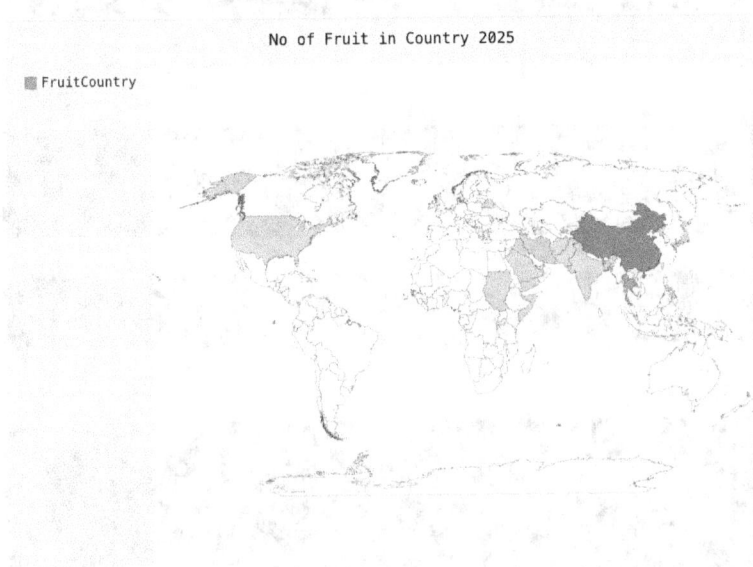

Figure Project III- 13:Map graphing example 1

For more information how country are defined in the app, go to:

https://www.pygal.org/en/3.0.0/documentation/types/maps/pygal_maps_world.html#country

Example Program
```
# import pygal
import pygal

# import Style class from pygal.style
from pygal.style import Style

# create a Style object
fruit_style = Style( colors = ('#40E0D0' , '#DE3163' ,
```

```python
                    '#FF7F50' , '#CCCCFF',
                    '#FFD700','#6495ED'))

# create a world map,
# Style class is used for using
# the fruit colours in the map,
exportFruit =  pygal.maps.world.World(style
                = fruit_style)

# set the title of the map
exportFruit.title = 'No of Fruit export 2025'

# hex code of colours are used
# for every .add() called
exportFruit.add('"Mango" ',
       ['ec', 'fi', 'eh','pg', 'ph',
        'er', 'et'])

exportFruit.add('"Banana" ',
       ['fr','ee', 'eg' ])

exportFruit.add('"Coconut" ',
       ['pa', 'pe', 'es', 'pk',
        'pl','pr', 'ps', 'zw' ,'af', 'al'])

exportFruit.add('"Orange" ',
       ['zm','pt', 'au', 'az'])

exportFruit.add ('"Durian" ',
       ['ad','ae',  'am', 'ao',
        'aq', 'ar', 'at', 'py','in'],
        color = 'black')
exportFruit.add ('"All" ' ,
       ['th','cn'],
        color = '#6495ED')
```

```python
# save into the file
exportFruit.render_to_file('exportFruit2025.svg')

print("Finished saving exportFruit2025.svg")
```

Results
open exportFruit2025.svg with browser.

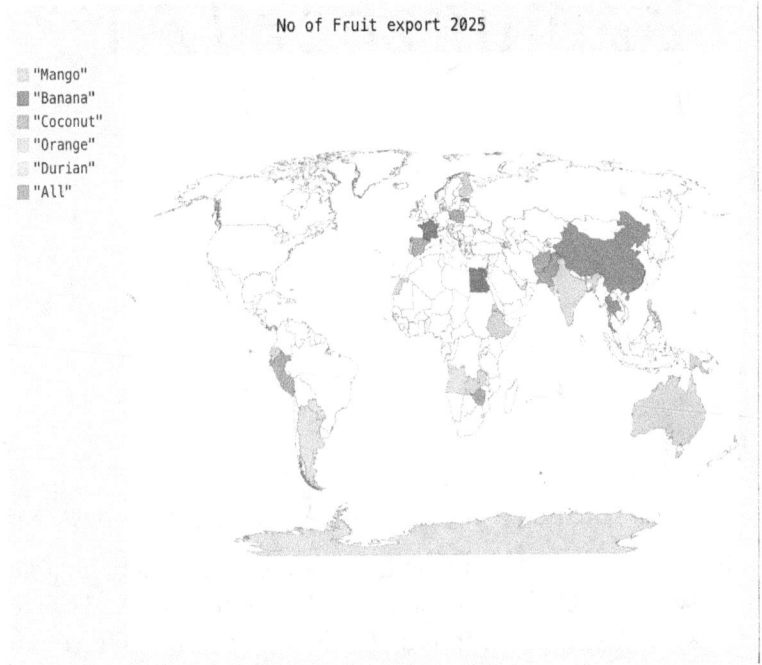

Figure Project III- 14:Map graphing example 2

Project IV
Artificial Intelligence (AI)

Artificial intelligence (AI) is a technology that allows machines to simulate human intelligence and be able to use their intelligence to solve various problems like humans. Using perception to learn information about images, sounds, letters, temperature, smell, and taste according to the 5 human senses: sight, taste, smell, sound, and touch. With a large enough amount of data, you can create an intelligence that replaces human intelligence in decision-making, planning, executing, solving problems, reasoning, analysis, and synthesis, which uses various algorithms such as Mathematics and data mining. It requires reviewing whether the intelligence generated by the machine can replace human intelligence in performing tasks. The advantage of using artificial intelligence is that the machine will learn more to become more intelligent as it performs its task, such as using machines to compete with humans in chess. After playing, the machine will learn more about its opponent and use it in the next match. Therefore, it becomes more and more difficult to play and win against machines. Another example could be using computers to interact linguistically. When a human asks a question, an intelligent machine can answer in such a way that is as intelligent as a human. Therefore, the most important factors for an AI are its **training data,** which is what the machine uses to learn, and its **testing data,** to determine its efficacy. Artificial intelligence can be categorized according to its complexity, from the lightest colors indicating the lowest level of artificial intelligence (Narrow AI) to dark colors showing the highest level of artificial intelligence (Strong AI).

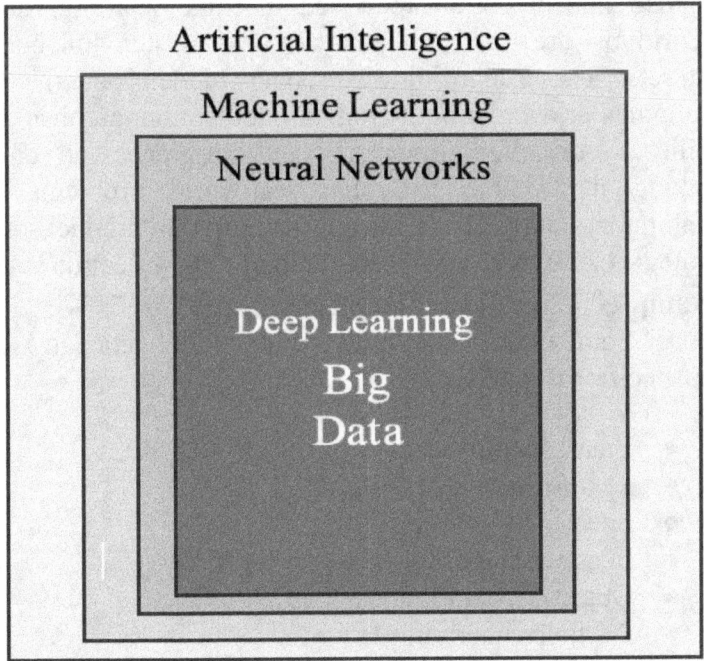

Figure Project IV- 1: Various AI Levels

For artificial intelligence, there are two basic forms of learning:
1) Supervised learning
   Also known as supervised machine learning, is the use of machine learning algorithms that use labeled datasets to train as input to form an intelligence model that is used to classify data or predict outcomes. The system adjusts the weight (w) until the intelligence model reaches an appropriate value. It is reviewed using a testing process. Supervised learning can help solve real world problems at various levels, depending on labels given to information used in its teaching, such as separating spam emails. If enough characteristics of spam email were given as input data, it can automatically separate spam emails and store them in the spam folder.
2) Unsupervised Learning
   Also known as unsupervised machine learning, uses algorithms are used to analyze and cluster unlabeled datasets. These algorithms discover hidden patterns or groupings in data without Human intervention, and has the ability to discover similarities and differences in data, making it possible to solve real-world problems in exploratory data analysis, such as determining product sales strategies, customer grouping and image classification.

Examples of artificial intelligence usage

Some examples of how artificial intelligence is used for specific tasks today are:

- Email spam filtering
- Text to speech
- Speech-recognition
- Image-recognition
- Object-recognition
- Predictive analytics
- Customer sentiment analysis
- Driverless car

- E-Payments
- Spell checking
- automatic language translation
- Answering questions instead of humans (Chatbots)
- Social Media
- Face Detection
- Identifying what the image is (Visual Perception)
- Searching for words, images, etc. (Search Algorithms)
- Robots
- Automated investment in stocks
- Natural Language Processing (NLP)
- Self-flying drones
- Finding customer personas
- Anomaly detection
- Find abnormalities from medical imaging

Various companies that use artificial intelligence include:
- **IBM:** has **Watson**, a high-level artificial intelligence system used in various tasks, such as helping doctors diagnose diseases or as an astronaut's assistant. It is still continuously self-learning and developing, and even expresses itself using a facial display.
- **Apple:** has **Siri**, a system that allows users to give voice commands instead of typing.
- **Microsoft** has **Cortana**, a desktop assistant for Windows users.
- **Amazon** has **Alexa**, that can help perform various household tasks.
- **Netflix** uses artificial intelligence to recommend movies to it users.
- **Google** uses artificial intelligence in various apps, such as Google Maps, Google Assistant, or Google News.

Learn Python with Projects

Machine Learning

Machine Learning (Machine Learning) is a subfield of artificial intelligence which uses processing power for the sake of learning. This method of using data to learn and create algorithms is very different from projects 1-3, which use data and algorithms predetermined by the programmer.

Neural Networks

Creating an artificial neural network is a programming technique that uses machine learning along with software that learns from its mistakes. By imitating the work of the human brain in which neurons send messages to each other while solving problems, repeating actions over and over to achieve success and reduce errors. This will result in an artificial neural network called a perceptron, which is the first step in creating a neural network, where a single neuron has a single layer, has only one layer of input and has no hidden layers, as shown in the picture.

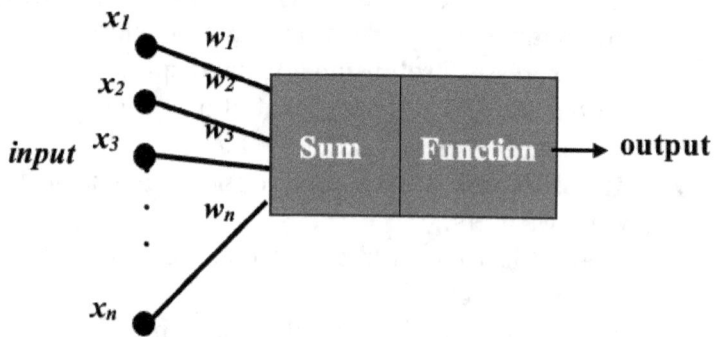

Figure Project IV- 2: Neural Networks

Discovered in 1957 by Frank Rosenblatt, an American psychologist famous for his work on artificial intelligence, the perceptron model was originally designed to input and output a single binary data (either 0 or 1), and uses the idea of using different weights(w) to show the importance of each input data *(x)* and the sum of the values should be greater than the threshold value before making a decision such as yes or no. (True or False) (0 or 1)

Perceptron Algorithm

The perceptron algorithm proposed by Frank Rosenblatt has the following principles:

1. Set threshold (Threshold)
2. Multiply the input data*(x)* with weight*(w)* for every value that carries information into the nerve cell.
3. Sum all values in item 2.
4. Compare the results from item 3. If it is greater than item 1, the results will be output.

For artificial intelligence in project 4, Python will be used to create artificial intelligence from scratch.
Creation of tools used for artificial intelligence as follows.

1. Mathematical tools

Statistics

1) Mean
2) Median
3) Mode
4) Standard Deviation
5) Percentiles

Creating data for testing

6) Create data in a uniform distribution
7) Create normal data distribution

Data analysis

8) Scatter Plot Analysis
9) Linear Regression Analysis
10) Polynomial Regression Analysis
11) Multiple Regression Analysis
12) Categorical Data Analysis

Data mining tools

13) Decision Tree
14) Hierarchical Clustering
15) K-Means
16) Association Rules

2. Teaching and Testing Tools

Developing artificial intelligence programs using Python

Developing an artificial intelligence program using Python using the tools mentioned above. There are 4 types of data used to create intelligence:

- **Nominal Data** refers to data that must be labeled with real-world data labels or names that are used to identify characteristics or properties that **cannot** be sorted, as shown:

Table Project IV- 1: Example Nominal Data

Label of data (label)	information
sex	male, female
occupation	Soldiers, farmers, company employees, actors, teachers, executives, singers
nationality	Thai, Chinese, American, French, Khmer, Burmese, Vietnamese, Singaporean, Philippines
color	White, black, red, orange, green

- **Ordinal Data** refers to data that must be labeled with real-world data labels or names that are used to indicate characteristics or properties that **can** be sorted, as shown:

Table Project IV- 2: Example Ordinal Data

Label of data (label)	information
study	Kindergarten, primary school, high school, bachelor's degree, master's degree, doctorate degree,
academic results	A+, A, B+, B, C+, C, D+, D, F
ability to speak English	Excellent, good, fair, bad, very bad
Preference for brand name products	most, a lot, moderate, a little, very little

- **Discrete Data** refers to data that has discrete values that are integers, numbers that can be counted, as shown

Table Project IV- 3: Example Discreet Data

list	information
Number of students who graduated	12,000 people
Number of times visited Japan	3 times
Number of cars parked in the hotel	123 cars

- **Continuous Data** refers to data that has continuous values that are not integers, as shown:

Table Project IV- 4: Example Continuous Data

Features or properties	information
student height	155.54 centimeters
Distance from Bangkok to Chonburi	81.38 kilometers
Measurable body temperature	35.32 degrees Celsius

Mathematical tools

Statistics

1) **Mean(μ)** is the sum of all values and then divided by the number of values, such as the mean average height of students. If there are 10 students, measure the height of every student as follows.

Table Project IV- 5: Example Height of Student Table for finding Average

No.	1	2	3	4	5	6	7	8	9	10	11
Height (cm)	150	210	156	170	168	156	168	168	165	172	170

Average = (150+210+156+170+168+156+168+168+165+172+170)/11

= 1853/11 = 168.45454545454547 cm.

Example of writing a program to find the mean average

```
import numpy
```

```
studentHigh = [150,210,156,170,168,156,168,168,165,172,170]

x = numpy.mean(studentHigh)

print(x)
```

Result

168.45454545454547

2) **Median** is the value that is in the middle of all values by arranging the values from lowest to highest. For example, to find the median height of students in a classroom of 11 students, measure the height of every student as follows.

Table Project IV- 6: Example Student height Table (amount of data is odd)

No.	1	2	3	4	5	6	7	8	9	10	11
Height (cm)	150	210	156	170	168	156	168	168	165	172	170

Arrange the height from lowest to highest as follows.

Table Project IV- 7: Example Student height Table after sorting

No.	1	2	3	4	5	6	7	8	9	10	11
Height (cm)	150	156	156	165	168	168	168	170	170	172	210

The middle order is 6 and the median height value is 168 cm.

Example of writing a program to find the median

```
import numpy
```

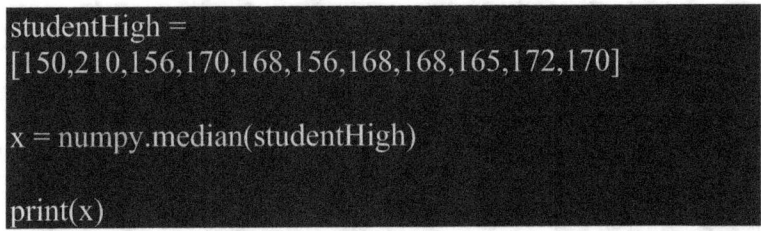

Result

168.00

In the case where the sums are even numbers:

Table Project IV- 8: Example Student height Table (amount of data is even)

No.	1	2	3	4	5	6	7	8	9	10
Height (cm)	150	210	156	170	168	156	169	170	165	172

Arrange the height from lowest to highest as follows.

Table Project IV- 9: Example Student height Table after sorting

No.	1	2	3	4	5	6	7	8	9	10
Height (cm)	150	156	156	165	168	169	170	170	172	210

The middle order are 5 and 6, resulting in height values of 168 cm and 169 cm. Add the 2 middle orders and divide by 2 as follows: (168+169)/2 = 168.5 cm.

Example of writing a program to find the median

```
import numpy

studentHigh = [150,210,156,170,168,156,169,170,165,172]

x = numpy.median(studentHigh)

print(x)
```

Result

168.50

3) **Mode** value is to find maximum frequency number of data. For example, to find the mode of the height of students of 11 students, measure the height of every student as follows:

Table Project IV- 10: Example Student height Table for finding mode

No.	1	2	3	4	5	6	7	8	9	10	11
Height (cm)	150	210	156	170	168	156	168	168	165	172	170

Find frequency of student height. Maximum frequency number of student height is 168 cm, at 3 people.

Table Project IV- 11: Frequency of Example student height

Height (cm)	150	156	165	168	170	172	210
Number of students	1	2	1	3	2	1	1

To find the mode value, you must install the scipy package. Installation method is as follows.

VaritSris>pip install scipy

Or in the case of python3, use the command

VaritSris>pip3 install scipy

To check which packages or modules are installed, use the command:

VaritSris>pip3 list

Result
Package   Version
---------- -------
scipy   1.12.0

Example of programming to find mode values.

```
from scipy import stats

speed = [99,86,87,88,111,86,103,87,94,78,77,85,86]

x = stats.mode(speed)

print(x)
```

Result

ModeResult(mode=86, count=3)

4) **Standard Deviation** is a number that describes how different, or deviant, the values are, determined by how similar the distribution is to the mean average(μ), as shown in item 1. If the value is low, it means that most of the numbers are distributed close to the average. If it is high, it

means that the value of the number is spread out from the average using the following formula.

In the case of all data (population) using N to represent the population.

Equation Project IV- 1: Standard deviation

$$\text{Standard deviation } (\sigma : \text{Sigma}) = \sqrt{\frac{\Sigma(x-\mu)^2}{N}}$$

For example, you want to know the standard deviation of the height of students in the classroom. If there are 10 students in the classroom, measure the height of every student as follows.

Table Project IV- 12: Standard Deviation Example Data Table

No.	1	2	3	4	5	6	7	8	9	10	11
Height (cm)	150	210	156	170	168	156	168	168	165	172	170

average (μ) = (150+210+156+170+168+156+168+168+165+172+170)/11

= 1853/11 = 168.46 cm.

Table Project IV-13: Standard Deviation Example Data Table 2

No.	height (x)	$x - \mu$	$x - \mu$	$(x - \mu)^2$
1	150	150-168.46	-18.46	340.77
2	210	210-168.46	41.54	1725.57
3	156	156-168.46	-12.46	155.25
4	170	170-168.46	1.54	2.37
5	168	168-168.46	-0.46	0.21
6	156	156-168.46	-12.46	155.25
7	168	168-168.46	-0.46	0.21
8	168	168-168.46	-0.46	0.21
9	165	165-168.46	-3.46	11.97
10	172	172-168.46	3.54	12.53
11	170	170-168.46	1.54	2.37

$$\Sigma(x - \mu)^2 = 340.77+1725.57+155.25+2.37+0.21+155.25$$
$$+0.21+0.21+11.97+12.53+2.37$$
$$= 2406.73$$

$$\frac{\Sigma(x-\mu)^2}{N} = 2406.73/11 = 218.79 = 14.79$$

The lower the standard deviation of the height of students, the more similar that the students' heights are in the room. The higher the deviation, the greater the difference is in the heights of the students in the room.

Example of writing a program to find the standard deviation.
```
import numpy

studentHigh = [150,210,156,170,168,156,168,168,165,172,170]
```

```
x = numpy.sd(studentHigh)

print(x)
```

Result

14.791666181662976

5) **Percentiles** are used to calculate the percentage of the total amount of data.

For example, to find how tall 70 percent of the students in a classroom are, if there are 11 students in the classroom, measure the height of every student as follows.

Table Project IV- 14:For Find Percentiles Example Data Table

No.	1	2	3	4	5	6	7	8	9	10	11
Height (cm)	150	210	156	170	168	156	168	168	165	172	170

Example of writing a program to find the value of 70 percent.

```
import numpy

studentHigh = [150,210,156,170,168,156,168,168,165,172,170]

x = numpy.percentile(studentHigh,70)

print(x)
```

Result 170.00

If you want to know how shortest 5 percent of the students in this class are:

```
import numpy

studentHigh = [150,210,156,170,168,156,168,168,165,172,170]

x = numpy.percentile(studentHigh,5)

print(x)
```

Result 153.00

Creating data for testing

6) **Creating a Uniform distribution** is creating random data that has a uniform appearance for use in testing artificial intelligence algorithms to see if they are as desired or not, in order to simulate data to use instead of using real data. In a unified form with big data (Big Data), for example, if we need data of 300 values in the range 0.0 to 8.0, write a program as follows.

```
import numpy

x = numpy.random.uniform(0.0, 8.0, 300)

print(x)
```

Result

```
[3.82383204 0.37617145 2.04685942 1.28961761 0.85438479 3.30379211
 5.45857711 2.71858176 6.54949061 0.5691704  7.29647107 2.12520682
 7.07839641 5.0964222  6.01543721 1.23568283 2.64667886 0.70037905
 7.47005709 3.31436949 3.99421443 4.35947555 3.01973916 3.84754375
 4.24015637 4.90593778 1.22089739 6.77379249 7.47484991 5.86270205
 4.00979343 0.02866112 1.43358783 7.83367908 3.78533632 6.89068939
 1.65996657 4.70681216 6.37332297 0.62112514 7.42057561 5.95836013
```

```
0.40654364 2.83234122 2.88320302 5.65254161 5.96780324 2.78700856
5.35556635 2.93893217 7.21345896 1.16728459 4.21543249 7.80319343
3.72001739 7.55737917 4.80616263 6.59449096 4.21019189 5.89312068
1.7141691  7.00288688 3.71895251 7.79336448 4.43689902 1.90869171
6.68263282 4.15805964 2.74917635 6.92804349 5.28282676 7.26720508
3.69955479 2.39351805 7.46659553 6.76203948 0.57499984 6.8984019
1.57857742 5.39106438 0.68214713 4.5533673  1.87688313 6.61643953
4.41972986 6.85879227 0.74710435 6.45305939 7.52303475 4.19945612
2.66961582 7.50149776 7.76564851 7.95791088 4.05052078 2.19607697
2.20890068 5.07482241 1.88995009 7.51618845 5.09939645 5.53377847
6.06874111 2.86396853 6.54895697 1.67341447 4.4244924  2.92951505
3.91127005 1.23008107 6.70098547 6.28837611 1.93864183 6.25269377
2.08535804 7.97855975 0.88794311 4.90417186 5.40713614 2.23472581
2.11145597 7.48214294 5.55668961 3.32319289 3.11803028 0.76309292
2.2367794  7.89477305 2.96648861 4.1536348  7.11278923 1.65133419
3.5179201  7.86426626 5.63993653 2.83330109 0.5401149  0.72893579
4.72183512 6.50404543 1.88539174 5.80673736 1.09211963 2.86887494
6.12332814 7.71735079 3.6267719  3.59639837 1.68386953 7.01094347
1.57205513 5.32902138 2.44495539 2.69779549 3.21294393 7.64035114
7.77958914 4.36697814 5.98749285 5.00572885 2.46043398 0.74656352
0.76118195 2.13161571 7.36109768 0.83054726 0.24844939 6.77865805
3.23300261 3.80330906 4.24390893 6.88666644 7.67818315 3.47718791
7.44294519 6.19271309 3.14947002 4.81166635 4.40734946 3.70767549
3.2808053  5.71119439 7.5829086  2.028375   7.51357748 1.47246832
3.02076502 6.5699309  7.81601941 1.42851395 2.98143559 7.59695305
2.17174129 1.58425075 6.71796773 3.15725818 2.09473527 2.31589955
3.77905064 0.58033619 1.67152092 3.7281755  3.9615458  5.25541537
7.29958457 6.66767211 7.41397044 4.56972919 1.4034655  7.69258303
7.84481889 7.35490503 0.78707677 1.97542724 0.77198027 6.56587461
0.47427056 4.8404121  5.7415584  2.31309182 6.39603787 2.31341135
2.57460463 1.18185893 2.84603437 5.62323327 4.76088899 1.34352642
6.14249677 6.35408364 5.28533585 0.23161532 3.74801704 5.25283038
3.35432842 4.61901811 7.71377067 0.66069193 3.05652201 6.57506811
1.06558786 0.49849268 5.90733229 0.42868528 1.11720008 0.15793666
7.86893474 2.80640901 1.37049326 1.58551298 6.71554026 1.49868358
7.79340147 4.20495437 7.43391648 6.27770111 3.87345083 1.59799812
2.9077636  6.81195371 6.98467484 5.47965523 7.81045003 6.25171156
2.7439931  2.14872633 3.43192425 2.43299192 0.11562545 6.80306611
4.98062863 1.2687343  3.46975622 6.95446123 3.21139828 1.42175384
3.73952323 2.09834422 1.51230067 6.46722033 2.70890947 6.32138688
7.16071777 0.86552457 3.67343664 1.58134708 6.09518561 0.35046998
3.18813998 5.53872577 7.13540783 1.35716085 0.03378975 3.09884776
2.89878779 2.74185368 0.46417965 4.68969689 2.40319231 6.38314018]
```

To display a Histogram graph, write a program as follows. You must use the matplotlib package, which the installation method is as follows.

VaritSris> pip install -U matplotlib

Or in the case of python3, use the command

```
VaritSris> pip3 install -U matplotlib
```

```python
import numpy
import matplotlib.pyplot as plt

x = numpy.random.uniform(0.0, 8.0, 300)

plt.hist(x, 8)
plt.show()
```

Result

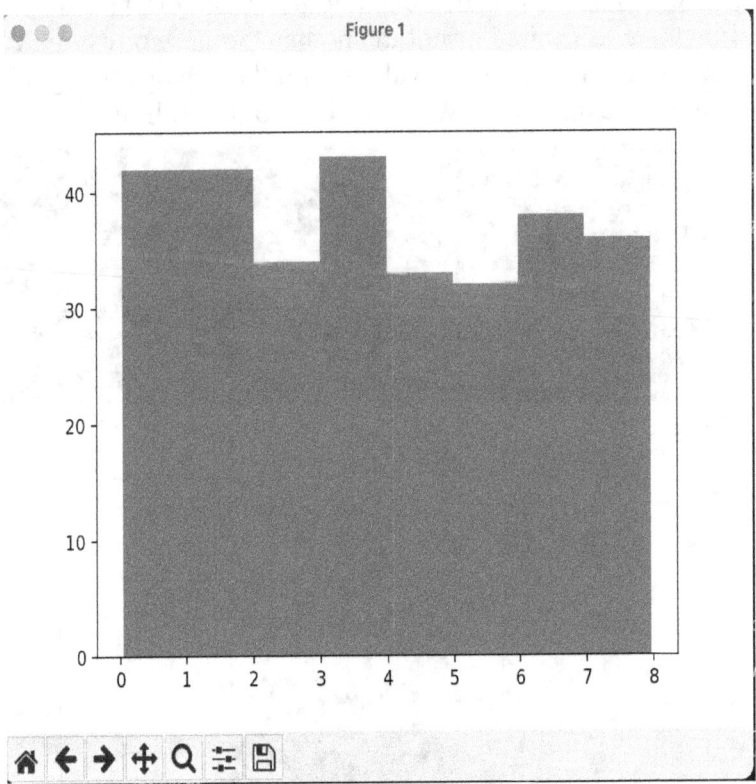

Figure Project IV- 3: Example Uniform distribution histogram

Every time the program is run, a new value will be randomly assigned every time. Therefore, programmers will be able to use it to test the developed artificial intelligence system to see if it meets the desired goals or not.

7) **Creating normally distributed** data (Normal data distribution) is creating random data that has normal characteristics or Gaussian (Gaussian). The nature of data in the real world is that the data is distributed in a symmetrical manner by using the average. Specified in the form of a bell curve (Bell Curve), with the data having the greatest value equal to the average. then descending to the left and right Data that is distributed like this is therefore used to simulate nature in order to test artificial intelligence algorithms to see if they are as desired or not in another format. For example, if we need data of 10,000 values with the average being 8.0 Standard deviation 2.0 Write the program as follows.

```
import numpy
import matplotlib.pyplot as plt

x = numpy.random.normal(8.0, 2.0, 10000)

plt.hist(x, 100)
plt.show()
```

Result

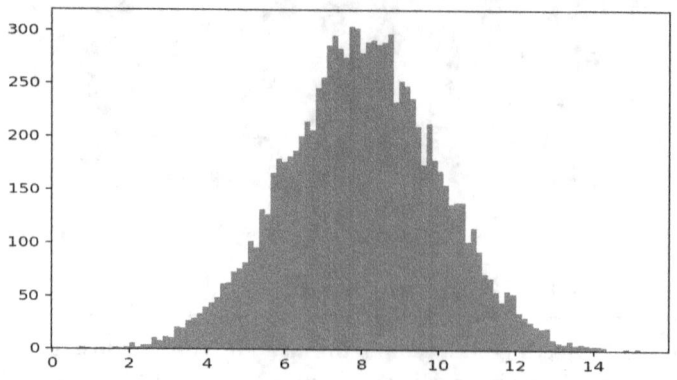

Figure Project IV- 4: Example Normal data distribution histogram

data analysis

8) **Scatter Plot analysis** is the analysis of data used in artificial intelligence to see how it is distributed. For example, you want to know the age of a person and the maximum weight that they can lift, as shown in the table.

Table Project IV- 15: Example Maximum weight lifted by subject weight

age	Weight that can be lifted (kg)
10	10
15	20
16	20
30	30
40	30
45	30
50	35
36	32
41	35
12	12
11	10
10	9
15	22
16	18
30	28
40	28
45	29
10	12
11	13
5	6
6	8
7	8

```
import matplotlib.pyplot as plt

age = [10,15,16,30,40,45,50,36,41,12,11,10,15,16,30,40,45,10,11,5,6,7]
weight = [10,20,20,30,30,30,35,32,35,12,10,9,22,18,28,28,29,12,13,6,8,8]

plt.scatter(age, weight)

plt.xlabel("Age(Year)")
plt.ylabel("Weight(Kg.)")

plt.show()
```
Result

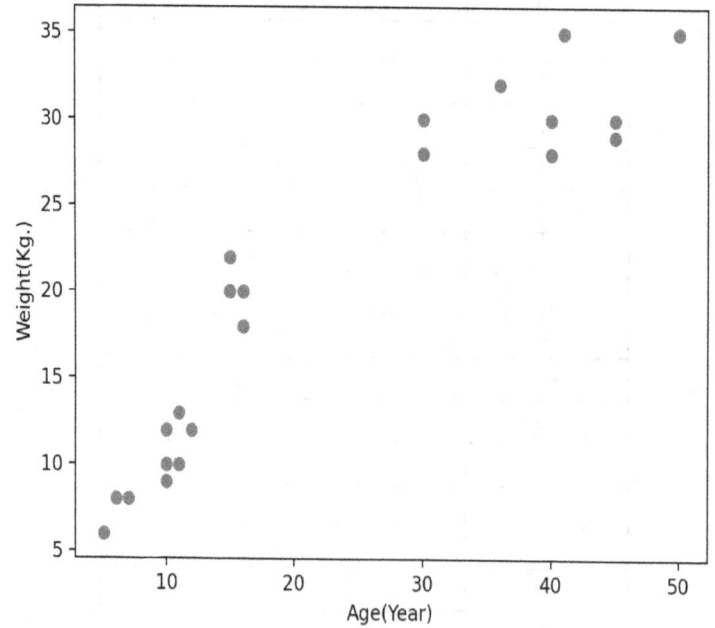

Figure Project IV- 5: Example Scatterplot analysis of age versus weight lifted

Looking at the graph, it can be seen that children will be able to lift more weight as they get older as teenagers and adults.

9) **Linear Regression analysis** is a data analysis used in artificial intelligence that has a linear equation with only 1 independent variable that affects 1 dependent variable, which can be used to predict the value of a dependent variable from an independent variable. For example, you want to know how a person's age, an independent variable, affects the maximum weight that can be lifted, a dependent variable, with the information obtained from a survey as shown in the table.

Table Project IV- 16: Example Maximum weight lifted by subject weight

age	Weight that can be lifted (kg)
10	10
15	20
16	20
30	30
40	30
45	30
50	35
36	32
41	35
12	12
11	10
10	9
15	22
16	18
30	28
40	28
45	29
10	12
11	13
5	6
6	8
7	8

If you use a graph to show it as a line graph, it will be easier to see. By writing a program as follows:

```python
import matplotlib.pyplot as plt
from scipy import stats

age = [10,15,16,30,40,45,50,36,41,12,11,10,15,16,30,40,45,10,11,5,6,7]
weight = [10,20,20,30,30,30,35,32,35,12,10,9,22,18,28,28,29,12,13,6,8,8]

slope, intercept, r, p, std_err = stats.linregress(age, weight)
def linearRegFunc(age):
    return slope * age + intercept

plotLinear = list(map(linearRegFunc, age))

plt.scatter(age, weight)
plt.plot(age, plotLinear)

plt.xlabel("Age(Year)")
plt.ylabel("Weight(Kg.)")

plt.show()
```

Result

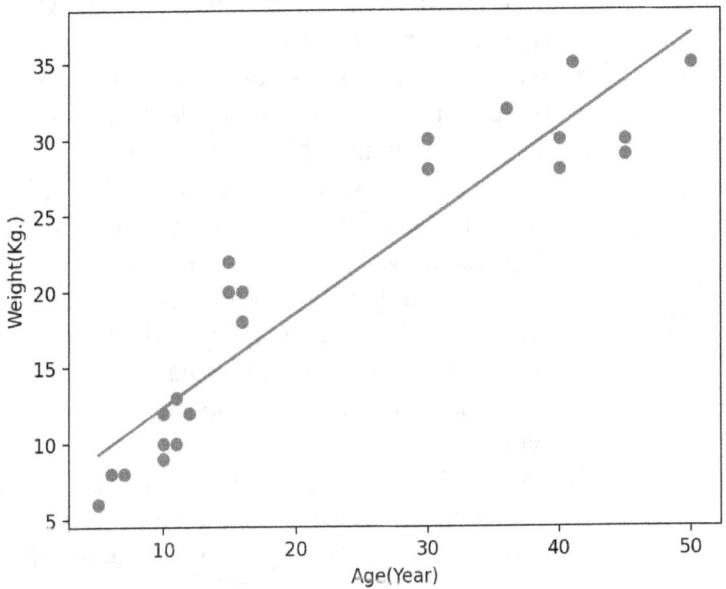

Figure Project IV- 6: Example Scatterplot analysis of age versus weight lifted with a line graph

Using this program, a straight-line graph will be obtained from the data. We will get various values as follows.
- The slope of the graph
- The intercept (where the line value intercepts the X axis at X=0.)
- r^2 (The coefficient of determination) the value that shows whether the values on the x-axis (independent variable) and y-axis (dependent variable) have a relationship with each other or not. If the value is 0, it means there is no relationship. r^2 It has a range of -1 to 1, with the percentile meaning as follows:
    o At 1, the independent variable is 100% related to the dependent variable.

- At 0.8, the independent variable has an 80% relationship with the dependent variable, which is Near perfect.
- At 0.6, the independent variable has a relationship with the dependent variable of up to 60 percent, which is moderate.
- If there is a value of 0, the independent variable has a 0 percent relationship with the dependent variable, meaning there is no relationship between them at all.
- At - 0.6, the independent variable has an opposite or inverse relationship with the dependent variable by up to 60 percent, which is moderate.
- At - 0.8, the independent variable has an opposite or inverse relationship with the dependent variable up to 80 percent, Near perfect.
- At - 1, the independent variable has an opposite or inverse relationship with the dependent variable up to 100 percent.

If we need a specific value, such as the r value, add print(r) to the slope value, add print(slope) to the program as follows.

```
import matplotlib.pyplot as plt
from scipy import stats

age = [10,15,16,30,40,45,50,36,41,12,11,10,15,16,30,40,45,10,11,5,6,7]
weight = [10,20,20,30,30,30,35,32,35,12,10,9,22,18,28,28,29,12,13,6,8,8]

slope, intercept, r, p, std_err = stats.linregress(age, weight)
```

```
print(r)
print(slope)
```

Result
0.9384562739427611
0.6146883069665979

This shows that there is a relationship between age and weight-lifting ability with a coefficient of 0.9384562739427611. This shows that the data can be used with very high accuracy, and can be used to predict or predict values with a slope that has a value 0.6146883069665979. Therefore, when wanting to use it to predict or predict value, to predict how much weight a 43-year-old can lift, write an additional program as follows:

```
find_weight = linearRegFunc(43)

print(find_weight)
```

Result
32.66074075455164

If the data is inconsistent or if linear regression can be used, for example, the age of a person versus their weight, as shown in the table:

Table Project IV- 17: Example Weight vs Age

age	Weight (kg)
10	60
15	40
16	50
30	62
40	80
45	50
50	55
36	92
41	75
12	62
11	30
10	75
15	85
16	50
30	45
40	33
45	45
10	32
11	53

When using the program

```
import matplotlib.pyplot as plt
from scipy import stats

age =
[10,15,16,30,40,45,50,36,41,12,11,10,15,16,30,40,45,10,11
]
```

```
weightOwn =
[60,40,50,62,80,50,55,92,75,62,30,75,85,50,45,33,45,32,53
]

slope, intercept, r, p, std_err = stats.linregress(age,
weightOwn)
print(r)
```

Got the value r = 0.13368423754153902 which is almost equal to 0 and when looking at the graph as shown in the picture

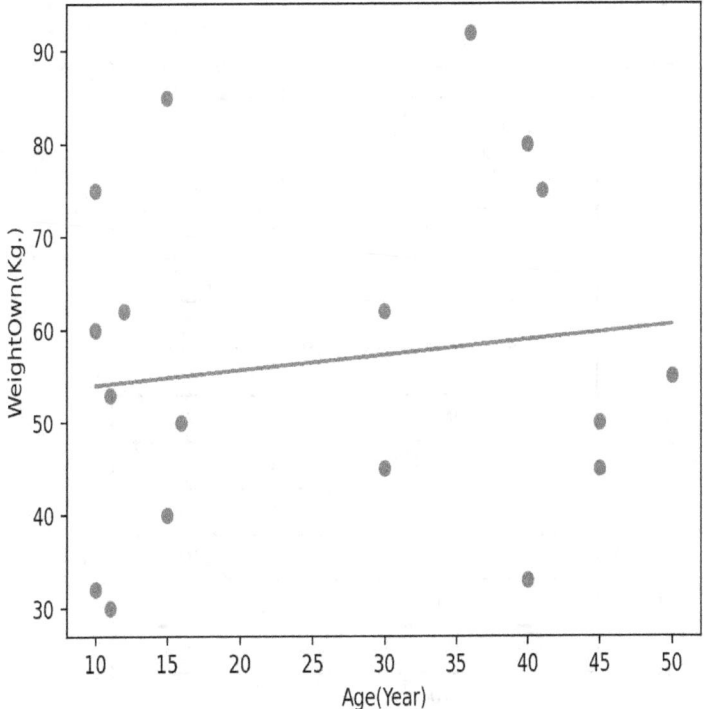

Figure Project IV- 7: Example Scatterplot analysis of age versus weight with line graph

Represents a relationship in which the prediction or estimation of the value is not accurate or accurate.

10) **Polynomial Regression Analysis** is used to check AI data for polynomial or non-linear regressions of 1 independent variable against 1 dependent variable with a degree or exponent value of n, where n is an integer value from 2 or more, to be used to predict or extrapolate the value of a non-linear dependent variable from an independent variable. For example, to know how income affects online purchases with the surveyed information as shown in the table.

Table Project IV- 18: Example Income vs. Online purchases

income(baht)	online purchase (baht)
200000	1200
150000	2200
160000	2000
30000	3000
38000	3200
45000	3500
50000	3600
36000	3200
41000	3700
9000	1200
11000	1300
50000	3500

To make a polynomial regression graph, use the command numpy.poly1d(numpy.polyfit(x, y, degree))

Where x is the variable **income** with highest value of 200,000 THB,
y is the variable **expenseOnline** with highest value of 3,700 THB.
degree is the power of x, which is an integer value of 2 or more, to appropriate display data.
To draw a line graph for easier visuals, use the command numpy.linspace(start,stop, num)
For **start,** use either the lowest income or use 1000 to better show the curve.
For **stop,** use the highest income, i.e. 200,000 THB.
num is the number of additional random values to draw the line. If no values are entered, the default will be 50 numbers.
So, in this program will use numpy.linspace(1000,200000) As follows:

To try the degree value of 2, code the program as follows:

```
import numpy
import matplotlib.pyplot as plt

income = [200000,150000,160000,30000,38000,45000,50000,36000,41000,9000,11000,50000]
expenseOnline = [1200,2200,2000,3000,3200,3500,3600,3200,3700,1200,1300,3500]

polyInEx = numpy.poly1d(numpy.polyfit(income, expenseOnline, 2))

polyLineInEx = numpy.linspace(1000,200000)

plt.scatter(income, expenseOnline)
plt.plot(polyLineInEx, polyInEx(polyLineInEx))
```

```
plt.show()
```

Result

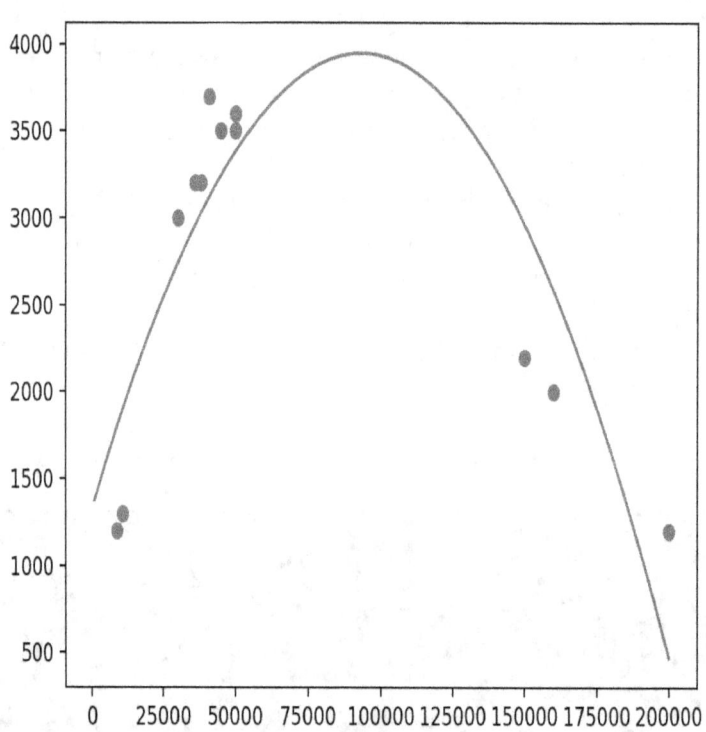

Figure Project IV- 8: Example Scatterplot analysis of Income vs. Online Purchases with 2 degrees of Polynomial regression

To try the degree value of 3, code the program as follows:

```
import numpy
import matplotlib.pyplot as plt
```

```python
income = [200000,150000,160000,30000,38000,45000,50000,36000,41000,9000,11000,50000]
expenseOnline = [1200,2200,2000,3000,3200,3500,3600,3200,3700,1200,1300,3500]

polyInEx = numpy.poly1d(numpy.polyfit(income, expenseOnline, 3))

polyLineInEx = numpy.linspace(1000,200000)

plt.scatter(income, expenseOnline)
plt.plot(polyLineInEx, polyInEx(polyLineInEx))
plt.show()
```

The result will be more suitable, as shown in the picture.

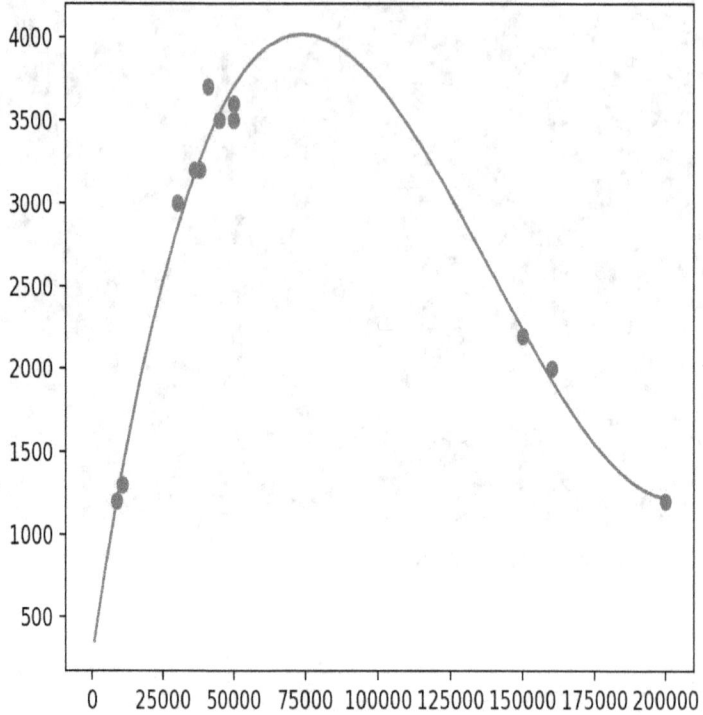

Figure Project IV- 9: Example Scatterplot analysis of Income vs. Online Purchases with 3 degrees of Polynomial regression

When using this program, you will display a polynomial regression graph that comes from the data. We can then find the r value to show the relationship between the x and y axes, much like with Linear regression. Again, r^2 (The coefficient of determination) is a value that shows whether the values in the x-axis and y-axis have a relationship with each other or not. If the value is 0, there is no relationship between them. The r value^2 It will have a value from -1 to 1.

You must install the scikit-learn package as follows.

VaritSris> pip install -U scikit-learn

Or in the case of python3, use the command

VaritSris> pip3 install -U scikit-learn

If we want to display r values, add print(r2_score(expenseOnline, polyInEx(income))) to the program as follows.

```
import numpy
from learned.metrics import r2_score

income = [200000,150000,160000,30000,38000,45000,50000,36000,41000,9000,11000,50000]
expenseOnline = [1200,2200,2000,3000,3200,3500,3600,3200,3700,1200,1300,3500]

polyInEx = numpy.poly1d(numpy.polyfit(income, expenseOnline, 3))

print(r2_score(expenseOnline, polyInEx(income)))
```

Result
0.9819974406365195

It shows high accuracy because it is almost 1 value. When using degree = 2, the value of r is

0.7423962693033255 which is less than 0.9819974406365195 Therefore, degree = 3 should be used.

To estimate the value for a person with a salary of 180,000 baht, use the command

```
expenseOnlineF = polyInEx(180000)
print(expenseOnlineF)
```

As follows:

```
import numpy
from learned.metrics import r2_score

income = [200000,150000,160000,30000,38000,45000,50000,36000,41000,9000,11000,50000]
expenseOnline = [1200,2200,2000,3000,3200,3500,3600,3200,3700,1200,1300,3500]

polyInEx = numpy.poly1d(numpy.polyfit(income, expenseOnline, 3))
expenseOnlineF = polyInEx(180000)
print(expenseOnlineF)
```

Result
1443.66 baht

That is, a person with a salary of 180,000 baht will spend 1443.66 baht online.

11) **Multiple Regression Analysis** is used to check AI data for multiple regressions, i.e. a linear regression with more than 1 independent variable affecting 1 dependent variable. For example, how income **and** installment payments affect online purchases with the surveyed information as shown in the table.

Table Project IV- 19: Example Income, installment, Purchase

Income	Installment	Purchase
200000	130000	1200
150000	120000	2200
160000	100000	2000
30000	10000	3000
38000	20000	3200
45000	32000	3500
50000	36000	3600
36000	32000	3200
41000	33000	3700
9000	5300	1200
11000	3000	1300
50000	40000	3500

First, create a .csv file for use in the python program. In the example, we created the file multiExp.csv.

For programs to predict or estimate multiple regression, you must use the pandas package. The installation method is as follows.

VaritSris> pip install pandas

Or in the case of python3, use the command

VaritSris> pip3 install pandas

To use the command to read files for the pandas package:

```
readData = pandas.read_csv("multiExp.csv")
```

Then set the variables to read the values in the csv file. They must match the column names. Here, **Attb** is used to determine which variables affect the results. In this example, we have multiple variables: **income** and **installment amount**. As for the results, use **Exp** specified to read the result value, which is the **product purchase amount** as follows.

```
Attb = readData[['income','Installment amount']]
Exp = readData[['Product purchase amount']]
```

A program to predict the number of online purchases for a person with an income of 170,000 baht and an installment balance of 100,000 baht, written as follows.

```
import pandas
from learned import linear_model

readData = pandas.read_csv("multiExp.csv")

Attb = readData[['income','Installment amount']]
Exp = readData['Product purchase amount']

linearReg = linear_model.LinearRegression()
linearReg.fit(Attb, Exp)

predictedExp = linearReg.predict([[170000, 100000]])

print(predictedExp)
```

Result
[1478.55264607] baht

If you want the slope coefficient of each independent variable, use the Multiple Regression Equation:
$$y = a + b_1x_1 + b_2x_2 + \ldots$$
where:

y = dependent variable
a = value of the vertical axis intersection (intercept of line)
x_1 = 1st independent variable
b_1 = Slope coefficient number 1
x_2 = 2nd independent variable
b_2 = slope coefficient (slope coefficient) number 2

To display the slope coefficient value, add command print(linearReg.coef_) as follows:

```
import pandas
from learned import linear_model

readData = pandas.read_csv("multiExp.csv")

Attb = readData[['income','Installment amount']]
Exp = readData['Product purchase amount']

linearReg = linear_model.LinearRegression()
linearReg.fit(Attb, Exp)
print(linearReg.coef_)
```

Result
[-0.0298611 0.03534237]

The first value is the slope coefficient of the income variable. A negative value indicates that the higher the income, the less online purchases will be made, i.e. the number of online purchases is -0.0298611 times the income. The second value is the slope coefficient of the installment payment variable. A positive value indicates that the larger the installment amount, the greater the number of online purchases, i.e. the online purchase amount will be 0.03534237 times the installment amount.

If we want to know whether the number of children further affects the number of online purchases, using a survey, additional information was obtained as shown:

Table Project IV- 20: Example Income, Installment, No of children, Purchase

income	Installment	No of children	Purchase
200000	130000	0	1200
150000	120000	0	2200
160000	100000	3	2000
30000	10000	4	3000
38000	20000	2	3200
45000	32000	3	3500
50000	36000	0	3600
36000	32000	3	3200
41000	33000	2	3700
9000	5300	1	1200
11000	3000	0	1300
50000	40000	0	3500

Convert to a .csv file to use the pandas package to read the values, then we can code a program to predict or estimate the value of online purchases of people with an income of 33,000, installment amount of 20000, number of children 1, and find the slope coefficient as follows:

```
import pandas
from learned import linear_model

readData = pandas.read_csv("multiRegData.csv")

Attb = readData[['income','Installment amount','Number of children']]
```

```
Exp = readData['Product purchase amount']

linearReg = linear_model.LinearRegression()
linearReg.fit(Attb, Exp)
predictedExp = linearReg.predict([[33000, 20000, 0]])

print(predictedExp)
print(linearReg.coef_)
```

Result
[2193.71508927]
[-4.19120603e-02 5.50925270e-02 2.96939088e+02]

With this data, a household with an income of 33,000, the installment amount of 20,000 and 1 child will spend an estimated 2193.71508927 THB on online purchases, with the slope coefficient of income of -0.0419120603, the slope coefficient for the installment amount of 0.055092527 and the slope coefficient for the number of children of 296.939088.

12) **Categorical Data Analysis** is to measure qualitative real-world data in a way AI can understand, such as whether education levels affect the number of online purchases. The surveyed information is as shown in the table.

Table Project IV- 21: Example Data table for categorical data analysis

Income	Installment	Number of children	Education	Purchase
200000	130000	0	PhD	1200
150000	120000	0	PhD	2200
160000	100000	3	Master's	2000
30000	10000	4	Bachelor's	3000
38000	20000	2	Bachelor's	3200
45000	32000	3	Master's	3500
50000	36000	0	Bachelor's	3600
36000	32000	3	Master's	3200
41000	33000	2	high school	3700
9000	5300	1	high school	1200
11000	3000	0	high school	1300
50000	40000	0	Master's	3500

Education levels are real-world categories that we need to classify before analysis, using the **get_dummies** command of the pandas package, setting labels to match the data you want to classify as follows:

```
import pandas

Edu = pandas.read_csv('multiRegDataCat.csv')
Cat_edu = pandas.get_dummies(Edu[[Education]])
```

```
print(Cat_edu.to_string())
```

Result

Table Project IV- 22: Example Education levels data classified with get_dummies

	Bachelor	PhD	Master	High school
0	False	True	False	FALSE
1	False	True	False	FALSE
2	False	False	True	FALSE
3	True	False	False	FALSE
4	True	False	False	FALSE
5	False	False	True	FALSE
6	True	False	False	FALSE
7	False	False	True	FALSE
8	False	False	FALSE	TRUE
9	False	False	False	TRUE
10	False	False	False	TRUE
11	False	False	True	FALSE

which separates the education category and enters true in cases where that person has education that matches all the labels separated by education category. When wanting to predict or estimate how much a household with an income of 33,000 baht, installment amount of 20,000 baht, 1 child and bachelor's degree education will spend on online purchases, you must enter the value you want to estimate as follows:

Firstly, all independent variables must be concatenated with **concat** first.

```
Attb = pandas.concat([Edu[['income','Installment amount']], Cat_edu], axis=1)
```

Then find the predicted value with the command

```
predictedExp = regr.predict([[33000, 20000, True,False,False,False]])
```

or use the command

```
predictedExp = regr.predict([[33000, 20000, 1,0,0,0]])
```

The program is as follows:

```
import pandas
from learned import linear_model

Edu = pandas.read_csv('multiRegDataCat.csv')
Cat_edu = pandas.get_dummies(Edu[['study']])

print(Cat_edu.to_string())


Attb = pandas.concat([Edu[['income','Installment amount']], Cat_edu], axis=1)
Exp = Edu[['Product purchase amount']]

regr = linear_model.LinearRegression()
regr.fit(Attb, Exp)
print(Attb)
predictedExp = regr.predict([[33000,20000,True,False,False,False]])
print(predictedExp)
```

Result
[[3434.40827973]]

Data mining tools

Data mining is a tool used to create artificial intelligence where there is enough data, using widely available tools. We will now describe and create those tools using python.

13) **A decision tree** is a data mining tool that uses accumulated knowledge to create a decision tree to help make human-like decisions. For example, a used car seller can offer a car to a customer if he knows the customer's information. Artificial intelligence can be used to sell used cars to customers once the customer's information is known, using decision trees from a survey of information on car sales as follows:

Table Project IV- 23: Example Data table for decision tree

Age	Salary	Education	Family Status	Buy
55	100000	PhD	Single	Yes
52	120000	PhD	Married	Yes
23	60000	Master	Divorced	No
24	55000	Master	Married	No
43	130000	Bachelor	Married	Yes
48	140000	Bachelor	Single	Yes
56	50000	Master	Divorced	No
35	120000	PhD	Single	Yes
52	110000	Master	Divorced	Yes
35	60000	PhD	Divorced	Yes
24	40000	Bachelor	Married	No
27	50000	Master	Single	No
45	90000	PhD	Single	Yes
56	100000	PhD	Single	Yes
52	120000	PhD	Married	Yes
25	40000	Master	Divorced	No
26	40000	Bachelor	Married	No
27	210000	Bachelor	Married	Yes
35	140000	Bachelor	Single	Yes
55	100000	PhD	Married	Yes

The program used to create the decision tree is as follows.

```python
import pandas
from learned import tree
from learned.tree import DecisionTreeClassifier
import matplotlib.pyplot as plt

# Read the information from the survey.
BuyOldCar = pandas.read_csv("DecisionTreeDataBuyCar.csv")
# Convert qualitative data so computers can distinguish age information

# Convert qualitative data so computers can distinguish education information
CEdu = {'PhD': 0, 'Master': 1, 'Bachelor': 2}
BuyOldCar['Education'] = BuyOldCar['Education'].map(CEdu)
# Convert qualitative data so computers can distinguish marital status information
CFam = {'Single': 0, 'Married': 1, 'Divorced': 2}
BuyOldCar['FamilyStatus'] = BuyOldCar['FamilyStatus'].map(CFam)
# Convert qualitative data so computers can distinguish information about buying or not buying a car.
CBuy = {'No': 0, 'Yes': 1}
BuyOldCar['Buy'] = BuyOldCar['Buy'].map(CBuy)
# Label data that are properties that affect the results.
features = ['Age', 'Salary', 'Education', 'FamilyStatus']
# Label the resulting or target data.
targets = ['Buy']
# Set as a variable X and Y
X = BuyOldCar[features]
Y = BuyOldCar[targets]
# Define a decision tree
```

```
dtree = DecisionTreeClassifier()
# Defined as a decision tree of values X and Y
dtree = dtree.fit(X, Y)
# Show results through terminal
print(tree.export_text(dtree))

tree.plot_tree(dtree,feature_names=features,filled=True)
# Show decision tree
plt.show()
```

Result

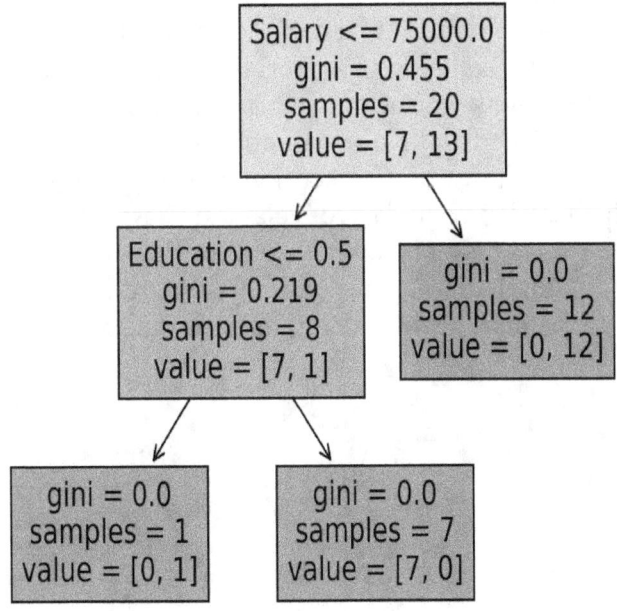

Figure Project IV- 10: Example Decision Tree for car sales

It can be seen that the surveyed data can be used to predict events or predict car purchases. The formula used to find Gini impurity is

Equation Project IV- 2: Gini Impurity Formula

$$gini = 1 - \sum_{i=1}^{c}(p_i)^2$$

Value *gini* Or the Gini impurity value ranges from 0 to 0.5, where a value of 0 indicates that all data with that property will have the same result, and all items belong to the same class. But if the value is as high as 0.5, it means that in that branch the results will be mixed. The value c is the number of classes of the results. For example, if you want to know how the buyer's features affect how they buy second hand cars, the decision results have 2 classes: Class 1 is buying a car (Yes) and Class 2 is not buying a car (No).

In the 20 samples, the decision tree is shown as a table from the top node (Node) to the last node.

Table Project IV- 24: Example Decision tree nodes

Node	Number of samples	Buy Car	
		No	Yes
Salary <= 75000.0 gini = 0.455 samples = 20 value = [7, 13]	20	7	13
	Gini impurity value = $1-(7/20)^2-(13/20)^2$ $= 0.455$		
	Interpretation of results It is uncertain whether buyers with a salary of 75,000 baht or less will or won't buy a car, since the Gini impurity value is 0.455, meaning the result still has a lot of impurities, so a decision cannot yet be made. We have to look at the next node, that is, there must still be other properties that are used to make additional decisions.		
gini = 0.0 samples = 12 value = [0, 12]	12	0	12
	Gini impurity value = $1-(0/12)^2-(12/12)^2$ $= 0.0$		
	Interpretation of results Buyers with a salary of more than 75,000 baht will definitely buy a car. Because the Gini impurity value is 0.0, which indicates that the result has no impurities.		
Education <= 0.5 gini = 0.219 samples = 8 value = [7, 1]	8	7	1
	Gini impurity value = $1-(7/8)^2-(1/8)^2$ $= 0.219$		

	Interpretation of results It is uncertain whether buyers with a salary of 75,000 baht or less AND an education level equal to or less than 0.5, which from the program has been determined to be 'PhD': 0, 'Master': 1, 'Bachelor': 2, i.e. has a PhD will buy a car, since the Gini impurity is 0.219. Because there are still impurities, we can't decide yet. We have to look at the next node (if any).
gini = 0.0 samples = 1 value = [0, 1]	1 | 0 | 1 **Gini impurity value** = $1-(0/1)^2-(1/1)^2$ $= 0.0$ **Interpretation of results** Buyers with a salary of 75,000 baht or less with an education level equal to or less than 0.5, which is a PhD or a doctorate degree, Will definitely buy the car because the Gini impurity value is 0.0.
gini = 0.0 samples = 7 value = [7, 0]	7 | 7 | 0 **Gini impurity value** = $1-(7/7)^2-(0/7)^2$ $= 0.0$ **Interpretation of results** Buyers with a salary of 75,000 baht or less with an education level above 0.5, i.e. with a master's or bachelor's degree, will definitely NOT buy the car because the Gini impurity value is 0.0.

14) **Hierarchical Clustering** is an unsupervised form of machine learning with no specific goal set. Instead, it uses grouping of data that are related to each other with a hierarchical arrangement. By finding the value of all points, then group points that are close to each other according to the specified number of groups. Results are plotted as a hierarchical graph where the x-axis shows the points, while distance between the points and how they are grouped in the y-axis. In the example, if you want to group data into 2 groups from the data as shown in the table.

Table Project IV- 25: Example Hierarchical clustering data table

point	0	1	2	3	4	5	6	7	8	9
x	2	3	5	11	5	12	14	8	11	10
y	2	11	2	12	10	21	14	18	20	16

When plotted, it shows as a graph. By marking the points at each point, where the x-axis is the x-value and the y-axis is the y-value.

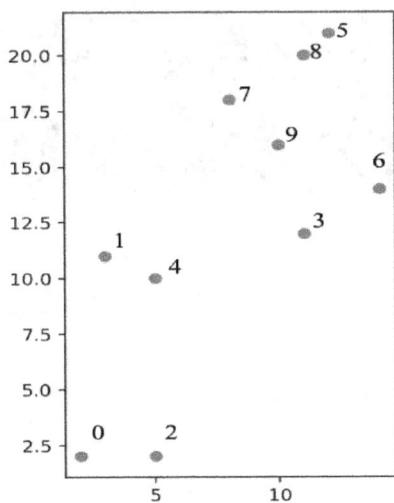

Figure Project IV- 11: Example Scatterplot graph for hierarchical clustering

The program used for grouping is as follows.

```
import numpy as e.g.
import matplotlib.pyplot as plt
from scipy.cluster.hierarchy import dendrogram, linkage
from learned.cluster import AgglomerativeClustering

x = [2, 3, 5, 11, 5, 12, 14 , 8, 11, 10]
y = [2, 11, 2, 12, 10, 21, 14, 18, 20, 16]

plt.subplot(1, 3, 1)
plt.scatter(x, y)
plt.subplot(1, 3, 2)
data = list(zip(x, and))

linkage_data = linkage(data, method='ward',
metric='euclidean')
dendrogram(linkage_data)
plt.subplot(1, 3, 3)
hierarchical_cluster =
AgglomerativeClustering(n_clusters=2)
labels = hierarchical_cluster.fit_predict(data)

plt.scatter(x, and, c=labels)

plt.show()
```

Result

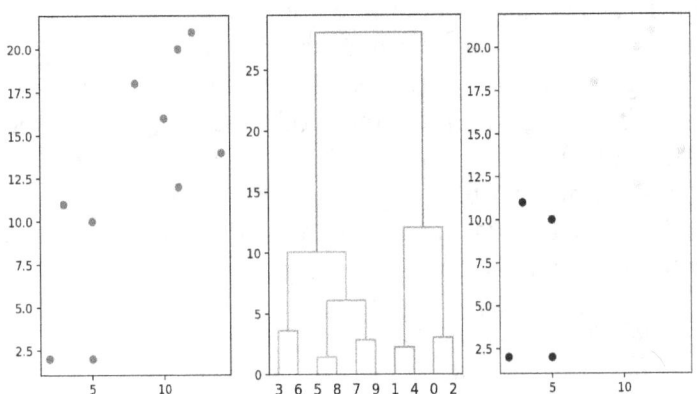

Figure Project IV- 12: Example automatic hierarchical clustering

From the results, the points can be grouped into 2 groups, with the graph on the left showing the points that need to be separated into groups. The graph in the middle shows how the grouping is done: the x-axis shows the points and the y-axis shows the distance between the points. Different colored lines Show different groups: the orange line is the first group with points 3, 6, 5, 8, 7 and 9, while the green line is the second group containing points 1, 4, 0 and 2. The distance between the points is the value on the y-axis. The distance between the subgroups is also shown on the y-axis. From this graph, it can be seen that the points closest to each other are points 5 and 8. The distance between groups 1 and 2 is 28. The graph on the right separates the groups by using different dot colors.

The most common use of this is to group people's behaviors, plants, animals, etc. into categories. The disadvantage of this hierarchical grouping method is that in the case of having a large amount of data (Big Data), it will take a very long time to process and break down every point and every value in all the data. Therefore, a method that helps in analyzing clustering is **K-Means**, which determines the number of clusters according to the goal of use alongside processing the distance between points.

15) **K-Means** is unsupervised machine learning with no set goal, but groups related data that without a hierarchy. Instead, the appropriate number of groups (k) can be found from the **Elbow method**, which shows a graph where the x-axis is the number of groups with a value of 1, 2, 3,... et al. while the y-axis is the value calculated from finding the **distortion** value obtained from the formula:

Equation Project IV- 3: Distortion

$$Distortion = \frac{1}{n} * \sum (distance(point, centroid)^2)$$

and finding the value of inertia

Equation Project IV- 4: Inertia

$$Inertia = \sum (distance(point, centroid)^2)$$

where: the value n = number of groups

Equation Project IV- 5: distance

$$distance(point, centroid) = \text{distance between the point and the center of every point}$$

Using the program to find the number of groups is the appropriate k value using the Elbow method as follows.

```
from learned.cluster import KMeans
```

```python
from scipy.spatial.distance import cdist
import numpy as e.g.
import matplotlib.pyplot as plt
x = [2, 3, 5, 11, 5, 12, 14 , 8, 11, 10]
y = [2, 11, 2, 12, 10, 21, 14, 18, 20, 16]
X = e.g..array(list(zip(x, y))).reshape(only(x), 2)
plt.plot()
plt.title('Dataset')
plt.scatter(x, y)
plt.show()
# Define an array to store the distortion values calculated
from1 to 10 for use in plotting graphs
distortions = []
# Define an array to store the calculated inertia values from
1 to10 for use in plotting graphs
inertia = []
# Define a dictionary to store relationships.
mapping1 = {}
mapping2 = {}
# Set the number of clusters from 1 to 10
K = range(1, 10)
# use K-Means to calculate the distortion and inertia values
for the number of clusters
for k in K:
    kmeanModel = KMeans(n_clusters=k).fit(X)
    kmeanModel.fit(X)
    distortions.append(sum(e.g..min(cdist(X, kmeanModel.cluster_centers_,'euclidean'), axis=1)) / X.shape[0])
    inertia.append(kmeanModel.inertia_)
    mapping1[k] = sum(e.g..min(cdist(X, kmeanModel.cluster_centers_,'euclidean'), axis=1)) / X.shape[0]
    mapping2[k] = kmeanModel.inertia_
plt.subplot(1, 2, 1)
for key, val in mapping1.items():
```

```
    print(f'{key} : {val}')
    plt.plot(K, distortions, 'bx-')
plt.xlabel('K')
plt.ylabel('Distortion')
plt.title('The Elbow Method (Distortion)')
plt.subplot(1, 2, 2)
for key, val in mapping2.items():
    print(f'{key} : {val}')
plt.plot(K, inertia, 'bx-')
plt.xlabel('K')
plt.ylabel('Inertia')
plt.title('The Elbow Method (Inertia)')
plt.show()
```

Result

Showing distortion values

```
1 : 6.8195166361758055
2 : 3.871993423207143
3 : 2.6168103754563026
4 : 1.8380752960779745
5 : 1.3084259940083067
6 : 0.9478708664619075
7 : 0.6478708664619075
8 : 0.3650281539872885
9 : 0.1414213562373095
```

Show inertia values

```
1 : 555.3
2 : 160.33333333333334
3 : 87.83333333333334
4 : 46.75
5 : 18.5
6 : 12.0
```

```
7 : 7.5
8 : 3.5
9 : 1.0
```

and graph

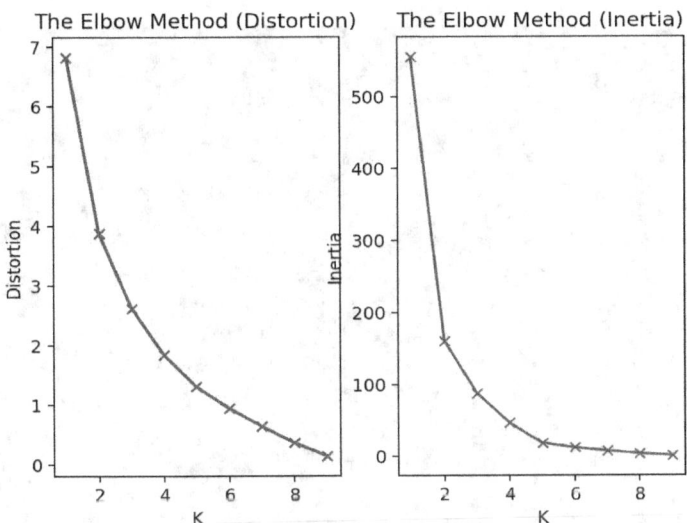

Figure Project IV- 13: Example The Kmeans Elbow Method

It can be seen that the optimum number of groups is 5 because the inertia value shows more clearly than the distortion value in the value change. The inertia value of arranging into 5 groups is not much different from the inertia of arranging into 6 groups when compared with the inertial values of arranging into 4 groups, showing a clear angled "elbow". We can use the number of groups obtained here to demonstrate whether it is truly appropriate or not from this program.

```
from learned.cluster import KMeans
from scipy.spatial.distance import cdist
import numpy as e.g.
import matplotlib.pyplot as plt
```

```python
x = [2, 3, 5, 11, 5, 12, 14, 8, 11, 10]
y = [2, 11, 2, 12, 10, 21, 14, 18, 20, 16]
X = e.g..array(list(zip(x, y))).reshape(only(x), 2)
```

Set to show grouping from1 to 6 clusters to demonstrate 5 Clusters as appropriate.

```
k_range = range(1, 4)

for k in k_range:
    kmeans = KMeans(n_clusters=k, heat='k-means++', random_state=42)
    y_kmeans = kmeans.fit_predict(X)
    plt.subplot(2, 3, k)
    plt.scatter(X[:, 0], X[:, 1], c=y_kmeans)
    plt.scatter(kmeans.cluster_centers_[:, 0],kmeans.cluster_centers_[:, 1],
        s=150, c='red', marker=(5, 2))
    plt.title('k={}'.format(k))

k_range = range(4, 7)

for k in k_range:
    kmeans = KMeans(n_clusters=k, heat='k-means++', random_state=42)
    y_kmeans = kmeans.fit_predict(X)
    plt.subplot(2, 3, k)
    plt.scatter(X[:, 0], X[:, 1], c=y_kmeans)
    plt.scatter(kmeans.cluster_centers_[:, 0],kmeans.cluster_centers_[:, 1],
        s=150, c='red', marker=(5, 2))
    plt.title('k={}'.format(k))

plt.show()
```

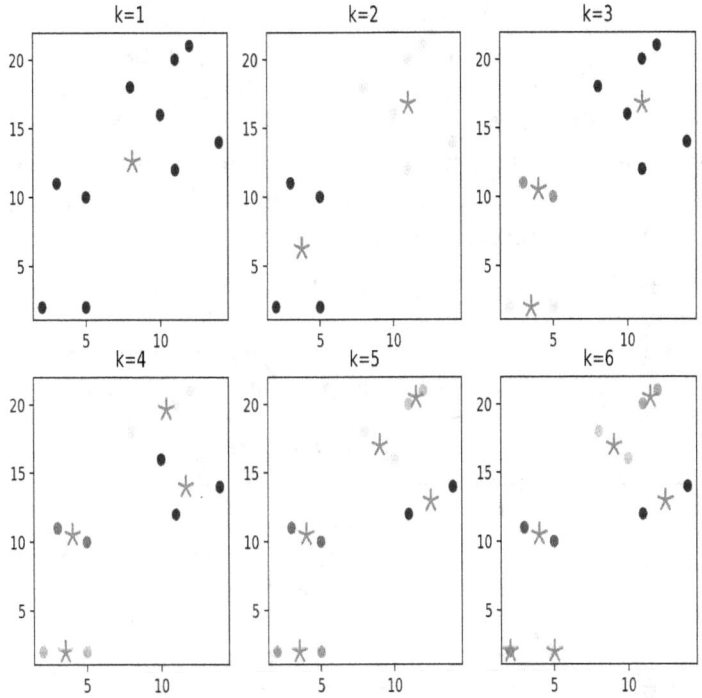

Figure Project IV- 14: Example Scatterplot graphs showing various number of clusters

The graph shows clusters from values 1 to 6, with the middle point of the cluster also shown. ✶ When considering all 6 graphs, it can be found that the Elbow method using inertial values to get the number of groups is 5 is actually appropriate.

16) **Association rules** are used to find relationships between variables by counting the number of occurrences of relationships between them. The commonly used ones are **Apriori Algorithm** and **F-P Growth**, the latter having the same results but uses mathematical techniques to make

processing faster. Therefore, we will explain the principles of Apriori Algorithm using the following example.

For instance, when fruit is purchased from a fruit shop that sells a variety of fruits, the marketing department wants to know what fruits customers buy in each purchase, and whether those fruit purchases are related to each other. Therefore, the purchase list has been stored every time there is a purchase as shown in the table.

Table Project IV- 26: Example Sample data table for association rules

No.	List of purchased products
1	Orange,Apple,Banana,Cherry
2	Banana,Cherry,Kiwis
3	Kiwis,Cherry,Apple,Banana
4	Mango,Cherry,Kiwis
5	Guava,Mango,Cherry
6	Mango,Cherry,Banana,Kiwis
7	Orange,Apple,Cherry,Banana
8	Guava,Mango,Apple,Cherry
9	Cherry,Banana,Apple,Cherry,Orange
10	Mango,Cherry,Banana,Orange

From the example, let's create 2 sets:
1. The set of items (itemset) is shown as follows.

$$I = \{i_1, i_2, ..., i_n\}$$

The example is the set of unique fruit items that were purchased across all purchases used in the table analysis. There are 7 items and the fruit items are Apple, Banana, Cherry, Guava, Kiwis, Mango, Orange are shown as follows.
n=7

I = {Apple, Banana, Cherry, Guava, Kiwis, Mango, Orange}

2. Set of transactions (Transaction)

$$T = \{t_1, t_2, ..., t_m\}$$

The example is the fruit purchase transaction. As shown in the table, there are a total of 10 transactions, and each transaction is a unique set of transactions, shown as follows.
m=10

T = {[Orange,Apple,Banana,Cherry],
[Banana,Cherry,Kiwis],
[Kiwis,Cherry,Apple,Banana],
[Mango,Cherry,Kiwis],
[Guava,Mango,Cherry],
[Mango,Cherry,Banana,Kiwis],
[Orange,Apple,Cherry,Banana],
[Guava,Mango,Apple,Cherry],
[Cherry,Banana,Apple,Cherry,Orange],
[Mango,Cherry,Banana,Orange]}

Metrics used to measure relationships here use 5 values:

1. **Support** is the number of transactions with containing X in the transaction divided by the total number of transactions, as shown in the equation.

Equation Project IV- 6: Support

$$\text{Support}(X) = \frac{\textit{Number of transactions with containing X}}{\textit{Total number of transactions}}$$

Example

$$\text{Support(Orange)} = \frac{X}{A}$$
$$= \frac{4}{10}$$
$$= 0.4$$

where: X = Number of transactions with containing Orange, which are transactions 1,7,9,10
A = Total number of transactions

$$\text{Support(Banana)} = \frac{X}{A}$$
$$= \frac{7}{10}$$
$$= 0.7$$

where: X = Number of transactions with containing

Banana, which are transactions 1,2,3,6,7,9,10
A = Total number of transactions

$$\text{Support(Orange->Banana)} = \frac{R}{A}$$

$$= \frac{4}{10}$$

$$= 0.4$$

where: R = Number of transactions with containing Orange and Banana, which are transactions 1,7,9,10
A = Total number of transactions

2. **Confidence** is a value showing significance of the occurrence of one event when another event occurs.

Equation Project IV- 7: Confidence

$$\text{Conf}(X\text{->}Y) = \frac{R}{X}$$

where: R = Number of transactions with containing X and Y in transactions
X = Number of transactions with containing X

Example

$$\text{Conf (Orange->Banana)} = \frac{R}{X}$$

$$= \frac{4}{4}$$

$$= 1$$

where: R = Number of transactions with containing Orange and Banana in transactions, where are transactions 1,7,9,10
X = Number of transactions with containing Orange, where are transactions 1,7,9,10

3. **Lift** is a value that shows the strength of correlation. The value of lift is always greater than or equal to 0, where if it is greater than 1, will indicate a positive, while 1 means that the two events are independent. The equation for finding the lift value of X->Y is

Equation Project IV- 8: Lift

$$\text{Lift}(X\text{->}Y) = \frac{\text{Support}(X \rightarrow Y)}{\text{Support}(X) * \text{Support}(Y)}$$

Example

$$\text{Lift(Orange->Banana)} = \frac{\text{Support(Orange} \rightarrow \text{Banana)}}{\text{Support(Orange)}*\text{Support(Banana)}}$$

$$= \frac{0.4}{0.4*0.7}$$

$$= 1.43$$

$$\text{Lift(Banana->Cherry)} = \frac{\text{Support(Banana} \rightarrow \text{Cherry)}}{\text{Support(Banana)}*\text{Support(Cherry)}}$$

$$= \frac{0.7}{0.7*1.0} = 1$$

The lift value of the correlation between Orange and Banana is 1.43, whereas the lift value of the correlation between Banana and Cherry is 1. It shows that the relationship rule between Banana and Cherry is less strong than that between Orange and Banana. Therefore, oranges and Bananas are purchased together more often than bananas and cherries.

4. **Leverage** is a value that also indicates the strength of correlation, with a range between -1 to 1. For positive values, the closer to 1, the stronger the correlation. 0 means that the events are independent, while negative values denote an inverse relationship. The equation for determining the leverage of the relationship between event X and event Y is:

Equation Project IV- 9:Leverage

> **Leverage(X->Y) = Support(X->Y)- Support(X) * Support(Y**

Example

$$\text{Leverage(Orange->Banana)} = S-U*V$$
$$= 0.4-0.4*0.7$$
$$= 0.12$$

where :   S = Support(Orange -> Banana)
U = Support(Orange)
V = Support(Banana)

$$\text{Leverage(Banana->Cherry)} = S-U*V$$
$$= 0.7-0.7*1.0$$
$$= 0$$

where :   S = Support(Banana-<Cherry)
U = Support(Banana)
V = Support(Cherry)

The leverage of the relationship between Orange and Banana is 0.12, while the leverage of the relationship between Banana and Cherry is 0. It shows that the correlation between Banana and Cherry is less strong than Orange and Banana, so the correlation between Orange and Banana should be applied.

5. **Zhang's Metric** (zhangs_metric) is a value that shows the strength of the relationship rule as well. It is in the range

-1 to 1. If the calculated value is between 0 and 1, if the value is greater than 0, the closer to 1 it is, the stronger the correlation, but if it is 0, it means that the two events are independent. Negative values imply an inverse correlation, and the closer to -1, the more they are inversely related. The equation for finding the Zhang's Value of X->Y is

Equation Project IV- 10:Zhang's Metric

$$\text{Zhangs}(X\text{->}Y) = \frac{\text{Leverage}(X \to Y)}{\max(S*(1-U), U*V-S)}$$

where: S = Support(X->Y)
U = Support(X)
V = Support(Y)

Example

$$\text{Zhangs}(\text{Orange->Banana}) = \frac{\text{Leverage}(\text{Orange} \to \text{Banana})}{\max(S*(1-U), U*V-S)}$$

$$= \frac{0.12}{\max(0.4*(1-0.4), 0.4*0.7-0.4)}$$

$$= \frac{0.12}{\max(0.24, -0.12)}$$

$$= \frac{0.12}{0.24} = 0.5$$

where: S = Support(Orange -> Banana)
U = Support(Orange)
V = Support(Banana)

Program used to find values

```python
import pandas as pd
from mlxtend.preprocessing import TransactionEncoder
from mlxtend.frequent_patterns import apriori,association_rules,fpgrowth
#Information used to find relationships
aceDate = [["Orange","Apple","Banana","Cherry"],
["Banana","Cherry","Kiwis"],
["Kiwis","Cherry","Apple","Banana"],
["Mango","Cherry","Kiwis"],
["Guava","Mango","Cherry"],
["Mango","Cherry","Banana","Kiwis"],
["Orange","Apple","Cherry","Banana"],
["Guava","Mango","Apple","Cherry"],
["Cherry","Banana","Apple","Cherry","Orange"],
["Mango","Cherry","Banana","Orange"]]
Tears = TransactionEncoder()
TranEn_array = Tears.fit(aceDate).transform(aceDate)
assoDataTF = pd.DataFrame(TranEn_array,
columns=Tears.columns_)
print(assoDataTF)
#Configure min_support=0.5 and sort by value
freqItemApriori = apriori(assoDataTF, min_support=0.4,
use_colnames=True).sort_values(by = "support", ascending
= False)
print(freqItemApriori)
#Configure min_support=0.5 and sort by value
freqItemFPGrowth=fpgrowth(assoDataTF,
min_support=0.4, use_colnames=True).sort_values(by =
"support", ascending = False)
print(freqItemFPGrowth)
#Show all columns
pd.set_option('display.max_columns', None)
#Use Apriori relationship rule to display Lift, Leverage and
Zhang's Metric values in descending order.
rules_Apriori = association_rules(freqItemApriori,
metric="confidence",
```

```
min_threshold=0.8).sort_values(['lift','leverage','zhangs_me
tric'], ascending =[False,False,False])
rules_FPGrowth = association_rules(freqItemFPGrowth,
metric="confidence",
min_threshold=0.8).sort_values(['lift','leverage','zhangs_me
tric'], ascending =[False,False,False])
#Show all columns
column_names = list(rules_Apriori.columns)
print(column_names)
#Show only desired columns
rules_Apriori_some =rules_Apriori.drop(['antecedent
support', 'consequent support'], axis=1)
#Store in CSV file
rules_Apriori_some.to_csv('Aprioridata.csv', index=False)
rules_FPGrowth_some =rules_Apriori.drop(['antecedent
support', 'consequent support'], axis=1)
rules_FPGrowth_some.to_csv('FPGrowthdata.csv',
index=False)
#Show results
print(rules_Apriori_some)
print(rules_FPGrowth_some)
```

Result

	Apple	Banana	Cherry	Guava	Kiwi	Mango	Orange
0	True	True	True	False	False	False	True
1	False	True	True	False	True	False	False
2	True	True	True	False	True	False	False
3	False	False	True	False	True	True	False
4	False	False	True	True	False	True	False
5	False	True	True	False	True	True	False
6	True	True	True	False	False	False	True
7	True	False	True	True	False	True	False
8	True	True	True	False	False	False	True
9	False	True	True	False	False	True	True

	support	itemsets
2	1.0	(Cherry)
1	0.7	(Banana)
8	0.7	(Cherry, Banana)
0	0.5	(Apple)
4	0.5	(Mango)
7	0.5	(Cherry, Apple)
11	0.5	(Cherry, Mango)
3	0.4	(Kiwis)
5	0.4	(Orange)
6	0.4	(Banana, Apple)
9	0.4	(Orange, Banana)
10	0.4	(Cherry, Kiwis)
12	0.4	(Orange, Cherry)
13	0.4	(Cherry, Banana, Apple)
14	0.4	(Orange, Cherry, Banana)

	support	itemsets
0	1.0	(Cherry)
1	0.7	(Banana)
6	0.7	(Cherry, Banana)
2	0.5	(Apple)
5	0.5	(Mango)
7	0.5	(Cherry, Apple)
14	0.5	(Cherry, Mango)
3	0.4	(Orange)
4	0.4	(Kiwis)
8	0.4	(Banana, Apple)
9	0.4	(Cherry, Banana, Apple)
10	0.4	(Orange, Banana)
11	0.4	(Orange, Cherry)
12	0.4	(Orange, Cherry, Banana)
13	0.4	(Cherry, Kiwis)

['antecedents', 'consequents', 'antecedent support', 'consequent support', 'support', 'confidence', 'lift', 'leverage', 'conviction', 'zhangs_metric']

	antecedents	consequents	support	confidence	lift \
4	(Orange)	(Banana)	0.4	1.0	1.428571
10	(Orange, Cherry)	(Banana)	0.4	1.0	1.428571
12	(Orange)	(Cherry, Banana)	0.4	1.0	1.428571
3	(Apple)	(Banana)	0.4	0.8	1.142857
7	(Cherry, Apple)	(Banana)	0.4	0.8	1.142857
9	(Apple)	(Cherry, Banana)	0.4	0.8	1.142857
0	(Banana)	(Cherry)	0.7	1.0	1.000000
1	(Apple)	(Cherry)	0.5	1.0	1.000000
2	(Mango)	(Cherry)	0.5	1.0	1.000000
5	(Kiwis)	(Cherry)	0.4	1.0	1.000000
6	(Orange)	(Cherry)	0.4	1.0	1.000000
8	(Banana, Apple)	(Cherry)	0.4	1.0	1.000000
11	(Orange, Banana)	(Cherry)	0.4	1.0	1.000000

	leverage	conviction	zhangs_metric
4	0.12	inf	0.50
10	0.12	inf	0.50
12	0.12	inf	0.50
3	0.05	1.5	0.25
7	0.05	1.5	0.25
9	0.05	1.5	0.25
0	0.00	inf	0.00
1	0.00	inf	0.00
2	0.00	inf	0.00
5	0.00	inf	0.00
6	0.00	inf	0.00
8	0.00	inf	0.00
11	0.00	inf	0.00

	antecedents	consequents	support	confidence	lift
4	(Orange)	(Banana)	0.4	1.0	1.428571
10	(Orange, Cherry)	(Banana)	0.4	1.0	1.428571
12	(Orange)	(Cherry, Banana)	0.4	1.0	1.428571
3	(Apple)	(Banana)	0.4	0.8	1.142857
7	(Cherry, Apple)	(Banana)	0.4	0.8	1.142857
9	(Apple)	(Cherry, Banana)	0.4	0.8	1.142857
0	(Banana)	(Cherry)	0.7	1.0	1.000000
1	(Apple)	(Cherry)	0.5	1.0	1.000000
2	(Mango)	(Cherry)	0.5	1.0	1.000000
5	(Kiwis)	(Cherry)	0.4	1.0	1.000000
6	(Orange)	(Cherry)	0.4	1.0	1.000000
8	(Banana, Apple)	(Cherry)	0.4	1.0	1.000000
11	(Orange, Banana)	(Cherry)	0.4	1.0	1.000000

	leverage	conviction	zhangs metric
4	0.12	inf	0.50
10	0.12	inf	0.50
12	0.12	inf	0.50
3	0.05	1.5	0.25
7	0.05	1.5	0.25
9	0.05	1.5	0.25
0	0.00	inf	0.00
1	0.00	inf	0.00
2	0.00	inf	0.00
5	0.00	inf	0.00
6	0.00	inf	0.00
8	0.00	inf	0.00
11	0.00	inf	0.00

This example shows that using the program to calculate the appropriate relationship rules to use in product sales, namely Rules 4, 10 and 12 that calculate lift, leverage and Zhang's metric values, we can see that according to Rule 4: Customers will always buy oranges along with bananas. As with Rules 10 and 12, customers always buy oranges, bananas, and cherries at the same time. Therefore, when arranging the three types of fruit, they should be placed close together to make it convenient for customers to purchase. But if you look at the support value, you will find that every customer will buy cherries because it has a value of 1. Therefore, the store must have cherries for sale in order to make customers buy them every time they enter the store.

Teaching and testing tools

Teaching and testing tools were created to assess whether the model created was good enough to be used as an artificial intelligence. Since there must be data used for teaching and testing the model before implementation, the data set must be divided into two parts accordingly. For example, such to know the age of a person and the maximum weight they can lift with 500 cases surveyed, we divided them into 75% teaching data and 25% test data, using the package

```
from sklearn.model_selection import train_test_split
```
With command:
```
x_train, x_test, y_train, y_test = train_test_split(x,y ,
                    random_state=10,
                    test_size=0.25,
                    shuffle=True)
```

You may use train_size = 0.75 instead by using the program as follows:

```
import numpy as np
import pandas as pd
import matplotlib.pyplot as plt
from learned.model_selection import train_test_split

AgeWeight = pd.read_csv('TrainTestData.csv')
```

```python
x= AgeWeight['age']
and=AgeWeight['weight']

x_train,x_test,y_train,y_test = train_test_split(x,y,test_size=0.25)

DataS = str(only(x))
trainS = str(only(x_train))
testS = str(only(x_test))

plt.subplot(1, 3, 1)
plt.scatter(x, y)
plt.title(f"Data Size :({DataS}) ")
plt.subplot(1, 3, 2)
plt.scatter(x_train, y_train,color = 'pink')
plt.title(f"Train Size : 75% ({trainS}) ")
plt.subplot(1, 3, 3)
plt.scatter(x_test, y_test,color = 'orange')
plt.title(f" Test Size : 25% ({testS}) ")

plt.xlabel("Age(Year)")
plt.ylabel("Weight(Kg)")
plt.show()
```

Result

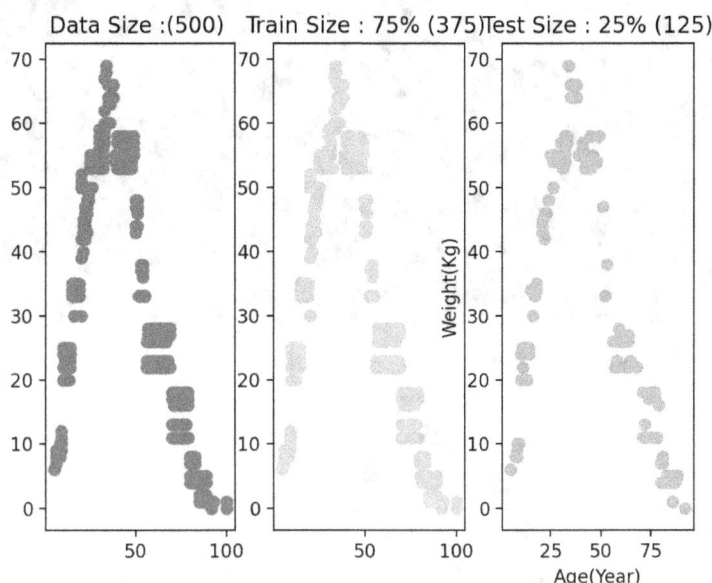

Figure Project IV- 15: Example Size of Total, Training and Testing Data

As for which model is appropriate for use in prediction, by observing the graph we can see that the data trends towards a polynomial regression, so let's try it. The program to find the model will be done using the teaching information as follows.

```
import numpy
import pandas as pd
import matplotlib.pyplot as plt
from learned.model_selection import train_test_split

AgeWeight = pd.read_csv('TrainTestData.csv')

x=AgeWeight['age']
and=AgeWeight['weight']
```

```
x_train,x_test,y_train,y_test =
train_test_split(x,y,test_size=0.25)

AWModel = numpy.poly1d(numpy.polyfit(x_train, y_train,
3))

AWline = numpy.linspace(0, 100, 10)

plt.scatter(x_train, y_train)
plt.plot(AWline, AWModel(AWline))
plt.show()
```
Result

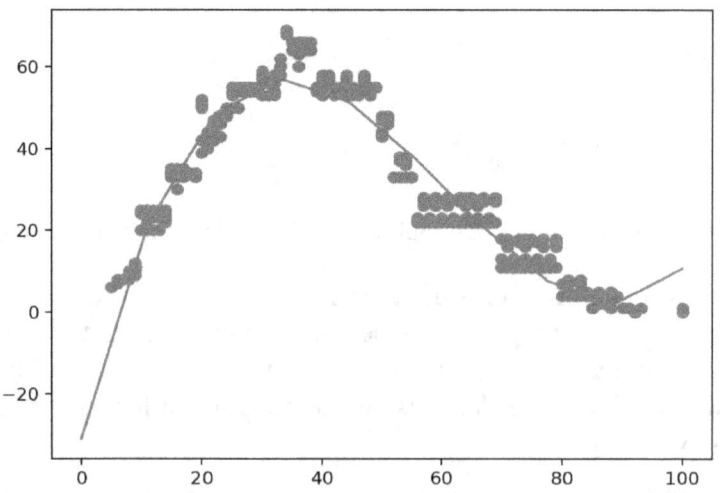

Figure Project IV- 16: Example Polynomial regression of training data

To check how accurate this model is, find the coefficient of determination. By adding a command

```
r2 = r2_score(y_train, AWModel(x_train))
print(r2)
```

The program is as follows.

```
import numpy
import pandas as pd
import matplotlib.pyplot as plt
from learned.model_selection import train_test_split
from learned.metrics import r2_score

AgeWeight = pd.read_csv('TrainTestData.csv')

x=AgeWeight['age']
y=AgeWeight['weight']

x_train,x_test,y_train,y_test =
train_test_split(x,y,test_size=0.25)

AWModel = numpy.poly1d(numpy.polyfit(x_train, y_train,
3))

AWline = numpy.linspace(0, 100, 10)

plt.scatter(x_train, y_train)
plt.plot(AWline, AWModel(AWline))
plt.show()

r2 = r2_score(y_train, AWModel(x_train))

print(r2)
```

Result
0.9271004387152981

The coefficient of determination has been shown to have very high accuracy.
When we want to test whether this model is accurate or not with test data, add a command to use the test data to find the decision coefficient of the model obtained from the teaching data:

```
r2_test = r2_score(y_test, AWModel(x_test))
print(r2_test)
```

Use the program as follows:

```
import numpy
import pandas as pd
import matplotlib.pyplot as plt
from learned.model_selection import train_test_split
from learned.metrics import r2_score

AgeWeight = pd.read_csv('TrainTestData.csv')

x=AgeWeight['age']
and=AgeWeight['weight']

x_train,x_test,y_train,y_test = train_test_split(x,y,test_size=0.25)

AWModel = numpy.poly1d(numpy.polyfit(x_train, y_train, 3))

AWline = numpy.linspace(0, 100, 10)

plt.scatter(x_train, y_train)
plt.plot(AWline, AWModel(AWline))
plt.show()

r2 = r2_score(y_train, AWModel(x_train))

print(r2)

r2_test = r2_score(y_test, AWModel(x_test))

print(r2_test)
```

<u>Result</u>
0.9291039427182437

It is almost equal to 1, so it has very high accuracy. And both the teaching and training data of this model have similar high accuracy, that is, the teaching data has a decision coefficient of 0.9271004387152981
and test data has a decision coefficient of 0.92910394271824377
So, this model can be used as an artificial intelligence tool if you want to know how much weight someone at any age can lift.

Learn Python with Projects

Files used in projects/Exercise Solutions

Go to : https://www.variitsris.org/learning-python/ Or Scan QR Code

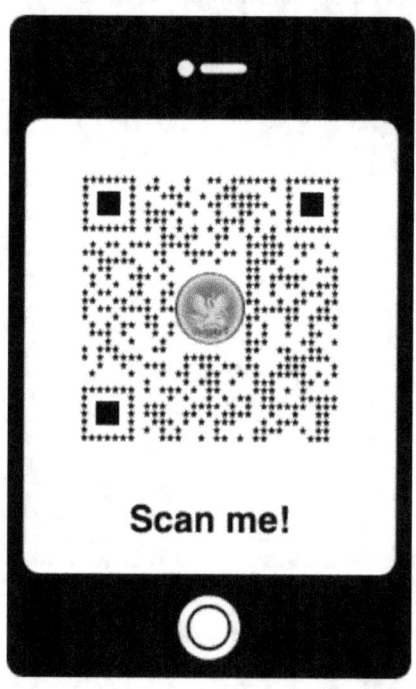

Learn Python with Projects

About The Author

Having written several bestselling textbooks, the author has experience in software development, research, teaching, and consulting in:

- Artificial Intelligence
- Customer relationship management
- Software engineering
- System analysis and design.
- Data warehouse
- Data mining
- Object-Oriented Technology (UML).
- Human-computer interaction.
- Image processing
- Big data
- Business intelligence

Experience in program and database development and giving advice :

- Node.js
- JavaScript
- Oracle
- Python
- HTML5
- MongoDB

Author certifications associated with this textbook are as follows:
1. Cybersecurity: Managing Risk in the Information Age, HARVARD University.
2. Digital Transformation: From AI and IoT to Cloud, Blockchain and Cybersecurity, MIT.
3. Data Science and Big Data Analytics : Making Data-Driven Decisions, MIT.

Learn Python with Projects